Francis Bugg

The Pilgrim's Progress from Quakerism to Christianity

Francis Bugg

The Pilgrim's Progress from Quakerism to Christianity

ISBN/EAN: 9783337294342

Printed in Europe, USA, Canada, Australia, Japan

Cover: Foto ©Lupo / pixelio.de

More available books at **www.hansebooks.com**

THE
Pilgrim's Progress,
FROM
QUAKERISM,
TO
CHRISTIANITY.

CONTAINING

A farther Discovery of the Danger of the Growth of *Quakerism*, not only in Point of Doctrine, but also in their Politicks, in what they call their Church Government, both from Matter of Fact, Practice and Experience; from the Connection of the Use and Design of their silent Meetings, their Monthly, Quarterly, and Yearly Meetings, &c. their Fund or Common Stock; with the Consequence of it. Together with a Remedy proposed for the

Cure of Quakerism.

To which is added an

APPENDIX:

SHEWING,

Wherein there is a most Damnable Plot Contrived and Carrying on by *NEW-ROME*, and that by a United Confederacy against the Reformed Religion, and the Professors thereof; both Magistrates, Ministers and People. With a Challenge to *Geo. Whitehead*, (HER CHIEF CARDINAL) to prove the same.

By *FRANCIS BUGG*, Sen.

Oh that my Words were now written! Oh that they were printed in a Book! (For) *these Men, the Sons of* Zeruiah, *be too hard for me*, Job 19. 23. 2 Sam. 3. 39.

LONDON: Printed for, and are to be Sold by *W. Kettleby*, at the *Bishops-Head*, in St. Paul's *Church-Yard*, 1698.

To the Right Worshipful, the *Vice-Chancellors*, and *Heads* of the *Colleges* of both *Universities*, and to all other, the *Reverend Clergy* therein, of what Title soever; the *Ensuing Discourse* is Humbly Dedicated, *&c.*

Honoured and Reverend Gentlemen,

Having herein collected my Experience, both of the Doctrine and Discipline of the Schism of Quakerism, shewing the Tendency thereof, from Matter of Fact, I thought it but my Reasonable Service to offer the same to your Judicious Perusal, and Christian Consideration; that so, according to the Apprehension you shall have, touching the Premises, you may put your helping Hand, not only to a farther Confutation of the Quaker Arguments, (which yet is needful enough) but also for the regaining such as (who thro' the cunning Slights and Plausable Pretentions of these Seducers) are mislead, and carry'd away; and thereby not only vindicate the Christian Religion, but defend the Church of England from the most horrible Scandals, cast upon both, by the Quakers.

I need not acquaint you with the great Labour, and unwearied Pains, our Protestant Divines have taken to Regain such, who have been seduced to Adhere to the Romish Religion, and the vast number of Volumes, writ on that Account, and not without Good and Great Success, as we see this Day, Thanks be to God; but behold, here is a NEW ROME arising, which Builds on the same Bottom, i. e. INFALLIBILITY, &c. and whose Principles were first Hammer'd at that Forge, and Coyn'd at that Mint, and are carrying on by the same Craft and Unsuspected Policy, and as Dangerous to the Reformed Religion, which our Martyr'd Ancestors suffered in the Flames for, as Rome Her Elder Sister. (And this you should see, had they but Power; an Instance of which is their Proceedings in Pensilvania) But notwithstanding all this, how few are there concern'd hereat? How few lay it to Heart? This is Cause of Lamentation and Astonishment; and yet, when I consider how long I my self was deceived by them, I

do

The Epistle Dedicatory.

do the less marvel; especially, considering what *Equivocations and Reserve* they make in their *Arguments*, whether *Verbal*, or in *Writing*; how *Industrious* they are to hide themselves, and their *Tenets*, expressing themselves in *Dubious Terms*, that want *Explication*; pretending to *Seriousness, Sincerity, Plainness*, &c. when none so *Insincere*, so *Deceitful*, and *False in the World*, as in a *Thousand Things* I could mention, whereby it is manifest, that they are the *false Prophets which Christ foretold of*, Matth. 24. 24. And therefore, if what I can contribute towards the *Discovery of this Painted*, as well as *Disguised Harlot*, may be useful to the *Church of God*, and the *Ministers thereof*, in bringing forth my known *Experience*, I shall be glad, and rejoyce therein.

I cannot but know, that herein you will meet with many *Deficiencies*, for want of *Parts* and *Learning*, requisite to such a *Work*: But since your *Generosity* is so mixed with *Christian Charity*, as to accept the *Will* for the *Deed*, as in my former *Essays*, I have at this time presumed to present this *Rough Draught* to your *Perusal*, and as my *Mite*, to cast it into your *Treasury*, hoping, that until the *Quakers can justly charge me with a false Quotation*, (which, as they never yet could do, so I hope they never shall) this may pass under your *Patronage*, as a *Defence against* the Quaker's *Invectives*; and it may be, when I cannot speak for my self; especially, when there is not a *Man of you*, but are *Sharers with me in the same Reproaches for the Gospel's sake*. Thus, Reverend Sirs, begging your *Pardon* for this my *Presumption*, I Humbly Subscribe my self,

Milden-Hall, *August* the 10th. 1698.

Your most Humble,

And Devoted Servant,

Francis Bugg, Sen.

A N

AN
ADDRESS
TO
Private Gentlemen and Tradesmen, &c.

Courteous Readers,

IT is certain, *That the Wicked Plotteth against the Righteous* *, as *David* said. This was and is the Churches Malady; and 'tis as certain, that the Lord Laughs at these Plotters, *Ver.* 13. This is the Churches Remedy. Now whilst God Laughs at the Plots of the Wicked, his People have little cause to Cry; especially considering that he would have us rejoice with him, saying, *The Righteous shall see and fear, and laugh at him* †. But do you think that we of the Laity ought to see this Plot carrying on by a united Confederacy against the Church, and say nothing, nor be at all concerned in the discovery of it; for saith *David*, *They have consulted together with one consent; they are confederate against thee* (*a*). Do you think, that because God has promis'd, that Kings shall be as * Nursing-fathers to the Church*; or because he has Commanded his Servants that wait at the Altar, to cry aloud, to give notice of these Seducers, that therefore we are wholly excused and unconcerned, I tell you nay; Christ's Mystical Body consists of many Members, but all the Members have not the same Office; yet the Eye cannot say to the Foot, I have no need of thee; so that there is some use and service for us, if we be Living Members, and sensible of the Churches Calamity; and if so, give me leave to remind you of what I conceive to be every private Christians Duty, which is, to use all Lawful Means to discover this Plot; to put Books into the Hands both of the *Quakers*, in order to regain them; and to others who lean that way; for it's probable some of you in your Shops, and by Commerce, may have that Opportunity your Minister have not; there are many such useful Books now extant *; by this means the *Quakers* in time will be capable to judge, how they have been impos'd upon, by their Leaders, by comparing the Books: And herein will the Burden and Weight of this Discovery be taken somewhat off the Clergy; who,

* Psal. 37. 12.

† Psal. 52. 6.

(*a*) Psal. 83. 5.

* Isa. 49. 23.

* *The Snake in the Grass*, &c. *Sathan Disrob'd*, &c. *Primitive Heresie*, &c. *A Discourse of Water-Baptism*, &c. *The Third Narrative*, per G. K. &c.

to

An Address, &c.

to study the Point, and disperse all Books at their own Charge, is too heavy: And if we be concerned in the Dishonour which this Heresie brings upon our Holy Religion; if we be concerned at the Blasphemies and Indignities cast upon our Saviour, his Death and Sufferings, we shall not think our selves wholly unconcerned, in the Vindication necessary. If you tell me, That it is my Duty to do what I can, to make amends for the Damage I did to the Church when I was a *Quaker*, and thereby an Enemy to the Church; I grant what you say; and I have, and yet shall do, what lieth in my power: But in regard I did it in my Mistaken Zeal, I hope my Ignorance thereof may extenuate my Offence; and thereupon I purpose to Bind up some of my former Books with this, as also some wrote by *Geo. Keith, Tho. Crisp, &c.* But if you find any Passage in our early Writings, not consistent with what we now set forth, we Retract the same: And this being wrote all with my own Hand, (Quotations excepted) is to be taken as my present Judgment, not only in Points of Doctrine Controverted, but also respecting the Design of the *Quakers* Politicks, in what they call their Church Government; yet in all the Books Bound up with this, something of the Design of *Quakerism* may be seen; at least, some of their Errors discovered. And when we consider the many Books wrote against the Papists, and the good Effect they have had, it may lead us to consider the Usefulness of Books against this *NEW ROME*, who follow the Steps of her Elder Sister: And the more we come to consult the Holy Scriptures, and to consider of that Benefit we (if obedient to those Evangelical Doctrines, and Holy Precepts laid down therein) shall enjoy, this; yea, this, will put us upon a Necessity to be concerned in our several Places, Stations, and Callings.

I remember that one Chief Method by which *Quakerism* Advanced, was by spreading Books*, and the same they still use; see p. 41, 70, herein: For before their Government was set up, their Books were carried on Pack-horses up and down the Nation; I my self have given away 20 s. worth at a Meeting; and all this to spread *Quakerism*: And shall we be less Zealous in detecting Errors, than they are to spread them? Oh! let it not once be said so of such as love God, and his Church, and Worship. Thus have I imparted my Mind, and I hope, without Offence; who am,

Your Humble Servant,

Francis Bugg.

Marginal notes:

And *Jeffery Bullock*, tho' a right *Quaker*, yet his Printing the 66 Judges and 67 Opposers, shews how Infallibility oppose Infallibility.

As is apparent; see p. 50, to 55, herein. Ibid. p. 57, to 90.

* I lately did Administer of the Goods of a Poor Widow a *Quaker*, whose Substance was not 10 l. yet she had more than 200 *Quaker* Books and Pamphlets.

THE

THE CONTENTS.

Chap. I. *An Account of the Author's Education.*   Pag. 1
Chap. II. *And his Falling from the Church to Quakerism.* 3
Chap. III. *Of the Quakers Silent Meetings.*   4
A Comparison between the Quakers *and* Muggleton.   9
Chap. IV. *Their Church Government Erected, and how.*   10
The *Convocation,* Anno 1666.   15
George Fox's *Ten Commandments.*   17
Chap. V. Fox *the Quakers Moses.*   20
George Fox *his Exaltations.*   21, 29
The Quakers *Adorations to him.*   23
Distrust the Quakers *in all they say; and why.*   25
Chap. VI. *The* Quakers Mysterium Maximum.   30
Chap. VII. *The* Quakers *Yearly Convocation; and how.*   37
W. Rogers *Condemned; and why.*   41
Chap. 8. *The Executive Part of the* Quakers *Government.*   49
Their Manner of Excommunication; and for what.   51
Chap. IX. *Their Fund, or Common Stock.*   58
Ann Docwra's *Lie to the Government.*   59
Her Verses on G. Fox.   64
Chap. X. *Their Six Week Meeting for Suffering.*   65
Tho. Ellwood, *Tom. Tell-troth.*   66
7000 Quakers *Petition the Parliament against Tythes.*   68
Their not Signing the Association; and why.   93 to 99
Their Care to spread their Books.   70
The Quakers *Never Addressed King* William III.   86
A Ministers Letter to the Clergy.   71
Chap. XI. *Their Second Day Meeting, where Satan dwells.*   72
Their Averseness to Monarchy, and Affinity with O. Crom.   78
Their Suppressing Joan Whitrow's *Books.*   88
A Proclamation against Mr. Penn.   89
Chap. XII. *Their Battle-door for the Clergy.*   104
Their Epistle or Liturgy for Churches; and why.   105
Chap. XIII. *A Sermon for* G. W. *suiting their Principles.*   107
Londoners *look about ye.*   112

Their.

The CONTENTS.

Their Contempt of the Scriptures.	109
They pretend to own them to the Parliament; and why.	111
The Authority of their own Books; and how.	112
Confession of Sin denied; and why.	115
Their Self-Exaltation; and how.	116
Their Testimony against the Clergy.	120
G. W's Prayer Pharisee-*like*	126
Sam. Fisher's *Prophesie.*	122
Baptism, Supper, Ten Commandments, &c. denied.	118
Chap. XIV. *A Cage of Unclean Birds.*	127
Geo. Fox *an Impostor.*	131
Letters to F. B. *in Verse and Prose.*	146
The Quakers Idolizing Geo. Fox.	133
Geo. Smith *their Favourite.*	143
My Lord Bishop of Norwich *his Certificate.*	149
Mr. Meriton's *Letter.*	152
F. B's *Six Queries, wrote* 1678.	155
Chap. XVI. *The Quakers directed to Christianity.*	156
G. W's *Challenge Answered.*	159
An Appendix; G. W's *Proposition Explained.*	164
Mr. Samuel Grove, *&c. their Subscription.*	164
F. Bugg's *Challenge to* G. W. *Renewed.*	172
The Church of God both Jewish and Christ. Exem. and how.	162
Four Warnings from the Quakers of an Horrible Plot.	167
Against whom this Damnable Conspiracy is.	168
The only way to discover this Plot, and prevent it.	175
Not by Persecution; no; far easier, and more safe.	169
Geo. Whitehead's *Innocency not Triumphant; and why.*	172
F. B. *renews his Challenge, pitches his Standard, and holds out the Flag of Defiance against* Geo. Whitehead.	173
The only way to Cure Quakerism, both easie and safe.	171
Is to Summons F. Bugg *and* G. Whitehead; *and why.*	170
They undervalue the Blood of Christ; and how.	26
They undervalue the Death and Sufferings of Christ.	163
And that the Name Jesus and Christ belong to every Believer, (i. e. Quaker) *as well as to Christ the Head.*	27, 173
William Penn's *Error Confuted,*	159
The Fear of the Quakers *Gulph Remov'd.*	156

THE

THE
Pilgrim's Progress,
FROM
QUAKERISM
TO
Christianity, &c.

CHAP. I.

Giving an Account of my Education in the Profession of the Christian Faith; and how I came to Apostatize from it, and fall in with the Schism of Quakerism.

I Was Born at *Milden-Hall*, in the County of *Suffolk*, on the 10th Day of *March, Anno* 1640. and Baptized into the Church of Christ, the 14th of the same Month; promising then by my Sureties, to Fight manfully under Christ's Banner. My Father's Name was *Robert Bagg,* second Son of *Francis Bagg* (and *Margaret* his Wife,) who was Chief Constable many Years; my Mother's Name was *Joan*, the Fourth and Youngest Daughter of *Thomas Holman*, and *Mary* his Wife, (who was Baptized the 16th Day of *March*, 1619.) living at *Ishenheath Hall:* My Parents were of good Yeomen-Family, and liv'd in good Repute, and brought me up in the Profession of the Church of *England*; and when I came to Years capable of Instruction, they Taught me the *Lord's Prayer,* the *Ten Commandments,* and the *Apostles Creed*; and very severe they were, in Teaching me the Rudiments of the Christian Religion. I remember my Mother, who was a very good and pious Woman, and religiously inclined, would not suffer me to Sleep, when I went to Bed, e're I had said my Prayers, and sometimes, part of my Catechism: And on the *Lord's Day*, she made me to frequent the Church, and at Home on that Day, as well as most other Days, to read some Portion of the Holy Scriptures: They brought me up to School-Learning, until I attained to the Age of about Fifteen Years, whereby I was capable to Write, and Read *English* very well; as also to cast Account, few Lads went beyond me: As also the *Grammar*, wherein I was well Instructed in the Rules thereof, insomuch that I began to make a Piece of *Latin*; but my Father living in a great Farm at *Undley-Hall*, in the Parish of *Lakenheath*, of 200 *l.* a Year; besides a *Fen-Farm* in his hands of 100 *l. per Ann.* more; he had, in the Summer time, great occasion for my Assistance, and thereby was prevented, of attaining to that Degree they once designed: And afterwards being an Apprentice, and so fell into Business, that I soon lost a great part of that Learning, I once had attained.

I must also confess, I was in my Youth inclined to Company, especially to Dancing and Musick; yet, I had in my early Years, a love to Religion; and delighted much in Reading the Holy Scriptures, sometimes 8 or 10 Chapters together; I also lov'd much to hear good Preachers. I very well remember, that sometimes I went to *Milden-Hall*, (where we formerly liv'd,) on the *Lord's Day*, on purpose to hear Mr. *Watson*, who was accounted a famous Preacher, being four Miles from my Dwelling. Thus much briefly touching my early Education.

Observations on the First Chapter.

Reader, I am the more particular in these Remarks, for that the *Quakers* [how much soever I was in esteem whilst with them] since I left them, have traduced me, and laid all the Reproaches on me which Malice can invent, (*a*) as shall be shewed hereafter; as well as to shew, how excellent a thing it is, for Parents to bring up their Children in the Nurture and Fear of the Lord, to instruct them in the Principles of Christianity; teach them the *Lord's Prayer*, the *Ten Commandments*, the *Apostles Creed*, and the *Church Catechism*: These Things, together with Reading and Hearing the Scriptures Expounded, being instilled into them, in their young Years, they will scarcely forget it when they are Old: But, if they should, yet at one time or other, the remembrance of them may so far be brought to mind, that they may thereby, be brought to a sense of their Condition. And I speak what I know by Experience; for the first Sermon I heard, after I was about 25 Years amongst the *Quakers*, the very hearing the *Lord's Prayer*, the *Ten Commandments*, the *Apostles*

(*a*) *Non patitur Ludum famæ, Fides, Oculus, i. e.* A Man's Good Name, his Faith, his Eye will not be dally'd with, said *Luther* in his Commentary upon *Gal.* p. 51.

From Quakerism *to* Christianity.

stles Creed, and *Confession of Sin,* did so strike me, and bring things to my Memory, that it shak'd all my Self-Confidence, and brought me to the consideration of Times past.

CHAP. II.

An Account of my Apostacy; and how I came to be carried away by the Quakers Dissimulation.

ABOUT the Year of our Lord 1657, *Thomas Symonds* of *Norwich* came to *Laken-heath,* and appointed Meetings; and many *Quakers* came from *Thetford,* and other Places: And tho' I went to Church on the Forenoon, yet I had itching Ears to hear the *Quakers*; and my Mother being dead, and much of my Restraint thereby taken off, I went to their Meetings in the Afternoon, and gave great heed to what was spoken; whose chief Subject was, *The Light within every Man,* and this Light to be Christ: And their great Argument was from Christ's telling the Woman of *Samaria* her Thoughts, saying, *Come, see a Man which told me all things that ever I did; is not this the Christ?* &c. Therefore, said the Quakers, this *Light within* must needs be the Man Christ, and no other Man Christ, do they now own to this Day, if they would speak their Thoughts: However, their Writings prove it; and till they condemn them, all they alledge to the contrary, is nothing worth. *John* 4. 29.

Well, however, I and others, were catched by these and the like fallacious Arguments, not being well grounded in the Principles of the Christian Religion, nor understanding the Wiles of Satan; and by their smooth and fair Carriage, by their suffering patiently the Affronts they then met with. I cannot but still remember how our Minister warned us of the Doctrine of the Quakers, and told us, they were Deceivers and Antichrists; even those very Deceivers which Christ foretold us should arise, shewing Signs and Wonders; insomuch, that if it were possible, they should deceive the very Elect. (b) But by this their pretended Patience in Suffering, by their so much insisting on the Dictates of our Consciences, which prompts to good, and checks for some Evils; with other fair Words, and seeming, nay, real Truths, with which they covered over their poysonous Pills of Schism and Heresie, many of us were deceived. *Matth.* 24. 24.

(b) Which I now also believe.

Again, when I saw so much Plainness and seeming Sincerity in the Quakers, and consider'd, how our Minister lived, it was another Motive to induce me to go after the Quakers; for Mr. *Swanton,* our Minister, lived with my Father, I do think some Years: my Father was the chief Man that got him into the Place: But, both then,

B 2

and

and afterwards, he was such an ill Example, and I not being capable to judge of the Doctrinal Part, I was carried away in my Affections; being more apt to be led by Example than Precept, which is not always safe: However, I do believe it was the scandalous Practice of our Minister, which I beheld in divers Particulars, which was one cause of my Stumbling, whereby I fell unhappily into that Schism.

Observations on the Second Chapter.

NOW therefore, I intreat all concerned in the Ministerial Office, as Fathers, That they beware they give no ill Example to their Flock, contrary to what becomes their Sacred Function; but, when they Preach well, let them Practice so, as believing what they say, so will their People believe them to be in earnest. But, if they Preach never so Orthodoxly, and tho' their Sermons be never so much Learned, yet if they do not live in some tollerable sort answerably, their People will Question, Whether they believe what they teach; and as a consequence thereof, will take that liberty in Living, which is not becoming Christians: Or else, if Seducers come, will be apt to seperate themselves, in hopes to get under a purer Ministry; which, when they come afterwards to examine, they may find it to be only in Shew.

CHAP. III.

Gives an Account of the Quakers *Silent Meetings, and the Tendency of them: In which, I shall speak sometimes in the Person of a* Quaker, *respecting the time I was one.*

HAVING by this time fallen in with the *Quakers*; in a few Years, I became very zealous that way, and to silent Meetings I went; and sometimes we had a few Words spoken, sometimes none; sometimes an Epistle of *George Whitehead*'s, *George Fox*'s, *Sam. Cater*'s, or some others, read in our Meetings; and sometimes none: But the chief of what we did hear, either from our inspired Infallible Teachers, or from our Friends Epistles, in those private Silent Meetings, was, To exhort us to wait in the Light, out of our Selves, out of our Thoughts, out of our Willings and Runnings, in that which is invisible; and then we should receive the hidden *Manna*, yea, *Manna* from Heaven, which the World knew not of; and that we should feel Christ to come the second time to Judgment; and that Judgment was to begin at the House of God,

which

From Quakerism to Christianity.

which House was our Bodies: And from hence, divers of us fell oft into a Trembling and Shaking. I have seen about five or six together in a Meeting, shake like a Leaf in Winter, namely, *Matthew Beesly*, *Jonas Skrook*, *William Eyfon*, and others; yea, they have shaken the Forms they sat on; and this, not once, nor twice, but frequently. I do very well remember, that *John Kilborn* the Elder, did one *Sunday* in our Meeting, fold his Arms, and stood upright; and by and by, leaped and jumped, about 18 Inches at a time, until he jumped round the Room. I know, that some are alive still, that know these things are true. But, let it be noted, Not a Chapter in the Bible was ever read amongst us, but all exhorted to adhere to the *Light within*, to obey the *Light within*, and to follow the Teachings thereof, as a Guide sufficient to lead us to Salvation; yea, above Scripture, above Fathers, above Councils, and above Churches: This I now confess, was a Paradox; not Orthodox, but absolutely Heterodox: For let the Scripture command Subjects to be obedient to Magistrates, Children to obey their Parents, Wives to reverence their Husbands, and live in subjection to them, Servants to obey their Masters, Christians to obey their Pastors, all this signified little; the *Light within* (our Teachers taught us,) was Christ, and Christ the Power of God, the higher Power to which every Soul was to be subject; yea, all Power in Heaven and in Earth, was committed to the *Light*; (a) and that no Command in Scripture was any further binding, than as we were convinced of the Lawfulness thereof, by the *Light within us*. (b) So, that all our Obedience to God, and his Commands, were bottomed and founded on our Conviction, by the *Light within*; that being the only Rule, Judge and Guide, both superior to the Scriptures, Fathers and Councils. For, said they to us, That *what is spoken from the Spirit of Truth* (c) *in any, is of as great Authority as the Scriptures and Chapters are, and greater.*

Fra. Howgill's Works. p. 602. to 627.

Perverting John 5. 23, 24. Acts 17. to 31. See Josiah Coal's Works, p. 93.

(a) Ed. Burrough's Works, p. 47.

(b) Quakerism a New Nick-name for Old Christianity. Per W. Penn. p. 71.

(c) Truth Defending the Quakers, &c. p. 7.

By which, it is self-evident, That these Silent Meetings were designed to wean us off from so much as the remembrance of all external Religion, and also, to prepare us to receive the false Notions of *Quakerism*; for, had they indeed exhorted us, to have regard to our *Light within*, and the Dictates of our Consciences, which prompts to good, and checks for many Evils; in obedience to the Commands of Holy Scripture, this would have been safe, for I believe we ought so to do, and 'tis the same the Ministers of the Church of *England* press and exhort us to. Oh! but this would not do our Teachers Business; they must bring us off from the Scripture Commands, as inferior to their Sayings and Speakings; for the Book last quoted, is said, to be given forth from the Spirit of Truth, in *George Whitehead*, and *George Fox* the Younger: And being Questioned by a Minister, *p. 7*. Whether the *Quakers* Speaking

See Title Pag.

ing was of as great Authority as any Chapter in the Bible? *George Whitehead* reply'd, saying, *That which is spoken from the Spirit of Truth in* ANY, *is of as* GREAT AUTHORITY *as the Scriptures and Chapters are, and* GREATER. So that, the plain consequence of this Doctrine, is, That the Authority of this little Pamphlet of *Whitehead*'s and *Fox*'s Writing, is of Greater Authority than the Bible; and not only that, but all their other Pamphlets which they give forth (as they pretend,) from the Spirit of Truth, or Light within. The said Minister proposed another Question to *Whitehead*, viz. Is the Moral Law, or Ten Commandments, a Rule to the Christian's Life, or is it not? To this G. *Whitehead* reply'd, saying, *Thou might as well ask, If the Moral Law be a Rule to Christ, for the Christians Life and Rule is Christ*; meaning, their *Light within*: From whence it's plain, that the Ten Commandments are not the *Quakers* Rule: No, no, not unless they be convinced by their *Light within*, of the reasonableness of their Obedience, as Mr. *Penn* teaches, and *Edward Burroughs*, their great Prophet. And by these, and the like Arguments, our Teachers brought us off, from believing the Scriptures to be the Word of God: And as such, to have Authority over us, and Binding to us, whether convinced or not convinced; by these means, they brought us from the Practice of repeating the *Lord's Prayer*, the *Ten Commandments*, and the *Apostles Creed*, in our Families: By these cunning Slights, they by degrees brought us off the Ordinances of Christ, as *Baptism* and the *Lord's Supper*, asking Forgiveness of Sin, and the like Christian Duties, in which many of us had been Educated, and which the Scriptures command and exhort to. And by reason of this, and the like Doctrine, together with not reading the Holy Scriptures in our Meetings, but their Epistles only, as in my former Books I have at large shewed; we came to forget, and not regard, nor have Faith in the Crucified Jesus, who died for our Sins, and rose for our Justification; and that in these Fundamental Points following, namely,

1. That Faith in Christ, as he outwardly suffered at *Jerusalem*, was necessary to our Salvation, provided we hearkened diligently to our *Light within*.

2. That Justification and Sanctification, is by the Blood of Christ outwardly shed.

3. That there shall be a Resurrection of the Body that dieth.

4. That Christ shall come without us in his Glorified Body, to Judge the Quick and the Dead at the last Day; even the same Jesus that was born of the Virgin, died, rose, ascended, and now sits at the Right Hand of God in Heaven, making Intercession for us; I say, by our Teachers thus slighting the Scriptures, as Death, Dust, and Serpents Food, of which I have largely treated elsewhere; and by their other Doctrine scattered up and down their Books, they

brought

From Quakerism to Christianity.

brought us off from the Belief and Expectation of these Things, as *George Keith* by his Third Narrative, has clearly made to appear; and as a pregnant instance thereof, with respect to my self, see my first Book I printed; which, altho' it Treat of the best part of *Quakerism*, and gave a mortal Wound to the Jurisdiction of their Female Government, yet it set not forth any one of these four Fundamental Points: For, as their Hypocrisy in pretending to be plain, sincere, simple and innocent, was a means to attract and draw me after them; so, the like Hypocrisy in pretending to gather to the Light, leave people to their Light, as a sufficient Rule, Judge, and Guide,*&c.* was one Reason why I left them. I do not look upon it so eminently my Business, to set forth the admirable Advantage and Use of the *Lord's Prayer*, the *Ten Commandments*, the *Apostles Creed*, *Baptism*, and the *Lord's Supper*; no, every Booksellers Shop is furnished with plenty of such Books, which are writ by Men of great Learning and Skill; which, should I write after them, it would be next to light a Candle at Noon-day, when the Sun shines in its Brightness. Tho', if I lived in a Country where such Arguments were not, I thank God, I could, through the Study of the Scriptures, (and the Knowledge I have of the Doctrinal part of Christianity thereby,) speak somewhat to the Point, and which might be useful too: No, I take it to be my Business and Office, amongst others, to unmask and discover the Errours and pernicious Principles of the *Quakers*; and therefore refer to Bishop *Andrews* upon the Commandments, Bishop *Pearson* upon the Creed, Dr. *Cumber* upon the Lord's Prayer, and indeed, what else the Church teach.

De Chris. Lib. Part 2.

* Yet acting quite contrary, as anon will appear.

And to make it yet more evident, if more can be, that the very Design of these Silent Meetings, was to bring us off, and wean us from the Articles of the Christian Faith, and the Principles of the Christian Religion; and thereby, to mould us, and square us, as fit Tools for their turn, to supplant and overthrow it. And this I know, that the more we obeyed the Doctrine of our new Teachers, the more we grew dead to all Instituted Religion.

For, as Universities, and other Schools of Learning, as well amongst the Jews as Christians, had a tendency to prepare Men, and (thro' God's assisting Grace) were a means, and a help to such as were to be Consecrated, and set apart for the Work of the Ministry; so I do affirm, and that from an Experimental Knowledge, That these Silent Universities tends only to empty the mind of all true and solid Notions of the Christian Religion, and only to prepare them for the wild Notions of *Quakerism*, which hath such a sandy Foundation, that to this day they have not been able to produce their Articles of that Faith they pretend to; but are, as Mr. *Baxter* said, *i. e.* 'The *Quakers* are amongst us, a disgraced broken Sect. *&c.* notwithstanding their pretence to Unity, Uniformity, and to be of one mind,

Penitential Confession. p. 63.

mind, referring oft to their Beginning; when, alas! some will pay Tythes, some not; some shut up their Shops on Fast Days, some not; some for Thee and Thou still, but most of them not; but are like other People: some wet *Quakers*, some not; some for this, some for that; and some for neither this nor that, as in a hundred things I could shew.

But, least any should think me partial in stating the Case, and in shewing the Consequences of our Silent Meetings, or Schools of Ignorance, I shall now proceed farther, to prove my Matter, and that from plain matter of Fact; that so it may appear, as well from our printed Books, as from our known Practice, what a strange Effect these Silent Meetings had upon us; and, how we thereby, became not only levened into a Temper, to throw off all Instituted Religion, but to a degree higher, even to throw contempt both upon the Scriptures, Ordinances and Ministers, and all things Sacred, crying down all Forms and Constitutions, how ancient and profitable soever they were, and all under a pretence of a higher Dispensation, even the *Light within*, &c.

(*a*) The Guide mistaken, p. 32.

For saith *W. Penn*, (*a*) 'We [Quakers] being withdrawn from 'every Form and Constitution, to wait [in Silence] for Life from 'God, and not from beggarly Elements, and therefore made a Prey 'to all Parties; against whom every hand have been lifted up, and 'forsaken by all Civil Power, *&c.*

A Musick-Lecture, p. 25.

To this, let me add the Testimony of one of our greatest Prophets; his Words are these, (*i. e.*) 'I dare not daub (saith *Solomon*) with 'untempered Mortar; for where they (*i. e.* Professors of Christianity) 'are, I was, *viz.* in Performances in Ordinances, in Family-Duties, 'in Hearing, in Reading, in Prayers and Fastings, in my own Will; 'and all this is Will-worship. But when that one thing (the *Light*) 'came, which was needful, I then began (waiting in Silence,) to 'learn to be a Fool, insomuch, that I durst not give God thanks for 'the Victuals that were set before me.

Thus it is plain, that our Teachers led us into this Silent way of pretended Worship, which never was known before since the World began. Indeed, Consideration and Meditation are good, and ought often to be the Exercise of Christians; but then, they have an Object to Meditate upon; either the Works of Creation and Providence, which affords much Comfort, and cause to praise God our great Creator; or else, on our Lord Jesus Christ his Death, and Sufferings, and perfect Obedience, and the like. But, I say, to go on purpose to a Meeting, and there sit starving in the cold three or four hours together, speaking never a word, nor as near as we can, think a Thought of our own, this is such a new, and non such way of Worship, as neither Prophets, Christ's Apostles, nor any Christian Church to this day, ever gave Countenance to, or President for; I grant,

That

From Quakerism *to* Christianity.   9

That *John Reeve* and *Lodowick Muggleton*, who came forth with *George Fox*, and their Books bear the like face, *viz.* 'Tho' all visible Joyful News 'Worship is now become of no value in the Eyes of the Lord, yet it from Heaven. 'may be truly said, that Christ is with his Apostles always to the end p. 61. 'of the World, in all those that Worship him in Spirit and Truth; 'I mean, those sober Silent Saints, whose Language and Practice 'speaketh forth the Spirit and Power of the Scriptures in them; 'these Silent Saints I speak of, pag. 72. from an unerring Spirit,—— 'from an infallible Light which I have received from the Divine 'Majesty, &c.

Reader, I have by me *Lodowick Muggleton*'s Journal, or Works, bound up in one Volume, containing eleven distinct Books in *Quarto*, and above One thousand pages; and so, like to *George Fox*'s, that I intend they shall stand together in the Library of *Christ's-Church* Colledge in *Oxford*, with the Works of *Burroughs, Bayly, Smith*, and others, that so any who are concerned with the Quakers Errors, may be furnished, &c.

Thus Reader, you see, that *Muggleton* and *Fox* stand on the same bottom; *Fox* was unerring, so is *Muggleton*; *Fox* was for an Infallible Light, so was *Muggleton*; *Fox* was for Silent Saints, so was *Muggleton*, only *Muggleton* keeps close to his Principles; for as he denies all Ordinances, so he does not Preach, Pray, nor Baptize, nor Administer the Sacrament: But the Quakers, as in the instance of *Solomon Eccles* above-quoted, pretend to be against all Ordinances, and yet own Preaching and Praying, and deny Baptism and the Supper, &c. However, since I have no Author, nor never read of any but *Lodowick Muggleton*, that justifie the Quakers Silent Meetings, I will produce one Passage more, *i. c.* 'That the p. 41. 43. *Ibid.* 'Worship required by him from his Saints, was an inward Stilness, 'by which their Souls were made willing to hearken to the Voice or 'Motion of his most Holy Spirit, speaking in them. —— Thus from 'an unerring Light, I have remonstrated to the Elect, what is the 'very true God, and his spiritual Worship accepted of him; 'tis not 'outward Praying, Preaching Fasting or Thanksgiving, to be seen of 'Men, but it is an Inward, Spiritual, Silent Praying and Praising, 'Fasting and Feasting, upon the glorious Things of Eternity, which 'is only seen by Divine Eyes, &c.

Thus I have shewed, that *Lodowick Muggleton* was a better Quaker of the two than *Solomon*: But, that it may appear, that as the *Quakers* have testified against the Christians for owning the Authority of the Bible, so let them see they have a Partner, namely *Muggleton*, who says, 'Again, in the next place, I shall demonstrate the p. 49. *Ibid.* 'Vanity of the Ministry of the *Baptists*; I need not tell you the Foun- 'dation upon which they build their Worship, because it is founded 'on the Letter (*a*) of the Scripture, and their own lying Reason, (*a*) The Qua- 'which is the Devil in them: All true Christians are now under the kers Language
C   'Ministry to a Tee.

'Miniſtry of the Holy Spirit, and therefore are no more bound in
'Conſcience to Apoſtolick Worſhip; I ſay again, that above this
'1000 Years there hath not been a Man ſent to Preach or Propheſy,
'*p.* 50. How then canſt thou poſſibly become a Miniſter of Divine
'Ordinances, by Authority from another Man's Words or Writings,
'unleſs without their Letter, thou wert immediately moved to ſpeak
'by the Holy Spirit, as they were? Moreover, tho' the Scriptures in
'themſelves are true, yet there is nothing but Death in them to a
'Carnal Spirit: The Letter killeth, but the Spirit giveth Life; And
'can a dead and killing Letter give the Power, to become a ſpiritual
'Miniſter of Chriſt's Ordinances to his Elect People? I trow not, &c.

Thus doth *Lodowick* profeſs the ſame Infallibility of Judgment the ſame way of Silent Meetings; the ſame Perfection and unerring Light to Guide, moved thereby immediately. Again, they join, like *Samſon*'s Foxes, againſt the Scripture, a dead Letter, a killing Letter, a carnal Letter. I think I have ſaid enough at this time, of the Harmony betwixt *Lodowick Muggleton*, and the Quaker Teachers; tho' I could bring many the like Inſtances.

Some Inferences from the Third Chapter.

IS it ſo, that whereas it is written, *John* 5. 23, 27. *For the Father judgeth no Man, but hath committed all Judgment to the Son, and hath given him Authority to execute Judgment alſo, becauſe he is the Son of Man:* Confirmed by the Apoſtle, *Acts* 17. 31. *Becauſe he hath appointed a Day, in which he will judge the World in Righteouſneſs, by that Man whom he hath Ordained, whereof he hath given aſſurance unto all Men, in that he hath raiſed him from the Dead.* I ſay, Is it ſo? And have the *Quakers* perverted theſe Texts in St. *John*, and put on a new Tranſlation, ſaying, *All Power in Heaven and Earth is committed to their Light?* Quoting *John* 5. 23. This is a bold Attempt; this is moſt Horrible, if not Blaſphemy, thus to ſubvert the Goſpel, to ſerve their Corrupt Ends. How wary then had People need be of receiving the *Quaker*'s Doctrine? Is it ſo, that People being thus caught in a Snare, and brought over to their Silent Meetings, and thereby weaned and drawn off from the Principles and Practices of the Chriſtian Churches in all Ages, as Baptiſm, the Lord's Supper, the Lord's Prayer, Ten Commandments, the Apoſtles Creed, Confeſſion of Sin, and reading the Scriptures in their Meetings, in the Worſhip of God? Oh! what care ought to be taken, that theſe People ſhould be ſhunned, and theſe falſe Worſhippers be rejected, as a contagious Diſeaſe? Is it ſo, that the *Quakers* hold, that what is ſpoken from the Spirit of Truth in any, is of greater Authority

Joſiah Coal's Works, p. 93.

than

than the Holy Scriptures, which was ever since the Days of Christ and his Apostles, brought as a Proof, to cast the Ballance in all Controversies? And do they indeed hold as their Books teach, That that is no Command of God to me, what he commanded to another; and that no Command in the Scripture is any further obliging upon any Man, than as he finds a Conviction upon his Conscience, as *W. Penn*, and their Prophet *Burroughs* teach: This surely is the Womb of all Iniquity in the World; this opens the Flood-Gates to all Error, Atheism, Deism, Socinianism, Arianism, and what not. This therefore ought to precaution all People, to beware how they receive the dangerous Pill of *Quakerism*, how excellently soever it is covered with some plausible Pretensions and fair Arguments. Is it so, that the *Quakers* have not, nor ever had, since the Days of *Symon Magus*, none like them amongst the Christian Churches, who denyed the Ordinances of Baptism, Supper, and Confession of Sin, but *John Reeve* and *Lodowick Muggleton*? How then does it behove their Followers, to examine the Doctrine and Practice of their Teachers, and to turn from them, and flee as for their Lives? *Burrows Works p. 47. Quak. a new Nick-name, &c. p. 71.*

CHAP. IV.

Shews that this Anarchy did not last long, but a Government was set up: Sometimes a Single Person, as Pope over us; and sometimes the Light in the Body of Friends, claimed a Power over the Light in the Particular.

FOR after we became dead to the Rudiments of the World, as we accounted those Christian Duties, commanded by Christ and his Apostles, and practised by Christian Churches downwards, as Baptism, Supper, Confession of Sin, &c. and became stedfast and fixed in the Notion of Quakerism; of which I gave only a Hint as I passed thro' my Pilgrimage in that Particular; then our Teachers began to bethink themselves of the necessity of a Government in our Church, as well as our Neighbours; and if a Government, then a Governour; and this Government must be either Inward, or Outward: The Inward we had tried, and found defective; for the Disciple pretended he was enlightned, as well as the Apostle; and he thought he had as much right to follow his *Guide*, i. e. his *Light within*; as to follow and obey the Light in his Teacher, or the Light in any Man.

Upon this, the Teachers met in Council at *London*, in the Month of *May* 1666, to settle this so necessary, as well as difficult Point; and many Arguments passed between the Clergy and Laity, between the Teachers and the Deputies. At last it was decided, That the Body should govern, and the Light in the particular should submit to the Body. But still this Body being without a Head, seemed like a Monster; so that there was a necessity to find a Head to clap upon this Body. Well, this Head must either be visible, or invisible; the latter it could not be, for then the least Hearer would plead his Light, his Guide, his Judge, his Leader; as the Teachers told them in the beginning, when they decoyed them over to them. So then it was resolved, it must be *George Fox*, he being the first, must become our Great Apostle; who, together with the Body, was to Govern from East to West, and from North to South. Since which time, it was in vain for any single Person to plead the Sufficiency of his Light, or the Authority of it, for to the Light in the Body was all Power in Heaven and Earth committed. (*a*)

(a) *Jos. Coal's Works*, p. 93.
(b) *A Brief Examinat. and State*, p. 3.

And to support this Glorious Cause, *W. Penn* (*b*) wrote a Book, wherein he affirmed, 'That it is a dangerous Principle, and pernicious 'to True Religion; and which is worse, it is the Root of *Ranterism*, 'to assert, That nothing is a Duty incumbent upon thee, but what 'thou art perswaded, [or convinced] is thy Duty, *&c*. This was Printed in 1681, and written by the same *W. Penn*, who in the Year 1673 wrote his Book stiled, *Quakerism a New Nick-Name for Old Christianity*; where he then judged it so far from *Ranterism*, to act as they were perswaded, that, *Pag*. 71. he saith, 'No Command 'in the *SCRIPTURE*, is any farther *OBLIGING* upon '*ANY* Man, than as he finds a *CONVICTION* upon his 'Conscience; otherwise Men (said Mr. *Penn*) should be engaged 'without, if not against Conviction; a thing unreasonable in a '*Man, &c*. Thus then it's plain, That with respect to the Commands of God recorded in the Holy Scriptures, Men are to be at liberty; they are to obey, if they be convinced or perswaded it's their Duty so to do; if not, they may by Mr. *Penn*'s Doctrine, be at liberty.

Burroughs Works, p. 47.

And so saith *Burrows*: 'That (says he) is no Command from God 'to me, what he commands to another; neither did any of the Saints 'that we read of in Scripture, act by the Command which was to 'another, not having the Command to themselves, *&c*. And if we read on in the same Page, we may find, that these Commands of God, thus rejected by the Quakers, unless they have them a-new, as the inspired Apostles and Prophets had, were Baptism, and other Ordinances.

And now let me return to see what things *Will. Penn* would have done and obey'd, Conviction, or no Conviction; and this will give us some Light into their *Mystery of Iniquity*; thus to reject the Commands of God, recorded in Scriptures, and teach that none need to obey them, unless convinced of the usefulness of them, as they have done these 40 Years. *GO TEACH ALL NATIONS, BAPTI-*

From Quakerism *to* Christianity.

BAPTIZING,&c. *DO THIS IN REMEMBRANCE OF ME, &c.* Matth. 28. 19, 20.
When you Pray, say, *FORGIVE US OUR TRESPASSES,* Luke 22.19,20.
AS WE FORGIVE, &c. Chap. 11. 4.

Well, I say let us hear what the Commands of the *Quakers* are, See also, *The* that whoever amongst them pleads for their Liberty, whether to obey, *Picture of Qua-* or not to obey, are *Ranters, Rebels,* and what not. See his *Brief kerism, drawn Examination,* &c. Pag. 11. 'And this I affirm, from the Understanding Part 1. Pag. 60, 'I have received of God, not only that the Enemy is at work to to 70. 'scatter the Minds of Friends by that loose Plea; What hast thou 'to do with me? Leave me to my Freedom, and to the Grace of God 'in my self, and the like. But this Proposition and Expression, as 'now understood and alledged, is a deviation from, and a perversion 'of the Ancient Principle of Truth. For this is the plain Conse- 'quence of this Plea; If any one shall say, I see no Evil in Paying 'Tythes to Hireling Priests, in that they are not claimed by Di- 'vine Right, but by the Civil Laws of the Land. I see no evil '(*saith another*) in marrying by the Priest, for he is but a Witness. 'I see no evil (*saith a third*) in declining a Publick Testimony in 'Suffering-Times, for I have *Christ's* and *Paul's* Example. I see no 'evil (*saith a fourth*) in respecting the Persons of Men; for what- 'ever others do, I intend a sincere notice, that I take of those I 'know. I see no evil (*saith a fifth*) in keeping my Shop shut, up- 'on the Worlds Holy-Days [Fast-Days,] for I would not willingly 'give Offence to my Neighbours, &c.

Reader, I have been the larger on this Quotation, because it may evidently appear, beyond all their Glossing, that like the Pharisees, their Forefathers, they make void the Commands of God, by exalting their own Traditions above them, saying, None are any further ob- liged to obey the Commands of God in the Holy Scripture, than they are convinced or perswaded by their *Light* to obey; but their own Commands, such as not paying Tythes, not marrying with a Priest, not putting off the Hat, not shutting up their Shop-Windows on Holy-Days, and Fast Days; this is highly Criminal, to plead their Liberty in these Things, is Ranterism and Rebellion.

To confirm this, *George Whitehead* said, in Answer to a Minister's Truth Defend-
Question, *i. e. Is the Moral Law, or Ten Commandments, a Rule to* ing the Qua-
the Christian's Life, or is it not? kers, &c. p.18.

I Answer, (says G. W.) *thou might as well ask, If the Moral Law* Quest. to Pro-
be a Rule to Christ? for the Christians Life and Rule is Christ, &c. fessors, &c.
meaning the *Light within.* And this is much like *Isaac Pening-* p. 27.
ton, who said, That the Name *JESUS* and *CHRIST,* belong to every Member, as *WELL* as to the Head; and if so, *Whitehead* is in
the right on't; they might as well indeed, carry the Ten Commandments to *Christ* as to the *Quakers:* For on their own Hypothesis,
there is as much reason, for the *Quakers* love to be equal with
Christ,

The Pilgrim's Progress,

p. 10. *Ibid.* Christ, if not above him. See *p.* 10. 'What is attributed to that 'Body, [meaning the Son of *Mary*,] we acknowledge, and give to 'that Body in its place, according as the Scripture attributeth it, 'which is THROUGH and BECAUSE of THAT which dwelt 'and acted IN IT, but that which sanctify'd and kept the Body

(a) Mark kept Christ's Body pure. 'pure, (a) and made all acceptable in him, was the Life, Holiness, 'and Righteousness of the Spirit; and the same THING which kept 'his Vessel pure, it is the same THING that cleanseth us; the va-'lue which the natural Flesh and Blood [of Christ] had, was from 'THAT, in its coming from THAT, in its acting in THAT, in its

p. 33. *Ibid.* 'suffering through THAT, *p.* 33. Now the Scriptures doth expres-'ly distinguish between CHRIST and the GARMENT which he 'wore; between HIM that came, and the BODY in which he came; 'between the SUBSTANCE which was VAILED, and the VAIL 'which VAILED it; there is plainly HE, and the BODY in which 'HE came; there was the OUTWARD VESSEL, and the INWARD 'LIFE: This we certainly know, and can never call the BODILY

(b) Viz. They can never call the Son of Mary Christ. 'GARMENT CHRIST, (b) but THAT which appeared and dwelt 'IN the BODY. Now if ye indeed know the CHRIST of God, tell 'us plainly what THAT is which appeared in the Body, whether 'THAT was not the Christ before IT took up the Body, after IT 'took up the Body, and for ever.

I am the larger on this Head, to shew first, *George Whitehead's* Pride, in saying, That the Commandments of God might as well be carried to *Christ* as the *Quakers*; next, that the *Christ* which the

Compare the last Quotation to G. W's. Sermon. *Quakers* own only, is the Light or Spirit which was in *Christ*, and is in them; lastly, that they can never call him that was born of the Blessed Virgin *Mary*, *Christ*, but a Vail or Garment, an outward Vessel, and the like: And for more of this tendency, I refer to *George Whitehead's* Sermon hereafter expressed, &c. Having by this time shewed, That the *Quakers* have rejected the Government and Guidance of the Light in the Particular to be sufficient, but that the Light in the Particular must vail to the Light in the Body, or Church. I am now come to set forth their Authority for it, which was the Sentence and Judgment of their Synod held at *London*, May 1666.

The Sentence of their London *Synod* 1666. *Contracted.*

First, 'We having a true discerning of the Working of that Spi-'rit, which under a Profession of Truth, leads into a Division from, 'or Exaltation above the BODY of Friends, who never Revolted

† Tis well they tacitly confess, it is not the Faith once delivered to the Saints. 'from their Principles, from the constant Practice of good ancient 'Friends, who are found in the Faith once delivered to US †. We 'do unanimously declare and testifie, That neither that Spirit, nor 'those that are joined to it, ought to have any Dominion, Office, or 'Rule, in the Church of God. *Secondly,*

From Quakerism *to* Christianity.

Secondly, 'We do declare and testifie, That the Spirit, and those who are joined to it, who stand not in Unity with the Ministry and Body of Friends, have not any true spiritual Right, nor Gospel Authority to be Judges in the Church, and of the Ministry, so as to condemn them or their Ministry; neither ought their Judgment any more to be regarded by Friends, than the Judgment of any other Opposers which are without; for of Right, the Elders and Members of the Church, ought to judge Matters and Things which differ, and their Judgment which is given, to stand good and valid amongst Friends. And we do further declare and testifie, That it is abominable Pride which goeth before Destruction, which so puffs up the mind of any PARTICULAR, that he will not admit of any Judgment to take place against him: FOR HE THAT IS NOT JUSTIFIED BY THE WITNESS OF GOD IN FRIENDS, IS CONDEMNED BY IT IN HIMSELF. *New Rome exactly.*

Thirdly, 'If any Difference arise in the Church, or amongst them that profess to be Members thereof, WE do declare and testifie, That the Church, with the Spirit of our Lord Jesus Christ, HAVE POWER, WITHOUT THE CONSENT OF SUCH WHO DISSENT FROM THEIR DOCTRINE AND PRACTICE, TO HEAR AND DETERMINE THE SAME. And if any pretend to be of us, and in case of Controversy, will not admit to be TRYED by the Church, (*i. e.* the Body,) nor SUBMIT to the JUDGMENT given by the Spirit of Truth in the Elders, and Members of the same, but kick against their Judgment, as only the Judgment of Man, WE testifie in the Name of the Lord, That if any Judgment so given be risen against, and denied by the Party condemned, then He or She ought to be rejected, as having erred from the Truth, and persisting therein presumptuously, are joined in ONE, with Heathens and Infidels. *All Property is now lost, unless there be Conformity and Submission, like the Star-Chamber, and High-Court of Justice, &c.*

George Whitehead	John Whitehead
Josiah Coale	Thomas Briggs
Stephen Crisp	James Parke
John Moone	Alexander Parker
Thomas Loe	Richard Farnsworth, &c.

Having by this time shewed, *First*, How our Teachers in order to bring us over to them, and to decoy us, told us, the *Light within* was a sufficient Guide, Teacher and Leader, even sufficient to lead to Salvation; yea, above Scriptures, above Fathers, above Councils, and above Churches: I have in the last instance, shewed the Fallacy of their so early, and smooth Pretences; and that from the beginning, they have been a false, perfidious, and treacherous Tribe of Deceivers, as ever the World produced. Well, now they appear plainly to be a

Body;

Body, and I having found who is the Head of this Body, namely *George Fox*, it will not be amiss to recite his Commandments; which whatever *Quaker* do not submit to, convinced or not convinced of the reasonableness of their Obedience, its now plainly seen what will befall them. I need not comment upon the recited Canon, it's barefac'd: I likewise shall recite the Ten Commandments of *Moses*, which the *Quakers* slight and reject, as not to be read in their Meetings, not to be taught their Children; nay, so proud is G. *Whitehead*, that he tells you as above, The *Jews* might as well have carried them to Christ in the days of his Flesh, *Viz.* the Ten Commandments for him to learn, observe, and obey them, as for the Christians to carry them to the *Quakers* to learn them, observe and obey them: † For saith he, What is spoken by the Spirit of Truth in any, is of as great Authority as the Bible and Chapters are, and greater. This is the Tenure and Purport of his Doctrine; and I do affirm, it's right *Quakerism*: For *Edward Burrough* said, † That was no command from God to me, what he commands to another: And *W. Penn* confirms the whole Saying, † 'No Command in Scri-'ptures is any further obliging upon ANY Man, than as he finds a 'Conviction upon his Conscience, otherwise Men should be engaged 'without, if not against Conviction; a thing unreasonable in a 'Man, *&c.*

But for their poor infatuated Disciples to plead, whether to conform or not, whether to obey or not, the Commands of *George Fox*, *i.e.* not paying Tythes, not to be Married with a Priest, not to put off the Hat, not to open their Shops on Feasts or Fast-Days; I say, to plead to be left to their Freedom herein, and the Grace of God in their Hearts; Oh! no: Says *W. Penn*, This is a dangerous Principle, this is a pernicious Plea, this is perfect Ranterism. What! to have Liberty, whether to obey the Commands of the Body given out by the Head thereof? This is wicked indeed, as by their Yearly Epistle above recited is plain: However, I shall recite both the Commands of *Moses*, and the Commands of *Fox*, in hopes, some of the Hearers at last, may adhere to Scripture Commands, and reject the *Quakers* Unscriptural Traditions, whereby they have endeavoured to make the Commands of God of none effect, *viz.*

Marginal notes:
Truth defending the Quakers, &c. p. 18.
† *Burrough's* Works, p. 47.
† *Quakerism* a new Nickname for old, &c. p. 71.

The Commandments of God by his Servant Moses, somewhat Abbreviated, referring to Exod. XX.	The Commandments of G. Fox, the Quakers second Moses, somewhat Abbreviated, and taken out of several of his Books.
J. Thou shalt have no other Gods but me.	I. Thou shalt not pay Tythes to the covetous Priests nor to the Anti-christian Improprietors.
	II.

From Quakerism to Christianity.

II. Thou shalt not make to thy self any Graven Image, or the Likeness of any thing that is in Heaven above, &c.

III. Thou shalt not take the Name of the Lord thy God in vain, for the Lord will not hold them Guiltless that taketh his Name in vain.

IV. Remember thou keep holy the Seventh Day, for it is the Sabbath of the Lord thy God; in it, thou shalt do no manner of Work, thou, nor thy Son, nor thy Daughter, thy Man-servant, nor thy Maid-servant, &c.

V. Honour thy Father and thy Mother, that thy Days may be long in the Land which the Lord thy God shall give thee.

VI. Thou shalt not Kill.

VII. Thou shalt not commit Adultery.

VIII. Thou shalt not Steal.

IX. Thou shalt not bear false Witness against thy Neighbour.

X. Thou shalt not covet thy Neighbour's House, thou shalt

II. Thou shalt not Marry by, or with a Priest.

III. Thou shalt not put off thy Hat in respect to thy Superiors.

IV. Thou shalt not shut up thy Shop on the World's Holy-Days, Fast-Days, &c. at the command of the Worldly Magistrates.

V. Thou shalt not pay towards the Repair of Parish-Churches.

VI. Thou shalt not pay towards the Trained-Bands, nor carry Guns in thy Ship.

VII. Thou shalt not wear Lace, nor Ribbons, nor Skimming-dish Hats, nor short Aprons, nor Slits on your Wastecoats, nor long Scarfs like flying Colours, nor unnecessary Buttons.

VIII. You shall have a Womans Meeting distinct from the Men, once a Month at the County-Town, about Ten a Clock, to get a little Stock.

IX. Thou shalt call the Days of the Week, First, Second, Third and Fourth Day, &c. and the Months, First, Second, and Third Month, &c.

X. I charge you all in the presence of the Lord God, That you shalt not covet thy Neighbour's Wife, nor his Manservant, nor his Ox, nor his Ass, nor any thing that is his, &c.

Exodus XX.

Verse 18. *And all the People saw the Thunderings and the Lightnings, and the Noise of the Trumpet, and the Mountain smoaking.* Verse 19. *And they said unto* Moses, *speak thou with us, and we will hear: but let not God speak with us, lest we die.*

you judge not one another, *i. e.* those that be in the Unity of the Ministry, and Elders in the Church, lest you fall into the Condemnation of the Monthly, Quarterly, Six Weeks, Second Day, or Yearly Meeting. *Amen.*

G. Fox's *Tryal at* Lancaster *Assizes,* p. 21.

'The thundering Voice An-
'swered, I have glorified thee,
'and will glorifie thee again;
'and I was so filled full of Glo-
'ry, that my Head and Ears was
'filled full of it; that when the
'Trumpets sounded, and the
'Judges came up again, they all
'appeared as dead Men under
'me.

I think it now necessary to insert two Passages out of two of the *Quakers* most learned Teachers Books; the one, to deter their Hearers from adhering to the Commands of *Moses*; the other, to confirm them in the belief of G. Fox's, *viz.*

The Quakers Refuge fixed, &c. p. 17.
'Whether the first Pen man of the Scriptures, was *Moses* or
'*Hermes*? Or, Whether both these, or not one? Or, Whether
'there are not many Words contained in the Scriptures, which were
'not spoken by Inspiration of the Holy Spirit? Whether some Words
'were not spoken by the Grand Imposture, some by wicked Men,
'some by wise Men ill apply'd, some by good Men ill expressed, some
'by false Prophets, and yet true, some by true Prophets, and yet
'false? This being suggested by *Robert Ruckhill*, an Eminent and Learned Man; I cannot blame his Hearers, who believe that he wrote by the Eternal Spirit; nor that they lay aside the Commands of God by *Moses*, and receive the Commands of G. *Fox*; at least not so much as I blame their Teachers. For if I did question whether *Moses* or *Hermes* were the first Pen-Man of the Holy Scriptures; or whether both of them had a Hand in it, or neither of both was concerned in the writing thereof; if I question'd the truth of what the true Prophets of the Lord said, and believ'd, that what the false Prophets said, were true; if I thought, that what good Men said, was ill expressed, and so insignificant, as hereby is suggested, truly, I should give as little heed to them as the *Quakers* do, and be ready with *George Fox* himself, to call them Death, Dust, and Serpents Meat.

From **Quakerism** *to* **Christianity.**

Meat †. But I thank God, I have been better taught, even from my Childhood: For, tho' by the Dissimulation of these Seducers, I was carried away into great Errours; yet the love of the Scriptures ever remained with me.

† See News coming up out of the North, p. 14.

The next Passage shall be from their Learned *Barclay*; 'It is no ways inconsistent with this sound and unerring Principle, to affirm, 'That the Judgment of a certain Person, or Persons, in certain Cases, 'is INFALLIBLE; or for a certain Person, or Persons, to give a 'positive Judgment, and pronounce it as Obligatory upon others, be-'cause the Foundations and Ground thereof IS; NOT because they 'are Infallible, but because in these things, and at that time, they 'were led by the Infallible Spirit.

The Anarchy of the Ranters, &c. p. 67. For more of this Quaker-Popery,see the Picture of Quakerism drawn to the Life, &c. p. 8. to 16.

By which 'tis plain, that as *Ruckhill* in the forecited Passage, render the Scriptures Uncertain, Fallible, and of no Authority; so does *Barclay* render *Quakerism* infallible Certain, and their Commands and Injunctions Obligatory upon others: And why forsooth? Why, because at such times as the *Quakers* thus Pronounce, thus Write, thus give out their Mandates, Commandments and Precepts, they (says *Barclay*,) are led thereunto by the Infallible Spirit.

Some Inferences from the Fourth Chapter.

IS it so then, that the tendency of the *Quakers* Doctrine is to undervalue the Holy Scriptures, to rob them of their Divine Authority, and thereby to exalt their own Horn? Let this then be a caution to their Hearers, to examine the Quotations, which I bring to prove my Assertions; and if they find it so, (as that they may; for I have ever been willing, and still am, to produce Book and Page, to prove matter of Fact,) then let them carry the said Books to their Teachers, to condemn and censure, as Heretical, and tending to overturn the Christian Religion; and if not, let them if they be wise, turn their Backs upon them, forsake their Errours, and imbrace the Christian Faith; so shall the end of all my Labour and Pains be Answered; but if they (after all the Pains my self and others have taken,) will still shut their Eyes, and stop their Ears, my Reward will be with me, and they shall bear their own Burthen in the Day of the Lord.

D 2 CHAP.

CHAP. V.

Giveth many Reasons, both Negative and Affirmative, That George Fox took himself to be a Second Moses; and that the Heads of the Quakers attributed to him Divine Honour, as Head of their Church, and Lawgiver to it.

TO come to a right Understanding of this, I shall first insert an Objection raised by *W. Rogers*, † [and by him taken out of a Manuscript, with Names to it:] next *George Fox*'s Answer; and then proceed to other particular Reasons and Demonstrations.

† The Christian Quaker distinguished, &c. Part I. p. 9.

Object. 'Tis true, Friends in the beginning were turned to the
'Light in their own Consciences, as their Guide; but when it plea-
'sed the Lord, to gather so great a Number into the Knowledge and
'Belief of the Truth, then the Heavenly Motion came upon *George*
'*Fox*, as the Lord's Anointed and Chosen, having the care of the
'Churches, as being the great Apostle of Christ Jesus; and as one,
'whom the Lord had ordained to be in that place, amongst the Chil-
'dren of Light in this our Day, as *Moses* was amongst the Children
'of *Israel* in his Day, to set forth Methods and Forms of Church-
'Government, and to establish Monthly and Quarterly Meetings of
'Men, and Women distinct from the Men; and these Meetings
'since, are called the Church, whose Counsel, Advice, and Judgment,
'is to be submitted unto by every one who profess himself a Member
'of Christ's Church; and that we ought to believe as the Church be-
'lieves, as *G. Whitehead* teacheth, † *viz.* I affirm, that the true
'Church is in the true Faith that is in God, and we must believe thus
'as the true Church believes, or else it were but both a Folly and Hy-
'pocrisy to profess our selves Members thereof.

†*G. Whitehead*'s Book, the Apost. Incendiary, &c. p. 16.

This Objection *W. Rogers* made, from the strength of divers Arguments he found in the Manuscript, from the Words and Writings of divers Persons, whose Names he did forbear to mention; but for the clearing up this Point, Whether *G. Fox* looked upon himself the Second *Moses*, the great Prophet and Apostle, see his Answer to *W. Rogers* †.

† The Christian Quak. distinguished from the Apost. and Innovator, in five Parts. See Part 4. p. 83.

George Fox's ANSWER.

'*William Rogers*, thou say'st, There is a Spirit risen at this day,
'that gives many occasion to be jealous, that I am look'd upon by
'some, as that Prophet which *Moses* testify'd of, that God would
'raise up, † but who they are thou hast not mention'd. And thou
'say'st, Christ is that Prophet that is to be heard, &c. and he is the
'only

† Deut. 18. 15.

From Quakerism to Christianity.

'only Lawgiver, and no outward Man †. Then is not this Prophet to be in Man, to give forth his Law, which comes after *Moses*? But I cannot deny that Prophet which *Moses* spake of, to be raised up; for I know, that it is he that is opposed, and his Law too, by many Talkers of him; and the Light of his Glorious Gospel, and the Order of it; and what I am, I am by the Grace and Love of God; and will not deny † the Prophet which came after *Moses*, nor the Election, before the World began, tho' all turn into the Jealousies in which they were before they were convinced; for I believe, few of them that does oppose, knows this Prophet that comes after *Moses*, tho' they may speak of him in Words; of which Prophet I am not ashamed.

† *So W. Rogers said; now mark his long-sided Answer.*

† *Deny, no; there was no body desired that: But if he had not owned himself to be that Prophet, he ought to have been plain, and denied himself to be that Prophet, as John did. I am not the Christ, said John, Joh. 1. 20.*

Reader, the Text and Context being duly consider'd, I mean *W. Roger's* Objection, touching the common Jealousies which was amongst us at that Day, besides the Letters in the said Manuscript, &c. I say, that duly consider'd on the one hand, and G. Fox's Answer on the other hand, which was so far from denying himself to be that Prophet which *Moses* prophesyed of, *Deut.* 18. 15. and St. *Steven* testified of, *Acts* 7. 37. and St. *Peter*, *Acts* 3. 23. and St. *John* the Evangelists, *John* 1. 45. These, and many others, gave witness to the fulfilling of the Prophesy of *Moses*, in sending the promised *Messiah*; I say, G. Fox's Answer was so far from denying himself to be that Prophet which *Moses* Prophesied of, that it confirmed us in that Day; and since, much more, that he did not deny, but rather owned the Charge.

But to strengthen my Argument, I shall give some small hints, (and but name them, having been heretofore more large,) first, What he said of himself; next, What his Followers said of him.

First, (a) Written from the Mouth of the Lord, from one who is naked, and stands naked before the Lord, cloathed with Righteousness, whose *NAME* is *NOT* known in the World, risen up out of the *North*, which was Prophesied of, (b).

Secondly, My Name is covered from the World, and the World knows not *ME*, nor *MY NAME*, (c).

Thirdly, HE that HATH the same Spirit that raised Jesus from the dead, is *EQUAL* with God, (d.)

Fourthtbly, All Languages are to me no more than Dust, who was before Languages were, (e).

Fifibly,

(a) *News coming up, p. 1.*
(b) *This is News indeed; What Prophet prophesied of Fox's Rising in the North?*
(c) *Several Petitions Answered, p. 30.*
(d) *Saul's errand to Damascus, p. 8.*
(e) *The Battle-door, &c. Introd.*

Fifthly, And the Thundering Voice Answered, I have Glorified thee, and will Glorifie thee again; and I was filled so full of Glory, that my Head and Ears was filled full of it, &c. (*f*)

(*f*) G. Fox's Tryal at Lan-caster, p. 21.

Reader, here was fulness of Glory, if his Head and Ears was so filled, &c. However, 'tis plain, it alludes to *John* 12. 18, 16, 14. and 17. 1. For nothing would please him, but to be equal, if not above Christ, as One hundred instances might be given.

Next, I may just name some few of those High Titles and Divine Attributes, which his Disciples and Followers (Men of greatest Note amongst them,) gave him, which are only due to Christ, who was the Prophet *Moses* Prophesied of, and not the subtle *Fox*, the doting *Quakers* so much admire and idolize.

First, † *George Fox*, the Father of many Nations, who's Being and Habitation is in the Power of the Highest, in which thou Rules and Governs in Righteousness, and thy Kingdom is established in Peace, and the Increase thereof is without end.

† *Judas* and the *Jews*, p. 44.

Secondly, † Dear and Precious one, in whom my Life is bound up, and my Strength in thee stand; by thy Breathings I am nourished, by thee my Strength is renewed; I cannot Reign but in thy Presence and Power; Glory unto thee Holy One † for ever.

† *John Audland's* Letter to *George Fox*.
† Holy *George*.

Thirdly, † *George Fox* (said *John Blaikling*,) is blessed with Honour above many Brethren, and thousands will stand by him in a Heavenly Record, that his Life Reigns, and is Spotless; whose eternal Honour and blessed Renown shall remain, yea, his Presence; and the Dropping of his tender Words in the Lord's Love, was my Souls Nourishment.

† The Christian disting. Part 5. p. 77.

Fourthly, † *George Fox*, a Prophet indeed; it was said of Christ, that he was in the World, and the World was made by him, and the World knew him not. SO it may be said of this Prophet G. *Fox*.

† The Quakers Challenge, p. 6.

Fifthly, To confirm all this, *William Mead* now living, when he gave *William Harris* one of *George Fox's* Journals, he said to him, Here *W. Harris*, I will give thee one of *George Fox's* Journals, it is a very good Book, yea, better than the Bible.

Object. 1. But some may say, this is only *W. Mead's* Judgment; surely, the *Quakers* do not hold, that either their Books, or *Fox's* Journal, is better, or of greater Authority than the Bible; for the

Fathers

From **Quakerism** *to* **Christianity.**

Fathers and Councils all submitted to the Test of Holy Scripture, as the Word of God.

Answ. To this I Answer, That *W. Mead* is a knowing Man; I will not say a wise Man, unless in that one Action of his, whereby he vigorously opposed *W. Penn*, and endeavoured to exclude him out of their Ministry, when he was proclaimed a Traytor to his Country, for being charg'd to be in the Plot with the Lord *Preston*, and others, and was therefore forced to hide many Months; [and for which, his Preface to *Fox*'s Journal, was not admitted to be bound up with the Journal, but waited upon it like a poor Lacquey with its Blue Livery;] I say, this Action of his excepted, I will not say he was a wise Man; yet, as I said, he is a knowing Man, and spake the Heart of *Quakerism*, in saying, *George Fox*'s Journal is better than the Bible.

First, As you have heard, 'tis question'd by the *Quakers,* Whether *Moses* or *Hermes* was the first Pen-man of the Scripture; indeed, Whether either or neither of them, †. † The *Quakers* Refuge fixed, &c. p. 17.

But as for what *George Fox* and Friends write, it is from and by the Motion of God's Eternal Spirit, and avouched so to be by a General Council of the Yearly Meeting †: And what any of our Friends speak from the Spirit of Truth, is of greater Authority than the Bible and Chapters are, †. Now, who can blame *W. Mead* on the *Quakers* Principles? Is not a certainty better than an uncertainty? † Held at *London*, May 1695. † Truth defending the Quakers, &c. p. 7. *Ibid.* p. 18.

Secondly, The Scriptures lay many Obligations upon us; it teacheth us the observation of the Ten Commandments, the Lord's Prayer, the Apostles Creed, Baptism, and the Lord's Supper, which the Journal do's not at all teach, nor inforce the Belief of; only to listen, adhere, and hearken to the *Light within,* and to obey its Dictates *. Therefore, as the Journal is most certain, so it is most easie, and therefore the best Book, and of most Authority, and on the *Quakers* Hypothesis, confirm all those Particulars above quoted. * Matth. 22. 21. Titus 3. 1. Rom. 13. 1, 2. 3. 1 Pet. 2. 13, 14, 17. See also *Tindal's* Works, *Obedience to a Christian Man,* &c. p. 111.

Thirdly, The Scripture teacheth to obey Magistrates as the higher Power, and that we should submit our selves to every Ordinance of Man for the Lord's sake, *.

But the Journal † (and our Friends Books) teach both by Precept and Example, That the *Light* in every Man is the higher Power, to whom all must submit and obey; for to it, all Power in Heaven and Earth is committed, †; and that this *Light* is one, in the Male and in the Female; but to a proud, heady, high-minded Man, there is no Honour due, tho' he be in a place to Rule, †. And if so, who can say, that *W. Mead* spake unadvisedly, in saying, The Journal of *Fox* is better than the Scriptures of the Prophets and Apostles? I think him a right *Quaker*, a knowing Man, and one that loves a certainty better than an uncertainty. † *Journal,* p. 40. to 400. † *Jos. Coal's* Works, p. 93. † *Smith's* Primmer, p. 43.

Fourthly, The Scriptures teach, That Women should obey their Husbands;

*Gen. 3. 16.
Numb. 30. to the end.
1 Cor. 11. 8.
1 Pet. 3. 1.
Titus 2. 5.
Colof. 3. 18.
Ephef. 5. 22.
* Smith's Primer, p. 13.
The Journal. p. 50. to 450.
† The Contem. Apoftate, &c. p. 5.
See their Marriage Certificate.

Husbands; yea, that they Reverence them, and live in Subjection to them as their Head, * quoting *Sarah* as an Example.

But the Journal teaches, That the *Light* is the higher Power, that it is one in the Male and in the Female, and 'tis the *Light* in each that is to be obeyed; for to that, all Power in Heaven and Earth is committed,* and that there is to be no respect of Persons; and if the Wife conceive her Husband to be gone from the *Light*, and the Guidance of it, and she be moved to rebel against her Husband, betray his Secrets to his Adversaries, yea, to give publick Testimony against him, she does well, and shall have praise of the same, †: And for this Reason, the *Quakers* do not put in, or make the Woman promise by their Certificate, to obey their Husbands; which, as it is contrary to the Tenure of the whole Book of God, both the Old and New Testament, so 'tis agreeable to G. *Fox*'s Journal, and their antient Testimony.

Fifthly, In a word, the Scriptures teach, That Children should obey their Parents, and Honour their Father and Mother, that Servants should obey their Masters, that Subjects should submit to their Governours, and obey Magistrates, that Christians should obey their Pastors, who are over them in the Lord, who watch for their Souls, as those that must give an account.

Journal, p. 20. to 320.

But the Journal teaches the contrary, both by Precept upon Precept, as also by the Practice of their great Apostle G. *Fox*, who not only broke the Laws in disturbing the Ministers in their Churches, but taught so to do; not only refused to pay Tythes, but taught so to do; not only slighted the Magistrates Command, (who oftentimes commanded a strict Fast to be kept,) but taught his Followers so to do: Nay, lately one *Thomas Mash* an antient *Quaker*, living at *Newberry* in *Berkshire*, was moved by his *Light within*, to open his Shop-Windows on the Lord's Day, as on Market-Days, and set out his Goods to Sale; this the Journal justifies,†; this *Whitehead* justifies, *: Nay,

† Journal, p. 200. to the end.
* Truth defending the Quakers, p. 18.
Fox's great Myft. &c. p. 77.
† Journal, p. 278.

Theft by *Fox* is likewise justified, who said, And as for any being moving the Lord, [meaning their *Light within*.] to take away your Hour-Glass from you, *BY THE ETERNAL POWER IT IS OWNED*, &c. Nay, their idolized Apostle, not only disregarded the Magistrates and their Laws, but declared in plain and significant Words, That he neither heeded, nor valued a Cart load of their Warrants, &c. †

Object. 2. But some Men will say, How then shall we reconcile the Doctrine of *W. Mead* and *G. Whitehead?* Mr. *Mead* saith, That G. *Fox*'s Journal is a better Book than the Bible; and G. *Whitehead* saith, † We prefer the Holy Scriptures above all other Books extant in the World.

† The Country Convert, &c. p. 16.

To which I Answer: Very well; for *p.* 72. G. *Whitehead* thus
saith,

faith, *viz*. *I MAY SEE CAUSE OTHERWISE TO WORD THE MATTER, AND YET OUR INTENTIONS BE THE SAME*, &c. Very well; now to make it appear, that *G. Whitehead* means one and the same thing that *William Mead* meaned, read his little Book, † *i. e. That which is spoken from the Spirit of Truth in ANY, is of as great AUTHORITY as the SCRIPTURES and CHAPTERS are, and GREATER:* And on the Title Page thus, *viz*. *WRITTEN FROM THE SPIRIT OF TRUTH*, in *G. Whitehead*, and *G. Fox* the Younger: Now, if this little Pamphlet in *Octavo* of 70 Pages, be of greater Authority than the Scriptures and Chapters are, how much more *G. Fox*'s Journal in *Folio*, of near 700 Pages? For that which is best, is of most Authority, generally speaking; and that which is of most Authority, is the best. Thus then is the Journal of *Fox*'s better, in the *Quakers* Esteem, than the Bible; and thus does *Whitehead* mean, even as Mr. *Mead* spoke.

<small>p. 72. ibid.</small>

<small>† *Truth Defending the Quakers*, &c. p. 7.</small>

Object. But some will say, How then shall we know a *Quaker*, if not by the import of his Words?

<small>Object. 3.</small>

I Answer, 'tis impossible to know them rightly, as it ever was for the Protestants to know the Jesuites; and therefore, you ought to do as the Protestants did, *TO DISTRUST EVERY THING THEY SAY*,†: For as the *Quakers* stand on the same Bottom, and are found in the same Steps, with the same Equivocations, Reserves and Double-meanings; and the same pretences to Miracles, Visions, Revelations, Perfection and Infallibility; they ought to have the same Answer, *viz*. To distrust them in all they say, until they retract Sentence, and condemn one sort of their Books; and this is highly reasonable on their part, if they would be taken to be at all, serious, sincere and honest: For many of their Hearers of the honest sort, begin to think *G. Whitehead* little better than a Jesuite already, he hath been so false in Fact, such a Glosser and Defender of every Errour the *Quakers* hold. †I have a Letter by me, which my Cousin *Ann Docwra*, Widow of *Cambridge*, sent me, dated 26th of 12th Month, 1682. *viz*. 'G. *Whitehead* have sent one of his Books for 'me to read, and there is the old Money Story in it, with I know not 'what besides: I was asked by an honest Friend, if he was not a '-Jesuite? I answered, nay, it is not solid enough for them to own, 'especially when they write to a solid People; there is pretty much 'airy conceited Stuff in it. ANN DOCWRA.

<small>Answer.</small>

<small>† *See the Book Entituled, The Missionary's Arts*, p. 32. printed 1688.</small>

<small>† *Ann Docwra* of *Cambridge*, her Letter, Dated 16th.12th Month, 1682.</small>

Thus it appears, how long the honest sort of *Quakers* have taken G. *W*. to be little better than a Jesuite, and my Cousin *Docwra* was of the same mind too, else she would not have given me her honest Friend's Judgment; only indeed, she is thus far of my mind, That Book was not solid enough; the Jesuites are more cunning than G. *Whitehead* then was, but he is come on finely since; for of late, he is grown so expert, as he can Vindicate or Excuse any

E Blasphemy,

Blasphemy, Idolatry, contempt of the Scriptures, contempt of the Magistrates, contempt of the Ministry, contempt on the Person and Sufferings of Christ; yea, and undervalue his precious Blood too: And how contrary soever their Sayings are to each other, yet they mean all one thing, referring to their Beginning. I have in my former Books shewed, how their Books are of two sorts, their Meetings of two sorts, their Doctrine of two sorts, carrying two Faces in all they do or say; and yet *Whitehead* can tell you, they mean all one thing. One Example more I may give, and so shall conclude this Chapter.

I find a Recital of a Letter, writ by *Solomon Eccles* to *Robert Porter*, in a Book of *William Burnet*'s, † *viz.* 'Robert Porter, take heed
'of Belying the Innocent; for I hear thou hast reported to a Friend of
'mine, that I should say, That the Blood of Christ is no more than
'the Blood of another Man; I never spoke it, but do very highly
'esteem of the Blood of Christ to be more excellent, living, holy and
'precious, than is able to be uttered by the Tongues of Men and An-
'gels; I *MEAN*, the Blood which was offered up in ‡ the Eternal
'Spirit, Heb. 9. 14. But the Blood that was forced out of him by
'the Soldiers after he was dead, who before that, bowed his Head
'to the Father, and gave up the Ghost; but thou say'st, that was
'the Blood of the New Covenant, which was shed after he was
'dead; which *I DO DENY.* Yet I did say, That was *NO* more
'*THAN* the *BLOOD* of another *SAINT:* These are my Words
'which thou art wresting, to thy own Destruction. I did [also] say,
'That the Baptists, Independants, Presbyterians and Pope, are all of
'one Ground; and none of you understand the Blood of Jesus Christ,
'no more than a Brute Beast: Therefore repent, for God will soon
'overthrow your Faith, and your imputative Righteousness too,
'for the imputation of Christ's Righteousness which he did at *Jeru-*
'*salem,* and without the Gates: The Pope, the Episcopal, the Pres-
'byterian, Independents and Baptists, shall fare all alike, and shall
'sit down in Sorrow, short of the Eternal Rest: But the true impu-
'tative Righteousness of Christ we own, but it is hid from you all,
'till the Lord open an Eye *WITHIN YOU,* &c.

Now comes *G. Whitehead* with his usual Paint, to cover, palliate, and excuse his Brother *Eccles,* saying, † 'Now whereas *Sol. Eccles,*
'in *p.* 41. is accused of little less than Blasphemy, about a Letter
'chiefly, of a Passage concerning the Blood, in these Words, *viz.*
'The Blood that was forced out of him by the Soldiers after he was
'dead, who before that bowed his Head to the Father, and gave up
'the Ghost; I did say, *THAT WAS NO MORE THAN THE*
'*BLOOD OF ANOTHER SAINT.* Now to these Words, *NO*
'*MORE THAN THE BLOOD OF ANOTHER SAINT,* his
'*INTENT WAS,* as to Papists, and you whose Minds are Carnal,
'who

† Entituled, *The Capital Principles of the Quakers,* p. 41. *printed* 1668.

‡ *Perversion; it's offered up, thro' the Eternal Spirit,* Heb. 9. 14.

† *See his Book,* i. e. *the Light and Life of Christ within,* &c. *Printed* 1668.

'who oppose the *Light within*, and ALSO SIMPLY as to the ES-
'SENCE of the BLOOD, &c.

Thus much by way of G. *Whitehead*'s Interpretation of *Solomon*'s Words and Meaning, which I take to be a fair Confession of the Charge of Blasphemy, exhibited by Mr. *Burnet* : But to confirm the the Reader, that the *Quakers* are defective in the Faith of the Christians in general, I will shew another Passage of the same Kind; thereby, shewing the *Quakers* Harmony about the Body of Christ, from another of their Eminent Authors, † *viz.* 'So, now this Christ was 'before the World began, and was a Seed † before any Name was 'given to it, who in process of time, was born of a Virgin; but none 'knows him born, or ever shall, but of a Virgin; (he that hath Ears, 'let him hear,) be thou [Man] but the Virgin, the Power of the 'most High shall over-shadow thee; and that HOLY THING which 'shall be born of thee, shall be called the Son of God; and saith 'Christ, a [Body] hast [thou] prepared for [me;] mark the distin-'ction, [thou] me] and [a Body,] this me that spake in the Body, 'was the Christ. They [his Disciples] loved his Person for the 'sake of the Frame and Quality of the Spirit that dwelt in Him ; 'or else, what was his Person to them, more than another Person? But 'for that that dwelt in him, they loved him; let none mistake, I do 'not slight it, nor the Person of any of his Brethren or Children, 'as they are prepared to do the Will of their Father, (*a*) &c.

† *W. Bayly's Works, p. 291, 292, 300, 307.*
† *i. e. A Principle within.*

(*a*) *As the Blood of Christ, so the Body of Christ, hath by their Doctrine no preference above the Body and Blood of another Saint.*

And hereupon, they do not only deny Christ, even the Lord that bought them, as in my Book, *Quakerism withering, and Christianity reviving*, &c. I have shewed beyond all their Glossing; but also, how they thereby take occasion to magnifie THEMSELVES, their OWN Blood, their OWN Sufferings, as I shall yet briefly shew: 'For saith *Isaac Pennington*, (*b*) The Name Jesus and Christ belong 'to the whole Body, and every Member in the Body as well as to 'the Head: Again, (*c*) saith *Josiah Coale*, his (*Edward Burrough*'s) 'Blood will be upon you as the Blood of 1000 Men : Again, saith '*Thomas Speed*, (*d*) Do not rashly draw your Swords against those 'harmless ones, [*i. e.* Quakers,] whom your bloody Teachers cloath 'and represent to you in the ugly Garb of Blasphemers; remember, 'that the Son of God who suffered at *Jerusalem*, was not Crucified 'by the strict Religious, as an innocent or just Man, but as a Blas-'phemer; be not [therefore] prevailed with, to release *Barabbas*, '(*e*) and give over Jesus to be Crucified, to gratifie the murtherous 'Appetite either of the Priests or the Multitude, considering, that 'tho' you may with *Pilate*, wash your Hands, (and to those Eyes 'that are dazled with Fury against Innocent Jesus;) [*i. e.* the Qua-'kers] appear clear from his Blood; yet, before the pure Eyes of the 'Lord, will the condemning Stain thereof be found upon YOU so 'fresh, THAT YOU WILL BY NO MEANS BE THENCE CLEANSED.

(*b*) *A Question to Professors, &c. p. 20, 27.*
( ) *Jos. Coal's Epistle to E. Burrough's Works, &c.*
(*d*) *See the Guilty-covered Clergy-Man, &c p. 16, 17.*
(*e*) *For the Name Jesus belonged to the Believing Quakers, as well as to Christ the Head; and so the whole Parallel holds good.*

'CLEANSED, BUT BY THE SAME BLOOD WHICH YOU SO
'CRUELLY SHED: Again, see *Burrough*'s Works, p. 273. 'The
'suffering of the People of God [call'd *Quakers*,] in this Age, is a
'GREATER Suffering, and MORE unjust than in the Days of
'CHRIST, or of the APOSTLES, or in ANY time SINCE; what
'was done to CHRIST and the APOSTLES, was CHIEFLY done by
'a LAW, and in a GREAT part by the DUE EXECUTION of a
'LAW, &c.

Now to close up this Head, let us hear, what Father *Penn* says; for none of them all express themselves more full to the Point in hand, *viz.*

(*f*) *The Christian Quaker, and his Divine Testimony,* &c. p. 107.
(*g*) *Within.*

'To conclude, We, (*f*) tho' this general Victory was obtained, and 'Holy Priviledges therewith, and that the Holy Body was not in-'strumentally without a share thereof; yet, that the efficient and 'chiefest Cause was, the Light and Life, (*g*) p. 102. so that the in-'visible Life was the Root and Fountain of all, which is sometimes 'ascribed in the Scriptures to the Body, by that common Figure or 'way of speaking amongst Men; the thing containing, which is the 'Body, for the thing contained, which is the Life, p. 209. Never-'theless, not to the Body, but to that holy Light and Life therein,

(*h*) *As in the Quaker's Body,* &c.

'(*h*) is chiefly ascribed the Salvation; and to the Body however ex-'cellent, but instrumentally, *p.* 97, 98. The Serpent is a Spirit; 'now nothing can bruise the Head of the Serpent, but something

(*i*) *Mark here, Christ the promised Seed,* Gen. 3. 14. *the Son of David, of Mary, is plainly denyed to be the Christ of God.*

'that is Spiritual; but if that BODY of CHRIST were the SEED, '(*i*) then could he not Bruise the Serpent's Head in all, because the 'the BODY of CHRIST is not so much as in any one; (*k*) and 'consequently, the Seed of the Promise is an Holy Principle of Light 'and Life, that being received into the HEART, bruiseth the Ser-'pent's Head; AND BECAUSE THE SEED WHICH CANNOT 'BE THAT BODY, IS CHRIST; as testifie the Scripture: The 'Seed is one, and that Seed is Christ. (*l*) They are false Ministers

(*k*) *Yes; by Faith.*
Read *Acts* 4. 10, 12.
Luke 2. 11.
(*l*) *Smith's Primer,* p. 8.
(*m*) *The Sword of the Lord drawn,* p. 5.
(*n*) *The People called Quakers cleared,* &c. p. 7.
(*o*) *Primitive Christianity,* &c. p. 53. *Printed* 1698.

'that Preach Christ without, and bid People believe in him, as he 'is in Heaven above: But they that are Christ's Ministers, preach 'Christ within. (*m*) Your imagined God beyond the Stars; and your 'carnal Christ is utterly denyed, that this Christ is God and Man in 'one Person, is a Lie, &c.

Reader, I have taken in enough, to shew the Marrow of the *Quakers* Divinity, and the Harmony of their antient Testimonies: And they tell you, in a late Print, (*n*) That God is the same, Truth is the same, his People the same, their Principles are the same, &c. And in another, (*o*) Our Principles are now no other than what they were, when we were first a People. So that, there needs no Comment; only for further satisfaction, I refer to my former Books, *New* Rome *unmask'd, and her Foundation shaken,* &c. *New* Rome *arraign'd, and out of her own Mouth condemned,* &c. *Quakerism Withering,*

From Quakerism *to* Christianity.

withering, and Christianity reviving, &c. *The Snake in the Grass,* &c. *Satan disrobed,* &c. *Primitive Heresie,* &c. And *George Keith's* Three *Narratives,* and Mr. *Crisp's Animadversions,* &c. to avoid repetition: Yet, least those Books may not come into some hands which this may, I thought it needful to give these brief Hints, for Information.

Object. 4. But still some may urge, What! Hath *W. Mead* no other Reason for his Saying, *Fox's* Journal was better than the Bible?

Answ. I do not grant, that he hath any good Reason that's far from me, neither do I know of any better; I know of some other, which with him may go far, which in brief, are,

First, George Fox's Miracles, which he writ in his own Name, like those of *Simon Magus,* and certain Vagabond *Jews,* Exorcists; (*p*) but these lying Wonders came too late, some 20, some 30 years after they were said to be done; no body knows where, nor when, nor who were cured, nor no Witness to attest the Truth thereof: Read the Margin for direction. [*Acts* 8.9, 10. cap. 19. 13. (*p*) *Journal,* p. 167, 170, 171, 103, 271, 28, 407, 258, 70, 370, 371, 373, 503.]

2*dly,* Because *Fox* pretended, that God sent a Trooper to him whilst Prisoner in the House of Correction, as he sent *Saul* to *Annanias,* (*q*). [(*q*) *Journal,* p. 45.]

3*dly,* Because he (*Fox*) pretended he had Visions, as had *Ezekiel,* (*r*). [(*r*) p. 69.]

4*thly,* For that *Fox* pretended, that the Keeper of the House of Correction came Trembling to him, as the Goaler did to *Paul* and *Silas,* (*s*). [(*s*) p. 37.]

5*thly,* That he saw the Heavens open, as St. *Stephen* did, (*t*). [(*t*) 47.]

6*thly,* That he spake like an Angel in *Beverly* Church, the wonderful things of God, (*u*). [(*u*) p. 55.]

7*thly,* That he was a Prophet like *Isaiah,* spake the Word, and it came to pass, (*w*). [(*w*) p. 67, 68.]

8*thly,* That he saw a Pool of Blood, and a Channel of Blood, in the Town of *Lichfield*; (*x*) when there was not a drop of Blood, much less a Channel or a Pool of Blood, &c. However, by these and the like lying Wonders, (*y*) the *Quakers,* like the deluded *Samaritans* of old, are made to believe with *W. Mead,* That the Journal of *Fox* is a better Book than the Bible; and, that *George Fox* as well as *Simon Magus,* was some great Man, even the Power of God; (*z*) and thereupon gave him Divine Attributes due only to Christ, which *Whitehead* their drudge, to help them at a dead lift, was forc'd to bring in his *Innuendo's,* to set forth the intents of *Coale, Eccles,* † &c. [(*x*) p. 53. (*y*) *As more large in the Picture of Quakerism,* Part 2d. (*z*) *See Journal, Third Index, under the Letter M.* † *Innocency against Envy,* &c. p. 18.]

CHAP.

CHAP. VI.

Shews George Whitehead, *&c. their Hypocrisie. Answereth an Objection,* Do not the Quakers *maintain their own Poor? Their Uncharity thereby discovered.*

Reader,

I Am now upon a fresh, yet a necessary Subject; for as the *Qua-ker*-Teachers have cry'd down all Protestant Ministers, as Covetous, lovers of filthy Lucre, and thereby raised their own Fame, as the Prophets of the Lord, called forth from their own Country, and from their Fathers Houses, from both Riches, Honours and Preferments, to come with their Lives in their Hands, for the good of Souls; this Noise I must confess, went a great way with me in my young Years, and I know it doth with many: And therefore, I think it needful to discover their deceit in this particular, as well as to shew, how far they maintain their own Poor; and, what they mean by those Words, THEIR OWN POOR; for as Hypocrisie is their *Misterium Maximum,* so it requires some time and Skill to unfold it; in order to which, I shall thus proceed:

Object. 1. But say some, G. *Whitehead* printed F. *Bugg* a conceited Fool, one that cannot write true English, † and also of little Credit; * likewise, that the Author of the *Snake in the Grass,* is a necessitous, malicious, expulsed Priest, one who writes for his Bread, a Villain, a venemous obnoxious sculking Vermin, *&c.* with abundance more of the like nature.

† *Judgment fixed,* &c. p. 233, 243. * *A sober Expost.* &c. p. 2. *Primitive Christianity continued,* &c. and G. W's *Letter to* G. Keith, *May* 3. 1698.

Answ. First, As to my self, tho' I had not that Learning, which I am satisfied my Parents once designed, yet I thank God and my Parents, for affording me both a competency of Learning and Judgment to deal with the *Quakers,* who are not over Learned; no, not *G. W.* when he came first amongst us; witness his Book, *Jacob found in a Desert Land,* &c. Printed 1656. which I am sure, is so Foreign from true School-Learning, that there is not in the whole Book, one Page good Grammar English, as well as some part meer Nonsence: Yet I will not call him Fool, nor yet nothing of a Scholar; for perhaps, he might be then entered in his *Accidence:* And I will also grant, that since that (having leisure enough, and lived with his Feet under other Mens Tables, whilst I was occupied in Trade and Worldly Business,) he has acquired a greater degree of Learning; yet not so much neither, as always to write true English, as in his Letter to Mr. *Archer,* is manifest; so that he might have pass'd by my want of Learning, *&c.*

2dly,

From Quakerism *to* Christianity.

2*dly*, As to his Reflection on my Credit, when I came first amongst the *Quakers*, I had sufficient to live upon, and to maintain my self in the rank I was brought up in; yea, to give, and not receive: At 16 Years old, I had by my Grandfather an Annuity given me of 6 *l.* *per Annum*, until I was 21 Years old, and then Thirty Pounds *per Annum*, besides what my Father gave me; and tho' I have met with many Losses, and that in divers Kinds, yet I thank God, who hath hitherto inabled me, to maintain my Post, and to defend my Faith and Christian Reputation, against the malicious Attempts of G. *Whitehead*, and his Confederates; besides, G. *Whitehead* might have forborn, since most of my Losses have been by the *Quakers*, having had eight or nine break in my Debt, some paying nothing, some paying 5 *s.* in the pound, some 2 *s.* 6 *d.* in the pound. † I will mention one more, namely *Tho. Plumstead*, [Brother to *Francis Plumstead*, at the *Cross-Saws* in the *Minories, London*,] and still an Eminent *Quaker* living in *Ireland*, but no Conscience he makes of paying me; and that it may appear true, I will recite the Note I have still under his Hand, *viz.*

† Viz. *Enoch Barwick* about two Years since, for *18 l.* I had but 4*s* *s.*

> *May* 12. 1696. *Reckon'd with* Francis Bugg *of* Milden-Hall, *and all Accounts being then cleared, there rests due to* Francis Bugg *Sixteen Pounds* ; *Four Pounds whereof is to be paid to him six Months after the Date hereof, and the Twelve Pounds remainder, not exceeding Four Years. Witness my Hand the Day abovesaid,*
>
> Tho. Plumstead.

However, he never had the Honesty nor Conscience to pay one Penny of it, which is now *Interest* and *Principle* between 30 and 40 *l.* and greater Sums than this, and of as Eminent *Quakers*, I can mention, if need be: But I understand the World so well, as not to make these things the Subject of my Discourse; nor did I ever mention any such thing in Print, only G. *W.* gives now occasion for it.

3*dly*, As to the Author of the *Snake in the Grass*, &c. I am sensible G. *W.* does as much abuse him, (and indeed, what Opponent ever had G. *W.* that he did not abuse?) However, he has been, and still is a Gentleman, a Man of great Learning and Piety, and cloathed with Zeal as with a Garment, for the Christian Religion, and well accomplished every way to display the Errours of the *Quakers*; and is preparing an Answer to G. *Whitehead*, wherein he (I believe) will trace him step by step, in all his crooked and by-paths.

But, G. *Whitehead*, I have not done with you yet; you tell us, in the History of your Call to the Ministry, saying, 'The Lord hath ' called me from my Native Country, and from my Father's House,

The Pilgrim's Progress,

† Jacob *found in a Desert-Land*, &c. p. 8.

'and from outward Riches, and the Honour of the World, † &c. I do well remember, that when I came first amongst you, this was a great part of your Cant; as if you had been some Lord's Sons, yea, Men of Breeding, Riches and Honour, and left all for the sake of Souls; when alas! upon a strict Enquiry (of which I have not been wanting.) I find you in this, as well as in almost every thing else, horrible Deceivers; for you left your poor Country for a Richer, and like *Yorkshire* Hostlers, are observed seldom or never to return thither again. You came from Penury to Plenty, from Labour and Toil, to Ease and Pleasure; you came from your Father's poor Cottage, which I have been told by them that saw it, that it is not worth 50 *s.* to Houses worth 500 *l.* (a good Exchange, believe me;) and you were so far from being possess'd with outward Riches, that you came a poor Boy on Foot, and liv'd upon Alms amongst us, sometimes a Month here, six Weeks there, more or less, as you could find Entertainment; the mean time, improving that little Learning you had, as well as to instruct the Children in the Family. But *George*, thou left thy Honour too; how came that to pass? What Worldly Honour wert thou endued with? Was it to carry a Letter to a great Person sometimes, for a piece of Victuals? Very well, I think that is as much as ever [during thy Dwelling in thy own Country,] thou didst arrive to; and for this, in time, thou hadst the Honour to send thy Servant, and ride thy self on Horse-back, with a *London* Linning-Draper

Benj. Antrobus.

riding before thee; and *John Kent*, worth some Thousands, (for ought I know,) riding behind thee, carrying thy Portmantle, and thy self *George* in the middle, like some Peer. Thus *George*, instead of lea-

Picture of Quakerism drawn, &c. p. 106, to 111. at large.

ving thy Riches, thy Honour, &c. thou left thy Penury and Contempt; and by Deceit, like thy Brother *Sam. Cater*, who pretended he suffered 20 *l.* when he suffered not a Groat; but by that pretence, got 10 *l.* clear into Pocket. But HARK *George*, I find you so deceitful, that I fear thou hast laid a Foundation, in this thy *Jacob found in a Desert Land*, (and with design too,) to have thy Friends after thy Decease, when they collect thy Works, to magnifie thy Call to thy Ministry, out of thy Father's Country, for the sake of Souls; when alas! it was for filthy Lucre-sake, in leaving thy outward Riches, when alas! it was to get Riches and Honour.

Object. 2. But may some say, What, will the *Quakers* give such notorious Accounts of their Call to their Ministry? And are they generally of such a mean Abstract, and yet so advanced? Where is the Self-Denial they so often boast of? And why do they debase the Clergy, as a Tribe of Covetous Worldly Teachers? Since, if others be like *Whitehead*, none exceed the *Quaker* Teachers in Worldly-mindedness.

Ansie. First, Well; to Answer this Objection, take G. W. for one instance.

2*dly*,

From Quakerism *to* Christianity.

2*dly*, *Sam. Cater*, who was a poor Journey-Man Capenter, and when he led *James Naylor*'s Horse into *Bristol*, crying, Hosannah to to the Son of *David*, and put in Prison, he was well acquainted with Vermin, Rags and Penury; however, 'tis believ'd he is worth now, besides Portioning out his Children, some Hundreds.

3*dly*, *John Kilborn*, another Journey-Man Carpenter, as poor as either *Whitehead* or *Cater*, when they first set up for Speakers, now a Wealthy Man.

4*thly*, *William Bingly*, a poor Taylor, wrought for 4 *d*. or 6 *d*. a day in the *North*, with *Tho. Denison*, or others, now a rich Man.

5*thly*, *Samuel Wallingseild*, a Glazier formerly; but since, a vast rich Draper in *London*.

6*thly*, *Tho. Green*, a Mason, or Bricklayer; now a Man worth many Thousands.

7*thly*, *George Fox*, a poor Journey-man Shoe-maker, died worth abundance, and liv'd in as much Plenty as most Knights in *England*.

8*thly*, *Stephen Crisp*, formerly a poor Weaver, but died very rich.

I have known most of these eight Persons near 30 years, some longer, and setting the Glazier and Mason aside, which possibly might make up jointly 100 *l*. if need were; but the other Six, I do verily believe, was not all worth 100 *l*. unless they had sold their Axes, Saws, Thimble and Needles, Beds, Stools, Shuttle and Awl: But such is the Art of their Preaching, how much soever they decry Gifts and Rewards in others; that put what *G. Fox* and *Steph. Crisp* died worth, to what the other Six now living [for ought I know,] together, and by the most modest Account that I can get, together with my own Estimation, their Estates thus got by Preaching, is not so little as Twenty thousand Pounds, but some think nearer Thirty thousand Pounds. Now then, I dare engage to produce 500 Clergymen, whose Fathers were Men of Estates, who brought them up at Schools and Colledges with great Expence and Charge; and that, since they came into the World, have been frugal Men, and liv'd as many Years in their Office of Preaching, and yet have not advanc'd their Fortunes to this degree: And yet to behold how their Books are fill'd with reproachful Language as well as their Sermons, against the Clergy, as a Tribe of mercenary Hirelings, Lovers of filthy Lucre, Followers of *Balaam* for Reward; seeking their Gain from their Quarter, greedy Doggs, *Babilon*'s Merchants, covetous Devils, Thieves, Robbers: Yea, says *W. Penn*, † ' And whilst the idle Gormondizing ' Priests of *England*, run away with above 150000 *l*. a Year, under ' pretence of being God's Ministers; and that no sort of People have ' been so universally thro' Ages, the very Bane of Soul and Body to ' the Universe, as that abominable Tribe; for whom, the Theatre of ' God's most dreadful Vengeance is reserved, to act their Eternal ' Tragedy upon, *&c*. And in the same Page, he tells us, that the

A brief Discovery of a threefold Estate, &c. p. 5, 7, 8, 9, 10.

† *The Guide mistaken*, p. 18.

F false

false Christians, (meaning the Church People,) are more intollerable than *Heathens*, *Turks* and *Jews*, saying, The equal Conversation of those Infidels, should make both Priest and People blush. †

(* And why not Quakers too?)

But Mr. *Clapham* the Minister, against whom *W. Penn* writ that Book, says, † 'It's a foolish thing to flatter the *Papists*, *Socinians* 'and *Quakers*, with the Hopes of Salvation: Upon which, Mr. *Penn* in his wonted carreer, first condemns the Clergy, then vindicates the *Socinians*; his Words are these, ' If [*Pap. Soin. Quak.*] be defe- 'ctive, they owe it to the idle, lying, covetous, ignorant, and murde- 'ring Spirit and Practice of the Priests, who's Interest it has ever 'been to enslave and obscure the Peoples Understanding; — it's not 'my Business to Apologize for Papists: As for the *Socinian*, I know 'him to have Wit and Learning enough; — his Exemplary Life, 'and Grave Deportment, I must acknowledge to be very singular; 'and if his Cause receive no greater Foil than this Person's bare Re- 'proaches, the discreet World will sooner acquiesce in the stronger 'Arguments of *Socinus*, and his quaint Adherents, †.

† p. 31, 32, ib.

† W. P. Vindicate the Socinians.

Object. 3. But may some object, If the *Quaker* Teachers be such thrifty Men, are they also charitable Men? We have heard, the *Quakers* maintain their own Poor.

Answ. I do not know many of their Teachers now, having been so long from them; but such of them as I do now know, and formerly have known, they were a sort of mercenary poor Men in their first Rise, (some few excepted,) but very uncharitable in their Language; the World never produced the like since *Noah*'s Flood; and I know not, nor never did, that the Ministers of that People were ever given to Hospitality; but what they got, commonly they held fast, and beside, ungrateful to their Benefactors. I remember, I met one of them in *London*, † sometime since, and he was so proud, being now grown Rich, that he would not speak to me, altho' I have entertain'd him and his Horse, yea, and Companion too, at my House divers times, sometimes a Week together; yea, when he has been thin, and thread-bare, I have taken him into my Shop, and at my own Charge have cloathed him; I will not say what I have done to others, both in Money and Cloathing; but thus much I will say, that 'tis the chargeablest Ministry this day in *England*, to some Particulars: For as Mr. *Croese* well observes, they range all the Nation round, and come like Mice uncall'd for, and like Flies unsent for; and both for their Horses, Themselves, and their Companions, fall upon their Provision, Oats, Hay, &c. insomuch that I can say, the Ministry of the *Quakers* has cost me as much in three Months time, nay, much more, than the publick Ministry have cost me this fifteen Years.

† John Kilborn.

But, as to their Hospitality and Charity, I never met with any of it; I remember, about 20 Years since, my Wife had a mind to see *London*, and I went with her to visit *Tho. Green*, who as well as ma-

ny

From Quakerism *to* Christianity.

ny others of them, made my House his Home when in our Country, *Brothers and* yet he never invited me and my Wife to a Meal; nay, his own Kin- *Sisters.* dred that have come to Visit him out of *Northamptonshire*, have scarce eat and drank at his House; but, which is still worse, for I can now spare none, where a Discovery may be made of this false Ministry and deluding Teachers; I say worse, for his own Brother *William Green*, who once was a chief Speaker amongst them; but poor Man! he was a wet *Quaker*, and they put him by Preaching; the Man Married, grew Poor; and notwithstanding his Brother *'Tis now judg-* *Thomas Green* was vastly Rich, and Application made to him time *ed, he is worth* after time, yet he held a deaf Ear so long, until his Wife was forced *8000 l.* to go to St. *Gregory*'s Parish for Relief for him, or else he might have † *I have been* starved, † for all his own Brother is worth many Thousands. *told, that he'll*

I shall give but one instance more of this kind, and then tell you *not allow his* who are their own Poor, and who they think themselves obliged to *Horse Litter,* maintain, *&c.* *but lye on the*

The instance is, touching *Sam. Cater*, whose Father was a poor *bare Flint-* Man, went about to sell Wings for three Two-pence, from door to *Stones.* door; but as you have heard, he by being a Preaching Quaker, is grown Rich: Well, he has a Kinsman that lives at our Town, and takes Collection, a Sweep-Chimney; this poor Man, sometimes in the Summer time, will go to *Littleport*, † *i. e.* about eight or ten † *Where S. Ca-* Miles, to Visit his rich Cousin, his Father's Brothers Son; but when *ter dwells.* he comes there, I have heard him say, that they will not so much as let him come in; I will not say, but sometimes he may have gotten something, but very little; no, they have very little Charity to God's Poor, but their own Poor, and such as they so esteem; and thereupon, look upon themselves obliged to maintain; are such as merit their Charity, by obeying their Doctrine, in Transgressing the known Laws of the Land, *viz.* such as are Sued and Imprisoned for Tythes, *Sam. Carter's* such as met in defiance of the Statute, made 22 of K. C. II. Yea, if *instance for one.* such could but make the Feoffees to the Fund at *London*, believe they did suffer, whether true or false, such were supplied: But if any one of their People happen to wear a 4 *d.* Lace on their Pinner, or pull off their Hat to a Magistrate, or break and violate the *Quakers* Laws, *Milton-H—ll.* such are turned to the Parish: I know but one poor *Quaker* in our Town; it may be, she is not so starch'd a *Quaker* as the rest; it may be, she may say *You* instead of *Thee* and *Thou*, or some such small Defect: Well, tho' she be a poor Widow with several small Children, and very Necessitous, yet she must starve, if our Parish did not sometimes relieve her; and for this seven Years, I believe, she hath lived in a little House of mine, and the Town pay me her Rent; no, they only take notice of their own Poor, *viz.* such as are made Poor thro' their Obedience to the *Quakers* unlawful Laws, or Laws against the Laws of the Realm.

F 2

I do not question but I have made the Friends angry; yet, if they take the boldness to stigmatize the Bishops, Magistrates and Clergy, and to reproach them with what is not true, why may not I tell them of their Faults? *G. Whitehead* wrote lately to *G. Keith*, i. e. 'I could further expose thee to thy Terrour and Shame, † than ever I have done; for I have been very sparing towards thee, in comparison of thy many Abuses, Scorn, and Injuries against me, &c. But, *Canes timidi vehementius latrant.*

'G W's Letter to G. Keith, May, 98.
† They'll tell you, they cannot seek Revenge.
Smith's Primmer, Part 2. p. 97.
An Account of the Children of Light, &c. p. 16.

I shall conclude this Head in the Words of *W. Penn* to the Clergy; and I shall only turn the Scales, and apply it to the *Quaker* Teachers, and hope it may be useful to their Hearers, as well as shew *G. Whitehead* thereby, how injurious, scornful and abusive, the *Quakers* have been to the Clergy, who yet never exposed them to Terrour; but I thank God, *England* is not *Pensilvania*, where the *Quakers*, tho' they cannot Fine, Whip, Imprison, and Fight as *Quakers*, yet they tell you they can as Magistrates. The Words are these, *viz.*

The Guide mistaken, &c. P. 43.

'Tho' manifold are the Stratagems of Satan, that old Serpent, by 'which he does surprize the Immortal Souls of Men, with most de-'plorable Woes, yet there is none that proves so generally effectual 'as HYPOCRISIE; it's his *Misterium Maximum*, a Study and Em-'ployment fit for none below the Form of his Arch-Angels; such 'make his archest Emissaries, and most subtle Meanders, sublime De-'vils, masqu'd with a Vizard of Sincerity, palliating themselves 'from what they really are, by seeming what as really they are not; 'out-side wash'd Platters, Wolves in Sheep's Cloathing, inside rotten, 'but outside whited Sepulchres; in short, the muddy Sensualist † re-'fin'd to a counterfeit Fidelity; and imitation of the Form of Godli-'ness, the more unquestionable to Deceive; and securely to insinuate 'candid Apprehensions of his Purpose, who is the most impudent de-'spiser of his God, destroyer of Souls, contemner of Laws, perver-'ter of Truth, and Treacherous to the end; against whom, the sharp-'est Woes are denounced, and Punishments reserved to Eternity: 'Now, how the *Quakers* † have rendered themselves obnoxious to 'the Corrector of a Hypocrite, has been my Business in this Chap-'ter, and will be in the ensuing Discourse farther to manifest, *&c.*

† T. G. and others, knew Crisp to be a great Sensualist, if not an Atheist.

† W. P. apply it to the Clergy.

And thus have I by answering these three Objections, shewed the *Quaker* Teachers their *Specialis regula triplex*, by which they are governed, *viz.* Pride, Hypocrisie and Covetousness, in which they all agree, in *Case, Gender, and Number.* I do grant, I have the content of some worthy Gentlemen in this my Undertaking; I also grant, I have met with Discouragement from some others of equal Worth and Merit, who are not so Apprehensive of the Danger of their Errours, both respecting the Church and State; but no Man hath been privy to, or viewed what I have wrote; and so I take it wholly upon my self, as what I think my self called to. And if *G. Whitehead,*

head, or his Associates, should threaten me with Terrour, as they do G. *Keith*, for his Christian Testimony against their vile Errours, I first let them know, they cannot bring me much lower than they have already done; next, that I am as willing to suffer three Years and four Months Imprisonment under their Rage and Fury, if God and the Government permit them to execute their Fury so far, as ever I was, to suffer the like Term when amongst them, in *Ely* and *Wisbech* Goal; and whatever I thought then, and what satisfaction I then had in my Sufferings, I have reason to believe, I have far more solid reason for the Cause I am now upon; and therefore, I shall not spare this painted Harlot, but lay her bare to the View of her Lovers; let her Fret and Fume, Rail and Rage never so much, for as she have dwelt by others, † by false Accusations without Mercy, so shall I by a true and faithful Testimony from Matter of Fact, deal by her, without all pity or compassion: For, why should *Jezebel* be suffered to seduce the Nation undiscovered? Why should she Dialogue the Bishops, contemn the Magistrates, revile the Ministers of the Gospel, at their own ungodly rate without contradiction? No, let *Gog* and *Magog* join together, yet shall there be War proclaim'd against them for ever, as long as the Sun and Moon endures.

† Viz. *the Magistrates, Ministers, and People.*

CHAP. VII.

Shew the manner of the Quakers *Yearly Meeting, or General Council; with the Use of it, and the Consequences thereof.*

Reader,

BY way of Introduction observe, that as I begin my Enterance into the *Quakers* Church-Government, with the manner of their ANNIVERSARY SYNOD, so I shall compleat the Discovery thereof in a distinct Chapter by it self, touching their Yearly Meetings. For as all Proceedings in our Courts of Judicature, in our Assizes, General Quarter-Sessions, Monthly Meetings of the Justices of Peace, Commissioned by his Majesty, are Authorized, and derive their Power from Acts of Parliament; so all the Proceedings of Monthly, Quarterly, Six Weeks, and Second-Day Meetings, of the *Quakers* Government, (which is a Government within the Government, and which is still worse against the Government,) derive their Power and Authority from their Yearly Meeting, where their Acts are made, their Orders are framed, and their Methods agreed upon, in a Parliamentary Way. And these in their Order, I shall briefly go thro', beginning with their YEARLY MEETING, shewing

ing their way and manner, and that part of their Busineſs which I ſtill remember when I was a Member thereof, and what elſe occur to my Memory, as well as by the beſt Information I can get; and ending with their YEARLY MEETING, ſhewing their Doctrine, by which they Influence the Deputies ſent from all Parts of *England* and *Wales*, to agree in Council, to maintain their ancient Teſtimony, &c.

As to the manner of their Houſe, and Meeting therein.

Firſt, They are Men choſen, and deputed by all the Quarterly Meetings of the Quakers in *England*, and *Wales*; and ſent up to *London*, to ſit in Council every *Penticoſt*, or *Whitſon-Week*, Annually, as the Repreſentatives of the Body of the People called Quakers; to which, there is reſort from *Scotland*, *Ireland*, *Holland*, *Penſilvania*, *Eaſt* and *Weſt Jerſey*, *Maryland*, *Long-Iſland Road*, *Iſland Virginia*, *Carolina*, *Friezland*, *Antego*, *Mevis*, *Dantzick*, *Germany*, *Holſteine*, and all other Places where-ever they have got footing; *London* being the Quakers Metropolis, as *Rome* is in *Italy*, where they hold their general Rendezvouſe from all Parts of the World, † to Negotiate their Affairs, ſettle their Orders, confirm as well as make Decrees, erect Canons, Repeal, not verbally, yet virtually, ſo far as their Power reaches, all Acts of Parliament which ſuit not with their *Light within*, which is the Higher Power, to which, together with the Body, * abſolute Obedience is required, and Submiſſion expected, may decreed; for to the *Light* (ſay they,) all Power in Heaven and Earth is committed, † and from whoſe Sentence there lyes no Appeal.

† *A notable way of Intelligence, and how to eſpy the Weakneſs of every Country as well as their own Strength.*
* *See the Fifth Chap. the London Edict, 1666.*
† Joſ. Coal's *Works*, p. 93. Smith's *Pimmer*, p. 13.

Secondly, As to their Convocation-Houſe, it is ſcituate, and being in *White-heart* Court in *Grace-church-ſtreet, London*, where there is a very large Room four ſquare, with a very large Table, which is covered in Convocation-time, with a curious Green Carpet; about which, may ſit forty or fifty of the principal Men; their Preſident being their *Light within*, which is to ſpeak thro' ſome or other infallibly, and ſo to be taken, &c. and round about, there are Seats ſet one above another, like the Houſe of Commons, where may convene about Six hundred; and their Speaker being below, they can all hear him, and he them, with eaſe and delight.

Thirdly, When this is done (the Doors being well ſecured, *i. e.* either lock'd and barr'd, or elſe 2 or 3 luſty Fellows to keep Guard,) then the Clerk opens his Baggs, and takes out his Books, opens the black Roll, and calls over all the Quarterly Meetings in *England* and *Wales*, and the Names of the Deputies; and is as careful to ſee that none be wanting, as Jehu was, who ſaid, *Call unto me all the Prophets of Baal, let none be wanting.*

2 K*ings* 10.19.

This

From Quakerism *to* Christianity.

This done, they proceed to examine, first the State of their own Affairs, next, that of the Nation, which any way affects them.

First, As to their own Church Affairs; it is to see that none Preach contrary to their ancient Testimony; if they do, they Excommunicate them, and expel them out of their Unity, as in the Case of *George Keith*; which, in regard it is made so Publick by several printed Books, particularly his three Narratives, I think I am the less concerned to be particular on that Head; as, *First*, To shew how they Summoned him to appear before them day after day, I think 10 or 12 days together, where G. *Keith* as readily appeared, as *Luther* did at *Wormes*; † and when they could not make him truckle, but that he manfully stood his Post, they then cast him out as a Troubler of their *Israel*, and called him Apostate, one seperated from the holy Fellowship of the Church of Christ, and one not fit to Preach and Pray in their Meetings, in that unreconciled Estate, until by a publick and hearty Acknowledgement of his Offence, and Condemnation of himself therefore, he return to Mother-Church, &c. as by the Words of his Excommunication, bearing Date *May* 17.1695. may more fully appear. Thus then is their boldness manifest, *First*, In presuming to Summons the King's Subjects to appear before them; and then to interrogate them, sentence and condemn them; yea, and that too, for holding no other Articles of the Christian Faith, than what every Orthodox Church holds. *Secondly*, That he is an Apostate, whilst no matter of Evil Fact, or false Doctrine, they could lay to his Charge; I say, this is bold in Fact.

† *And there was as much need for him; for New Rome is as fatal, and as dangerous to the Protestant Interest, as her Elder Sister.*

I will not deny, but that Dissenters have sometimes admonished scandalous Walkers; and if they have persisted therein, to the scandal of their Church-Society, rejected them, &c. But I deny that any, whether Presbyterians, Independants or Baptists, ever yet took upon them to call a General Council, and then, and there assume an Authority to call before them the King's Subjects, examine, try and judge them Apostates, for differing from them in matter of Faith and Doctrine, especially when G. *Keith* held no other Articles of the Christian Faith, than all sound Protestants hold. This then is a Figure of their Church-Government, respecting the Doctrinal Part thereof.

Next, As to their Interfering with the Government, and their calling in question Acts of Parliament, and absolving their Hearers from their Obedience to them; if this can be made appear, I think 'tis worth noticing, the dangerous Consequences thereof are so many, and so pernicious. And,

THEREFORE observe, what *W. Rogers* wrote, in Answer to an Objection, Whether it were lawful or no, to pay Tythes, † if the Supream Powers command it? &c.

† *The Christian Quaker distinguished from the Apostate, in five Parts. Part 2: p. 43. Printed 1680.*

Answ.

Answ. 'We are so far from condemning all those who freely pay
'them, (and not by constraint,) that we look upon it the Duty of
'all professing Christianity, to contribute towards the outward
'maintainance of such whom they usually hear, and account to be
'the true Ministers of Christ, in case they have need; and if the
'Charity of any should be such, as to bestow upon them one fifth
'part instead of a tenth, far be it from us to condemn it, &c.

This Book did so startle the *Foxonian* Quakers, that *Tho. Ellwood*, one of their best Tools, wrote an Answer to it; and fearfully complains of this extensive Charity of *W. Rogers*, and the Dissenting Quakers, called *Storians* for distinction, &c. saying,

† *An Antidote against the infection of* W. *Roger's Book*, p. 78.

'In this Answer (saith *Ellwood*,†) you discover an Errour of
'Judgment, otherwise you would not be so far from condemning
'all those who pay Tythes freely, as you say you are: FOR TRUTH
'ALLOWS NO PAYMENT OF TYTHES AT ALL, UNDER
'THE NEW COVENANT, BUT CONDEMNS IT: And so
'would you also, if your Hearts were right in Truth: THEY

* *This Proof of* Elwood's *out of 1* John 4. 3. *is like many of their Proofs; for there is not a word of Tythes, or that it is a mark of Antichrist to pay Tythes.*

'who PAY TYTHES, do THEREIN uphold a legal Ceremony
'abrogated by Christ, and THEREBY DENY CHRIST to be come
'in the Flesh, which IS a MARK of ANTICHRIST, 1 *John* 4. 3.
'* However, whether you condemn or approve it, the faithful Fol-
'lowers of the Lamb see and discern this Spirit, the nature of it, and
'the end it tends to, which is downright RANTERISM.

† *See what a sad thing it is to break one of* Fox's *Commandments.*

Again. *p.* 139. poor *T. Ellwood* makes a sad Complaint, of some that had been convinced ten, nay, some twenty Years, and yet can pay Tythes without any Acknowledgment of Evil therein: †'Is it 'not savoury Language, (says *Ellwood*) for such to say, I must stay 'until I be convinced? Can such as see not such manifest Evil, * be 'said to be faithful? &c.

* *Possibly the poor Men had not seen* G. Fox's *Commandments, at least not well con them.*

Well, these Differences grew high, and very difficult to decide, but in time the matter came up to the Terms of *W. Roger's* Objection, *viz.* the SUPREAM POWER, continued the Payment of Tythes, in that very Act of Parliament by which the *Quakers* claim their Tolleration; and therefore, 'tis worth the while, to see how the *Quakers* take this very Act of Parliament, and bring it to their Light, which is (say they) the higher Power; all Power in Heaven and Earth being committed to it; † and how they null, make void, and repeal that part of it relating to Tythes, repairs of Churches, &c. *viz.* so far as it concern the *Quakers*.

† Smith's *Primmer*, p. 13. *Jos.* Coal's *Works*, p. 93.

Anno

From Quakerism *to* Christianity.

Anno Regni Gulielmi & Mariæ Regis & Reginæ, Angliæ, Scotiæ, Franciæ & Hiberniæ, primo May 24. 1698. *this Act passed the Royal Assent.*

Provided always that nothing herein contained, Nº 308. *shall be construed to exempt any of the Persons aforesaid, from paying of Tythes, or other Parochial Duties, or any other Duties to the Church or Minister, nor from any Prosecution in any Ecclesiastical Court, or else where, for the same.*

Well, after much strugling between the *Foxonian* Quakers that hold it Antichristian to pay Tythes, tho' voluntarily paid; yea, a compleat Denial of Christ to be come in the Flesh, quoting 1 *John* 4. 3. yea, downright Ranterism, on the one hand; and the *Storian* Quakers who held it lawful to pay, if the Supream Power gave it them, nay, not only the Tenth part, but even the Fifth part, if the Party thinks his Minister want it; I say, great Struglings, and Writings, and Disputings, were on both Parts, about this so nice a Point, and so necessary to be decided: Wherefore at a Yearly Meeting held at *London, June* 1693. and by the Authority of the same, it was thus, amongst other things, Enacted:

'And therefore, that all due and godly Care be taken against the
'Grand Oppression and Antichristian Yoke of Tythes, That our Chri-
'stian Testimony born, † and greatly suffered for, be faithfully main-   † *Soft Words,*
'tained against them in all respects, and against Steeple-House rates: *and hard*
'—— That Friends at all their Monthly and Quarterly Meetings, be   *Names mixt.*
'reminded to call for the Record of the Sufferings of Friends, to see
'that they be duly gathered, truly entered and kept; and according-
'ly sent up (to *London,*) as hath been often advised, both of what
'Tythes, &c. are pretended to be due, and for how long a time, and
'the time when taken; and by, and for whom, and what Goods are
'taken, and the value thereof, as well those not exceeding, as those
'exceeding, the Sums or Quantities demanded, (it being a Suffering
'for both for Truth sake;) they being in these particulars found
'defective and imperfect in divers Counties, which is an obstructi-
'on to the general Record of Friends Suffering: And THEREFORE,
'the Monthly and Quarterly Meetings, are advised to take more care
'for the future, that all Friends Sufferings for Truth-sake, may be
'brought up (to *London*) as FULL and COMPLEAT in ALL re-
'spects as POSSIBLE may be.

G Thus

The Pilgrim's Progress,

† *Journal,*
p. 400, to 478.
* *The antient*
Teſt. p. 2.
† *The Anarchy*
of the Ranters,
&c. p. 42.
Ellwood's *Antidote, p. 78,*
139.

Thus Reader, you ſee, That this Act of Parliament being brought to the Quakers Light, the Higher Power, it is condemned as a GRAND Oppreſſion, and an ANTICHRISTIAN YOKE of Bondage, ſuitable to the Doctrine of *Fox*,† *R. Pye,* * *T. Ellwood,* and *Barclay,* †.

But ſtill there is another Clauſe in the ſaid Act of Parliament above-recited, which they take as little notice of as that of Tythes, *viz.*

Provided always, and be it Enacted by the Authority aforeſaid, That if any Aſſembly of Perſons, diſſenting from the Church of England, *ſhall be had in any Place for Religious Worſhip, with the Doors lock'd, barr'd, or bolted, during any time of ſuch Meeting together; all and every ſuch Perſon or Perſons that ſhall come to, and be at ſuch Meeting, ſhall not receive any Benefit from this Law, but be liable to all the Pains and Penalties of all the foreſaid Laws recited in this Act, for ſuch their Meeting, notwithſtanding his taking the Oaths, and his making and ſubſcribing the Declaration aforeſaid.*

Another inſtance I may recite, to ſhew the Preſumption of the *Quakers,* in their Yearly Convocations, *viz.*

In the xxii of K. *Charles* II. there was an Act of Parliament made, Entituled, *An Act to prevent and ſuppreſs Seditious Conventicles:* In which it was ſaid,

Be it Enacted, &c. That if any Perſon of the Age of Sixteen Years, and upward, being a Subject of this Realm, at any time after the Tenth day of May *next, ſhall be preſent at any Aſſembly Conventicle, or Meeting, under colour and pretence of any Exerciſe of Religion, in other manner than according to the Liturgy and Practice of the Church of* England, *&c.*

From **Quakerism** *to* **Christianity.**

&c. *at which, there shall be five Persons or more, Assembled together, over and besides those of the same Family, &c. shall suffer those and those respective Fines, &c.*

Now, tho' it be well known, that the Exercise of the *Quakers* Religion is not only otherwise than according to the Liturgy, but directly contrary to it, yet all must be Persecution that limit them: As first, the Liturgy teach the Practice of the Ten Commandments, the Lord's Prayer, and Apostles Creed, which the *Quakers* have not the least Shadow of, either in their Meetings, or in their Families; the Church Liturgy teach the Sacraments of Baptism and the Lord's Prayer, † together with Confession of Sin, which the Quakers reject as Idolatrous and Superstitious. † *See the Picture of Quakerism, p. 94, to 100.*

Well, no sooner did this Act take place, and some did forbear meeting in this Riotous manner, but their Preachers came thro' the Nation, and gave out their Epistles or Mandates, commanding, rather than exhorting the People, to meet in great Numbers, in spite of Law and Law-makers; I receiv'd many Letters to that purpose, one whereof I may recite, to shew, how presumptuous they were in Summoning the King's Subjects to meet and transgress this Law, which allow'd a moderate Tolleration, considering how retrograde their Religion runs to all Instituted Religion. For, there might four meet, besides those of the same Family, and 'tis probable, that many Families have 12 or 15 in a Family. Here then might have been satisfaction, to such as only mean to meet for their more private Edifying, either by Reading or Expounding some Portion of the Holy Scriptures, and which is Practised by the users of the Church-Liturgy; but alas! this was too mean, too low and contemptible, for these proud Boasters to submit too. The Letter is as followeth, *viz.*

This for Joshua Bangs, †. † *Poor Joshua felt the weight of their Entertainment, as well as Benj. Antrobus, and many others.*

Dear Friend,

By this thou may'st know, that God willing, Jonathan Johnson *and I, do intend to be at* Milden-hall *Meeting the next First-Day, and shall be glad Friends* GENERALLY *may know thereof, that we may have a good* LARGE MEETING, *I mean, Friends that are afar off in the Country.*   R. S.

The like I had from *John Hubbard,* and others, to appoint Meetings for *George Whitehead,* and others, tho' often therein precaution'd not to mention the Names of the Speakers; no, they must go like disguis'd *Ahab*'s, and the poor silly Sheep must suffer for them, and their own Transgressions too; insomuch, as that in the loss of 13500 *l.* by Fines and Distress, our Teachers never lost 50 *l.* where they were Strangers, and they had more wit than to Preach at home where they were known. Well, but as these Letters as well as their common Practice, was bottom'd upon an Edict made at a Yearly Meeting, which both repealed this Law, respecting the *Quakers* who adheared to them as the Higher Power, alienated their Obedience from the Magistrates, and the Laws of the Land: Which Edict is as followeth, *viz.*

Concerning our open Testimony by Publick Meetings, in times of Sufferings.

'That as it hath been our Care and Practice from the Begin-
'ning, that an open Testimony for the Lord should be born, and a
'Publick Standard † for Truth and Righteousness

† *High boasting Words; but the Snake lay in the bottom,* i. e. *Disobedience to Authority, their Light being the Higher Power.*

* *Meaning their Light, in opposition to the Doctrine and Practice of the Apostles, and all Christian Churches, as well as against the Commands of Jesus of* Nazareth: Go, teach all Nations Baptizing, *&c.* Do this in remembrance of me, *&c.* When you Pray, say, Our Father, *&c.* Forgive us our Sins, for, *&c.*
Read *Luke* 11. 14. *Matth.* 28. 19, 20. *Luke* 22. 19. *John* 1. 8. *Psal.* 38. 18. 50. 15. 51. 1. 2, 3. *Isa.* 64. 6. *Lam.* 3. 20. *Job* 7. 20. *Prov.* 20. 9. *Eccles.* 7. 20. *Nehem.* 1. 6. 1 *Tim.* 1. 15. *Dan.* 9. 4, 5, 10, 23.
See *Pist. of Quak.* p. 63, *to* 70.

'upheld in the Power and Spirit of God, by our
'open and known Meetings against the Spirit of
'Persecution, that in all Ages hath sought to lay
'waste God's Heritage; and that only thro' faith-
'fulness, constancy and patience, Victory hath
'been, and is obtained: SO IT IS OUR AD-
'VICE and JUDGMENT, That all Friends ga-
'thered in the Name of Jesus, * keep up those
'Publick Testimonies in their respective Places,
'and not DECLINE, FORSAKE or REMOVE
'their Publick Assemblies, because of Times of
'Sufferings, as WORLDLY, FEARFUL and PO-
'LITICK Professors have done, because of In-
'formers, and the like Persecutors: For such
'Practices are not consistent with the Nobility of
'the Truth, and therefore not to be owned in the
'Churches of Christ.

Subscribed by,

London, the 23d.
of the Third
Month, 1675.

. G. *Whitehead,*
Tho. *Salthouse,*
Jo. *Burnyeat,*

W. *Penn,*
Alex. *Parker,*
Stephen *Crispe.*

Thus have I given two Instances, as particular Demonstrations, That as their Books teach, so their Practice confirm it: That their Light is the Higher Power, to which they require Obedience, contrary to the Practice of God's Saints and Servants in all Ages, where nothing

thing that is sinful, and so against the written Word of God is commanded. Read *Matth.*22.21. 1 *Pet.*2.13,14,17. *Rom.*13.1,2,3. *Tit.*3.1. See *Tindall's* Works, *i. e.* The Obedience of a Christian Man, &c. p. 111. and compare these Holy Sayings with their Practice, unless where Idolatry or Things sinful are commanded, and then 'tis better to obey God than Man; but this the Quakers could never produce: But as they thus slighted and Trampled upon the Government, so did their great Apostle glory in it, saying, *He did not heed a Cart-load of Warrants.* Journal, p. 278.

And now I shall briefly run through several of their other Methods and Ways at their Yearly Meeting, reserving their Doctrinal Part, which support and influence them to a distinct Chapter by it self.

First, They oft refer to their last Yearly Epistle, that the Contents of it be seriously reminded in all Monthly and Quarterly Meetings, but not a word of Scripture referred to therein, as their Rule of Faith and Practice.

2*dly,* Against that grand Oppression and Antichristian Yoke of Tythes; yea, Antichristian in the Law-maker, in the Payer, and in the Receiver.

3*dly,* Against the Paying of Churchwardens Rates, by which we have much trouble in the Country, otherwise things might be easie; but from this Fountain spring their Antimagistratical Practices.

4*thly,* That all their Sufferings may be brought up to *London,* in order for a Martyrology, both full and compleat, that nothing may be wanting, to reproach the Magistrates, and extol their own Sufferings, which they are not already asham'd to say, are greater and more unjust than in the Days of Christ's Apostles, the ten Persecutions, and all the Massacres, for the Name of Christ, † tho' many of them are meer Shams, as in the Case of *Sam. Cater,* who pretended and got it Recorded, that he suffered 20 *l.* for Preaching at *Phakenham* in *Norfolk,* altho' he never did for that Meeting suffer a Groat; yet for that pretence, had 10 *l.* sent him out of their *London* Exchequer, or Fund: And yet this is not the whole of this Grand Cheat; but nine Years after he Printed a Book, * wherein he had the Impudence still to complain of Sir *Christopher Colthorp's* Injustice and Persecution, concealing his having his Goods again, and 10 *l.* to boot: And by this their Chronicles, they so much boast of, † may be measured.

† *See Burrough's Works* p. 273.

* *The Lamentable Cry of Oppression, &c.* p. 14, 44.

† *Yet no Cronicle appears: What, are they asham'd of their Shams Sufferings?*

5*thly,* Against their People using Guns in their Ships; which in 1693. when this Advice was given, His Majesty had need of such as would Fight, &c. But tho' the Quakers in *Pensilvania* can Fight as Magistrates, yet they cannot Fight as Quakers; and 'tis not time yet to throw off their Coats of Quakerism, and put on the Robes of Magistracy.

6*thly,*

6thly, To receive Applications, Epistles, and Embassies, from the Foreign Parts beyond the Seas, mentioned in the former part of this Chapter, and grant them Orders, Edicts and Laws, for the governing themselves in subjection to their Light, the Higher Power, especially when met in a Body, as the Epistle, *Anno* 1660. before recited shew.

7thly, To refer the Sufferings of their own Poor, *i. e.* such as by breaking the Laws, lying in Goal for Non-payment of Tythes, &c. For otherwise, tho' their own Brothers, they may starve e're they'll take any charitable notice of them; or if a Woman that wears a Lace of a Groat on her Head, or a Man that puts off his Hat; no, many of these are God's Poor, but the Quakers Poor are of another sort; and they having merited the *Quakers* Kindness, by obeying their Laws: These are plentifully rewarded; so that what they call their Unity, is rather a Confederacy, which ought to be noticed.

Nay, Father, as in the Case of Tho. Ellwood, who suffered his Father to go from door to door, as John Rauce's Relation is.

8thly, They take care, that all their erronious Books may be dispersed by all their Monthly and Quarterly Meetings, for the spreading of Truth, but not a word of dispersing the Bible; however, it may serve for a Motive to our Clergy, for to take care to Disperse such Books as discover the *Quakers* Errours and Hypocrisies; the neglect of it has been very hurtful.

9thly, They every Year order a Committee to be chosen, to view the Accounts, and to examine the State of their Cash, *i. e.* the Quakers Exchequer, which some say, now run over: They likewise nominate their Feoffees for the time being, who by the Order of their Superiors, give out sometimes 5 *l.* sometimes 10 *l.* sometimes 20 *l.* at a time to their Preachers; and such as have been ruin'd for Non-payment of Tythes, and the like, the Feoffees for *Anno* 1693. were *W. Crouch, J. Staploe, W. Macket, W. Chandler, W. Beech,* and *Nath. Marks.*

10thly, They give their Deputies fresh Orders, to bring (or send) up the Sum-Total of each County's Collection, for the relief of their Suffering-Friends, *viz.* such as have suffered against Tythes, &c. that such as Preach up G. *Fox*'s Commandments, Orders and Precepts, may not lose their Reward.

11thly, George *Fox* had a Saying in their Yearly Meeting, worth noting; *Pensilvania* had Experience of it; and when they get Power, *England* may also, *viz.* I do not like (*said* Fox,) the Words LIBERTY OF CONSCIENCE, for there is no Liberty out of the Power: What! Liberty to the Episcopals; no. What! Liberty to the Presbyter; no. What! Liberty to the Independant; no. What! Liberty to the Baptist; no. No Liberty out of the Truth. And for further Evidence, that they are against Liberty of Conscience, R. *Hubberthorn* and *Edw. Burroughs,* Men of note amongst them; in an Answer to the Baptists Declaration, wherein they did

Spirit of the Hat, p 12. R. Hubberthorn's Works, p. 228, 229. Printed 1695. Ed. Burrough's Works, p. 615. Printed 1659.

declare

From Quakerism to Christianity. 47

declare themselves against an universal Tolleration of all Miscarriages, whether in things Civil or Religious; nor are we for tollerating Popery, nor such as speak contemptuously of our Lord Jesus Christ, nor any that deny the Holy Scriptures to be the Word of God; and yet we are not against tollerating Episcopacy, Presbytery, or any stinted Form, &c. Now hear these two Eminent Doctors of the *Quakers* Answer. † 'What confusion is here! you will not tollerate 'Popery, nor any that Worship a false God, nor that speak contem-'ptuously and reproachfully of our Lord Jesus Christ, nor that deny 'the Holy Scriptures to be the Word of God; and yet you are not 'against tollerating Episcopacy, Presbytery, or any other stinted 'Form: Why will you not tollerate Popery as well as Episcopacy? 'And why will you tollerate the Book of Common Prayer amongst the 'Episcopals, and not the Mass-Book amongst the Papists, seeing the 'Mass was the substance out of which the Common-Prayer was ex-'tracted? Here is nothing but partiality, to tollerate one thing and 'not another of the same kind, &c. Thus then does it appear, what Friends the *Quakers* are to Liberty of Conscience, and how kind they were to Episcopacy, in 1659. and they are the same still; they tell you, they are not chang'd, and you may believe them, since they have given such a plain Demonstration thereof in *Pensilvania*, where they have both Fined, Whip'd, and Imprison'd *George Keith*, and others, for holding the same Faith, and Preaching the same Faith that the Episcopalians hold and teach.

† R. Huberthorn's *Works*, p. 228. Edw. Burrough's *Works*, p. 615.

12thly, and *Lastly*, And what I have heard with my Ears, That *George Fox* hath exhorted this Meeting, that when they return to their respective Habitations, that such in each County as had most interest, and thereby the most influence on the Members of the House of Commons, should resort to them, and work upon them, &c. And I do say, that the whole twelve Instances I have named, are not more Political than this one; for ten to one, if some Quaker be not himself, or some of his Kindred, some way related, either to the Members of Parliament to serve for that County or Burrough, or to some of his Friends; or ten to one, if some *Quakers* do not deal with him, or some near him, or is Tenant to him, or some of his Friends; if then, some one, or any of these, or all concur, then there is Application made to him time after time; and most English Gentlemen are apt to be kind, and they not knowing the Craft and Subtilty; besides, the Design of this People are apt to tell them, Well, if I can do you any good, consistent with a National Good, I shall not be against it: And if they meet one that is resolute, and from a knowledge of their erroneous Principles, that they are Enemies, and implacable ones too, to all instituted Religion;

And when at the House, they still by all the Interest they have, make fresh Suits; they have their Emissaries wait continually, to see what comes out; they are quick at their Answers; and a Fund or Common Bank to maintain all; none like them but the Jesuits.

then

The Pilgrim's Progress,

then they will fawn upon him, and flatter him, (as they did Coll. *Goldwell*,) and desire him to stand Neuter, *&c.* but, thanks be to God, the Parliament and whole Nation, begin to see them, and grow every day more sensible of the tendency of their pernicious Principles.

Some Inferences from the Seventh Chapter.

IS it so, that the *Quakers* hold their Anniversary Synods, and General Councils, thus Publickly in the View of the Nation, without the King's Letters of License, or Inspection, or Pattent, which is more than the Bishops of the Establish'd Church have power to do? How then does it concern the Legislative Power, to take notice of it, that in time they may prevent the danger of it? Is it so, that their Light is the Higher Power, to which every Soul is to be subject, and all Laws vail? Let us then begin to remember, how zealous our Kings and Parliaments have been, ever since the Reformation, against such as adhered to a Power superior to the King, Lords and Commons, which our Protestant Divines have held to be the Higher Powers, and which we are commanded (by the Apostles) to submit our selves. Now any People that adhere to a Foreign Power to be Supream in *England*, besides and above that of *KING, LORDS* and *COMMONS*, (who under God, are the Higher Powers,) are to be suspected to undermine the Government, whether they mean the *POPE* of *ROME*, or the *QUAKER LIGHT* in their *BODY* Assembled in *COUNCIL*, (the latter being the most dangerous, because not so obvious;) and thereupon ought to be prevented from holding such Councils, with Doors lock'd, barr'd, or by a guard of Men secured, that none can go in, to observe their Transactions: Again, is it so, that the *Quakers* are against Liberty of Conscience, and that they would as freely tollerate Popery as Episcopacy? † *&c.* What reason is there then, for the *Quakers* to expect, much less to presume, to take the Liberty, (under an Episcopal Government,) to hold these Convocations without License, which no other Dissenters either ask, desire, or pretend to; nay, what the Bishops themselves, of themselves, without the King's License, can do?

Rom. 13. 1, 2, 3.
1 *Pet.* 2. 13.
Tit. 3. 1.

† *Yea, see their Antient Testimony in* R. Hub. *Works, p.* 229. *Anno* 1659.

Luke 8. 17.

For *nothing is secret, that shall not be made manifest; neither any thing hid, that shall not be made known, and come abroad.*

CHAP.

CHAP. VIII.

Shews the Executive part of the Quakers *Laws and Government, in their Monthly and Quarterly Meetings.*

I Join the Use and Service of their Monthly and Quarterly Meetings together, for Brevity-fake; as also, because they are much the same in all respects, only the Monthly inferior to the Quarterly; because in one County, there may be three or four Monthly Meetings, much like Justices Monthly Meetings, where the Party offending need not be concluded, but entering his Recognizance to appear at the Quarter Sessions, he may have a more full hearing; so it is with the *Quakers*, he may Appeal from the Monthly to the Quarterly Meeting: This I know very well, not barely because I was Clerk in these Meetings many Years, but also during my Controversy with *Sam. Cater*; I Summon'd him, first, to the Monthly Meeting; and when I found no Justice, I Appeal'd from that to the Quarterly, and indeed from the Quarterly to the Yearly; and so twice or thrice round, as I remember: For it was the greatest Tryal that ever was amongst them, in regard it struck at the Ministry, *viz. WHETHER THEY OUGHT NOT TO TELL THEIR NAMES AND HABITATIONS, AND THEREBY SET THEMSELVES IN ALIKE SUFFERING CAPACITY WITH THE HEARERS,* † *&c.* since they advised us to be valiant, and give up all? *&c.*

† *At large in my Book,* The Painted Harlot both Stript and Whipt, *&c. And the Postscript, stiled* Reason against Railing, *&c.*

But to the matter:

When we came together, which is commonly about 9 or 10 a Clock, then we sate a while together Silent, unless we have a Teacher with us, and then it may be, we may have a short Exhortation, to keep to our antient Testimony; * so then the Doors being secured, they proceed after this manner: The Clerk calling over the Meeting, I mean the particular Meetings of every Town, which possibly may be forty Towns, more or less, *viz.*

* *i. e.* G. Fox's *Commandments, and some other things, which in the next Chapter you'll hear of.*

Clerk. Come Friends, How is it as to your Town of *Littleport?*

A. and *B.* [For there is to be two appear from every Town,] Things are pretty well with us, only *D. E.* is married with a Priest.

Meeting. Aye, How came that to pass? Did you not perceive his Relapse from the Truth, and the Order of it, till he made such a Revolt as to become an Apostate?

A. B. Truly, we found he declin'd; and some Friends in our Town spoke to him, and warn'd him of the Danger of it; but all would not do.

H *Meeting.*

Meeting. Well, let some body be ordered to go to him, and admonish him; if he Repent, and acknowledge his Fault, and confess to Truth, †.

† *i. e. To them, for if he confess his Fault to them, they Absolve him, and all's well again.*

Clerk. How is it at your Town of *Milden-Hall*?

A. B. Things are pretty well with us; but *Francis Bugg* still continues his Writing against Friends: And he being examined by *Samuel Fulbig*, Whether he owns *W. Roger's* wicked Book? (Which admits of Liberty of Conscience, to pay Tythes, or not; to marry with a Publick Minister, or not;) and he owns it: And therefore, we must take care about him, for he does much hurt to Truth, and lays Stumbling Blocks in the way of others.

Meeting. Course, we know not well what course to take with him; he will neither lead, * nor drive, †: Indeed we have suffered him too long Clerk, in this Meeting; but it may thank *R. S. J. A. E. L.* and some of you his Friends, or else he had been excluded long since, for his very owning *W. Roger's* Book, which admits of a voluntary Payment of Tythes; which, as our dear Brother *Ellwood* faith, * is a mark of Antichrist, a Denial of Christ come in the Flesh, yea, downright Ranterism: But notwithstanding, thro' such Arguments as *W. Rogers* use, † we have by woful Experience, seen, that some have been convinced ten, some twenty Years, and yet can pay Tythes without any acknowledgment of Evil therein; and altho' we grant, faith our Brother *Ellwood*, * That our great Apostle G. Fox, did say in his *several Papers given forth for spreading Truth:* 'Friends, to you all this is the Word of the Lord;
'† Take heed of judging one another; judge not
'one another I command you, in the presence of the
'Lord; and judge not one another behind one ano-
'thers backs, *I command you in the presence of
'the Lord; this is the Word of the Lord unto
'you: Neither lay open one anothers Nakedness
'and Weakness behind one anothers Backs, for thou
'that dost, art one of *Ham's* Family which is under
'the Curse, &c. This indeed (continues our be-
'loved Brother,) is a warning to Friends, not to
'judge one another: † But, it is not a warning to
'Friends, not to judge those that oppose Friends,
'being gone out of the Unity of Friends themselves,
'and endeavouring to draw others out also. and to
'divide and rend the Church; so that you have mist your Aim, and
'lost your Blow, &c. Thus Friends, you have the Judgment of the
'Church; and *Francis Bugg* has not only owned that pernicious Book,
'but has written two Books against Friends, as pernicious as that of
'*W. Roger's*; * nay, not only so, but hath wrote divers Letters, Re-
'monstrances and Queries, to particular Friends, to the Second-day
                                                'Meeting.

* *Into blind Conformity.*
† *Into an Implicite Faith.*

* *Antidote, p. 78. 139.*

† *Christ. Quak. disting. Part 2. p. 42.*

* *Antidote, p. 109.*

† *See, Fox's Papers are the Word of the Lord, whilst they say, 'tis Blasphemy to call the Letter, i.e. Scripture the Word. See his Book, Entituled, The Way to the Kingdom of God, pag. 4.*

* *Yet they passed Sentence on me behind my back, I not being there that Day, i. e. 4th June, 1681.*

† *No, let their Immoralities be gross, do but keep in the Unity of the Corrupt Body.*

* *De Christiana Libertate, &c. And the Painted Harlot both Stript and Whipt, &c.*

From Quakerism *to* Christianity.　51

'Meetings. And therefore, 'tis time to take some course with
' him, *&c.*

Meeting. Content; therefore, let us draw up a Paper against him,
and when we have view'd it, let us Record it, *&c.* This was done;
a Copy whereof is as followeth, *viz.*

At a Quarterly-Meeting in Hadenham, 7th Day,
4th Month, 1682.

' Whereas this Day, there was inserted † into our
' Meeting, several Papers subscribed by *Francis*
' *Bugg*, wherein he hath unrighteously and ungod-
' lily reflected upon Ancient Friends, and greatly
' abused faithful Ministers of the Gospel; * and also
' amongst the said Papers, was one subscribed by
' twelve Persons, directed to the Second-Day
' Meeting in *London*, wherein Friends are misre-
' presented and greatly abused; which said Paper,
' we believe the said *Francis Bugg* promoted. Now we being great-
' ly grieved in our Spirits, and truly sensible of his herein going from
' Truth, do testifie, We have no Unity with him, nor can have,
' whilst he is thus Acted.

† *Notable Scholars* INFERRED.

* *They can call other Ministers, Witches, Devils, Thieves, Robbers, Antichrists, Jesuits, Bloodhounds, Sodomites, and what not? But none must touch the Hem of their Garment. O Proud Hypocrites!*

OBSERVE, *First*, I was judged and condemned behind my Back,
without a Hearing: *Secondly*, The Papers subscribed by twelve
Persons, they only supposed to be of my promoting. Now if *John
Lilborn*'s Judges had been thus implicite in their Faith, at his Tryal at *Guild-Hall*, in *October* 1649. he must have been hang'd, for
writing the naked Truth in *Oliver Cromwel*'s time, *&c.*

The next Instance I shall recite, and which I think is to the purpose, is, to shew the *Quakers* implacable Malice, against not only *W.
Rogers*, but his Book too; and no Passage in his whole Book came under the like sad Sentence, as that of his admitting a Voluntary Payment of Tythes, if the Supream Powers bestowed it on a National
Ministry, *&c.* His Words are, ' We are so far from condemning
' all those who freely pay them, [*i.e.* Tythes,] and not by con-
' straint, that we look upon it to be the Duty of all professing Chri-
' stianity, to contribute towards the outward Maintainance of such,
' whom they usually hear; and account to be true Ministers of Christ,
' in case they have need: And if the Charity of any should be such,
' as to bestow upon them one Fifth part, instead of a Tenth, far be
' it from us to condemn it, *&c.* But this was such a horrible Tenate,
and so much of Liberty of Conscience in it, That as you have heard,
† *First*, It was an Errour of Judgment. 2*dly*, It came from an un-
sound Mind. 3*dly*, That Truth, [*i.e.* the *Quakers Light*,] allows
no payment of Tythes at all, under the New Covenant. 4*thly*, They

The Chr. Quaker distinguished, *&c.* Part 2. p. 43.

† *Ellwood*'s Antidote, p. 78. 139.

who do pay Tythes, tho' Voluntarily, do therein uphold a legal Ceremony abrogated by Chrift. 5*thly*, And thereby deny Chrift to be come in the Flefh, quoting 1 *John* 4. 3. which fpeaks not one fyllable of Tythes. 6*thly*, That it is downright Ranterifm, &*c*.

Well, but *W. Rogers* was fo modeft, as not to put this Book into the Bookfellers hands to fell, left thereby he might widen the Difference; which both he, and my felf, at that time, thought might have been compofed, † that he put it into the hands of *John Barnard*, a Merchant, (being one of the feparate *Quakers*,) for him to difpofe of, and to difperfe us he in Wifdom fhould fee meet; and fome hundreds of them he did difperfe. Well, he was Summoned time after time, to the Monthly Meeting in *Devonshire*-Houfe, *London*, to Anfwer for his Fault; and I think, he as often appeared:

† For I did not then underftand their Fundamental Errours; but thanks be to God, that as their fair and fmooth Pretences proved a Snare to catch me, fo their grofs Diffimulations proved a means to fee them.

But being of too Mafculine a Temper, to fubmit to their Arbitrary Authority, and Ufurped Dominion, he ftill continued felling and difpofing of this fo fad and fo lamentable a Book; of which, you have heard the greateft Crime, namely for admitting a Voluntary Payment of Tythes, &*c*. And to fay true, fo it was; for there is nothing upon Earth that the *Quakers* thirft more after, than the utter ruin of the Priefthood, and the abolifhing the Maintainance thereof: This is the Vein that runs fluently thro' all their Books and Sermons; nay, rather than the Priefts fhould have it, and that it might be a means to ftarve them, they are willing to pay Tythes to fecular ufe: 'For '(faith G.*Whitehead*,) if the King and Great Coun-

† The Cafe of the Quakers, concerning Oaths defended, &*c*. p. 50. per G. *Whitehead*.

'cil of the Nation were pleafed † to repeal thofe 'Old Laws, inforcing the payment of Tythes, and 'to convert them into fome neceffary civil Ufe; as

Oh fmooth *George!* Here is the Face of a Lamb, but the rough Paw of a Bare, and the Claws of a Leopard.

'for the Poor [Oh *Judas!*] or fome National Ser-'vice and Benefit, it would appear, whether we 'fhould not pay our parts; and whether the Roy-'al Exchequer would not be conveniently fupplyed, 'without the Tenths from the Priefts, &*c*. Thus they could pay Tythes into the Exchequer, to maintain a War, which they equally Difclaim: Oh! but do what you will with the Tythes, fo the Priefts do but ftarve, and their Miniftry fall, and their Religion over-turned; then HEY BOYS UP GO WE: But (bleffed be God) the fear of that is paft.

Well, but let us hear what became of this honeft *John Barnard*: Why, in fhort, he was Excommunicated *ipfo facto*. A Copy of it here followeth *verbatim*.

From

From Quakerism *to* Christianity.

From the Monthly Meeting at Devonshire-House, *the Fourth of the Eleventh Month,* 1681.

'Whereas there hath been some unruly Spirits gone out from
'Truth, and the Unity of the blessed Power of God, which hath ga-
'thered us to be a People, Writing, Printing, and Publishing things
'hurtful and prejudicial to Truth, by corrupting of Peoples Minds,
'tending also to draw them into Disesteem of many of the Lord's Ser-
'vants, † whose Faithfulness hath manifestly appeared amongst us, *† A Preserva-*
'with whom our Unity stands, to our mutual Satisfaction and Re- *tive for their*
'freshment. *Teachers decay-*
  ing Reputation.
'Upon consideration of these things, we find our selves conscien-
'tiously concerned, * to take notice of something of this Kind, be- * *Oh! Deep*
'fallen *John Bernard*, Merchant, formerly a Member of this Meet- *Hypocrisie.*
'ing, who having dispersed into several Parts of this Nation, divers
'of those pernicious Books, wrote by *William Rogers*, called, *The*
'*Christian Quaker distinguished from the Apostate and Innovator, in*
'*Five Parts*, &c. which hath manifestly been proved in many mate-
'rial Passages, Erroneous and False, both in the Historical and Do-
'ctrinal Part of it; was privately and publickly reproved for that un-
'righteous Action, by several Friends, at divers times, according to
'Gospel Order, as they found it on their Spirits from the Lord, † as *† Never was*
'also admonished against it; yet, after all the Labour and Travel, *God's Name*
'Friends have had on his behalf, being desirous, if possible, to re- *more propha-*
'claim him out of the Enemies Snare, into which he is fallen; he hath *ned by a People*
'from time to time resisted their Advice and Counsel: So that now, *ligion.*
'we being wholly clear, having used our utmost Endeavours in the
'good Will of God, to reclaim him as aforesaid, do not only testifie
'against that Spirit which hath led him into that disorderly Pra-
'ctice, but also against him, whilst join'd thereunto; * nor can we * *Both the Man*
'have spiritual Communion, or Fellowship with him, until unfeign- *and his Spirit*
'edly he shall return unto the Truth, by condemnation of that Work *condemned.*
'and Spirit, which in the Love of God we exhort him to, and desire,
'that for him a place of Repentance may be found.

Reader, What Person living, who is a Stranger to the *Quakers*
deep-dyed Hypocrisie, but that would think this *John Bernard* had
committed some more than ordinary Immorality, nay, some almost
unpardonable Crime? Here is such Indeavours said to be used, such
Gospel Order exercised, such Stiff-neckedness on his part, wilfully
persisted in; but behold all centre in a most profound Piece of Hypocrisie, as I shall shew, and that from divers Reasons: And,

FIRST, In that *Benjamin Clark* their Bookseller, a great Quaker
in their Unity, † sold at the same time Play-Books, Popish-Books, *† I should have*
Gypsie-Books, yea, Baudy-Books, such as I never saw before; and *said Confedera-*
yet *cy.*

The Pilgrim's Progreſs,

yet never Reproved, never Admoniſhed, according to Goſpel Order; never ſentenced and condemned, neither he nor his Spirit: By which, it may appear, how zealous they are for preſerving their own good Name, and Eſteem amongſt their Proſelytes, and their own Laws and Commandments, from being brought into diſrepute; and yet all theſe their Proceedings, they father upon the Lord, who hates Iniquity, and whoſe Laws condemn ſuch wicked Books, as their own beloved Brother ſold and vended every day. Thus do they Phariſee-like, make void the Law of God by their Traditions.

For, as ſoon as this Excommunication came to my hand, I (as a Country-Man,) went to the ſaid *Ben. Clarks*, and asked for ſome pretty Play-Books for Children; and he produced me a parſel of all ſorts, *ut ſupra*! of which I bought Eighteen-Pennyworth, and noticed it in my next Book; † which they never did deny, nor did they ever ſentence him as above.

† *De Chr. Lib. Part 2. p. 207.*

SECONDLY, In all the Records of Condemnation, that ever I made, or ever ſaw made, during the 16 or 18 Years I was their Clerk, I never knew of, or ſaw any Record of Condemnation againſt any Quaker, for the Breach of any Scripture Commands; but either for writing againſt their Teachers, * or for paying Tythes, or for diſperſing and ſelling ſuch Books, as allowed of the payment of Tythes, † or for not Marrying according to their Orders, or for the Breach of ſome one or more of *G. Fox*'s Commandments. An inſtance of the laſt followeth.

* *As my ſelf.*
† *As W. Rogers.*

Hadenham *Quarterly-Meeting, the Fourth of the Seventh Month,* 1678.

' We at this Quarterly-Meeting having the Buſineſs of *John Ainſlo's*
' taking his Wife, contrary to the Order of Friends brought BEFORE
' US; and Friends having ſeveral times ſpoke to him about it, and he
' not giving Friends ſatisfaction, WE do teſtifie, That WE have no
' UNION with him in this his ſo doing, &c.

THIRDLY, I never knew any Book wrote againſt any of their Teachers in the Unity, tho' guilty of notorious Immoralities; † no, here was no conſciencious Concern manifeſted, no Goſpel Order exerciſed, no Publick Condemnation ſent out againſt them, but againſt my ſelf, *George Keith*, *Tho. Criſp*, and others, for diſcovering their Errours: Here they pretend a great Caſe of Conſcience; and having ſhewed who they account ſcandalous Walkers, and who they frequently Record out of the Unity, and who they write their Books againſt, I ſhall conclude this Chapter with one of their Yearly Canons; and if any deſire to ſee more of them, I refer to my former Books, †.

† *As in the opening of the Cage, I ſhall ſhew.*

† *De Chriſ. Lib. &c. Part 2. p. 49. to 52. the Fifth and Seventh Chapter of this Treatiſe.*

London,

From Quakerism *to* Christianity.　　55

London, the 27th of the Third Month, 1675.

Concerning Recording the Church's Testimony, and the Party's Condemnation.

'That the Church's † Testimony and Judgment against disorder-　† The *Light*
'ly and scandalous Walkers, also the Repentance and Condemnati-　and the *Body*
'on of the Party's restored, be Recorded in a distinct Book, in the　join'd.'
'respective Monthly and Quarterly Meeting, for the clearing Truth,
'Friends, and our Holy Profession, to be produced, and published
'for that end and purpose, so far only as in God's pure Heavenly
'Wisdom they shall be needful: And 'tis our Advice in the Love of
'God, That after any Friend's Repentance and Restoration, he abi-
'ding faithful in the Truth, that condemns the Evil, none among
'you so remember his Transgression, as to cast it at him, or upbraid
'him with it; for that is not according to the Mercy of God.

Thus Reader you see, *First*, Who are the scandalous Walkers they Record out of their Unity. 2*dly*, You see, here is an Order from the Yearly Meeting, to get a Book distinct for that Use. 3*dly*, You see also, that here is a door open, that if any repent of Writing against them, of paying Tythes, of Marrying contrary to their Infallible Order, they may be restor'd to their former Dignity; for they have power to bind and to loose, † to condemn and to acquit ;† Yea, whom and that it may so evidently appear, I shall recite one of their final they please. Sentences, pass'd upon one of their Adversaries, Irrevocably, *viz.*　See *Judas* and the *Jews*, p. 85.

In the Name of that God, that spanneth the Heavens with Josiah Coal's *a Span, and measureth the Waters in the hollow of his Hand, I* Works, p. 243. *bind thee here on Earth, and thou art surely bound in Heaven,*　Was there *and in the Chain under Darkness, to the Judgment of the Great* ever the like: *Day thou shalt be reserved.*　Insolency.

　　　　　　　　　　　　　　Josiah Coale.

Some Inferences from the Eighth Chapter.

IS it so then, that these Monthly and Quarterly Meetings, who de-　† No, not one
rive their Power and Authority from the Yearly Meetings, as-　Scripture
sume to themselves this great boldness, to Arraign, Sentence, and　Proof was e-
Condemn Persons, for disregarding their illegal Laws, and for the　ver produced,
breach of their unscriptural Commands? † What need is there then　to strengthen
to suppress these Meetings, that thus alienate the Obedience of the　their Laws or
　　　　　　　　　　　　　　　　　　　　　　Subjects, Actions.　condemn

Subjects from their lawful Soveraign, and his Laws, and to limit this Arbitrary Government thus exercised in these new Spiritual Courts, whilst it may be; lest the time come, wherein they may capitulate with the Supreme Magistrate, and tell him with a carnal Weapon in their hand, that the *Light* is the Higher Power, and all Powers and Dominions ought to cast their Crowns down at its Feet in the Saints? However, I have given warning, by pointing at the Danger, and hope to prescribe a Remedy; and let not THE POOR MAN'S COUNSEL be rejected, lest the time come, wherein it may be said, *It is too late, for the* Gibeonites *hath deceived us with their Wiles*. Pray read the ninth Chapter of *Joshua* at your leisure, and think it not a strange thing to be deceived by the *Quakers* fair Shews, and innocent Pretences, when you see that good *Joshua* the Servant of the Lord, and Successour of *Moses*, he, and his Wise Men and Counsellors, were all deceived; the best of Men mean well, and thinking others do so too, are oft times the soonest deceived. A word to the Wise (as the Proverb is) should be sufficient.

Eccles. 9.14,15.
Joshua *the 9th.* read and ponder, I beseech all wise Men.

CHAP. IX.

Sheweth the Quakers *Fund, Exchequer, or Common Bank; and the Use and ill Consequences of it.*

I Considered, that as Blood is to the Veins, which by a frequent Circulation thro' the Body of Man, both refresh the Heart and support the Head; and that, as the Sinews to the Joints both unite the Members and strengthen the Body, so doth the *Quakers* Exchequer strengthen and support them, in the carrying on their whole Design: For as Money is said to be the Sinews of War, so it may be called the Nerves of Heresie; for Money answers all things. And to shew it to be so, with respect to the Quakers, I shall briefly shew, first, Their way and manner of raising their Bank; next, Their way of Distribution: In both which, it cannot be expected, that I should be exact in their very Words, having forgot great part of their Cant; nor the Particulars to whom they dispose of their Money; that's a Secret kept under Lock and Key: It sufficeth then, that I give some sure Marks of both, and which I hope, I shall so infallibly do, as never an infallible *Quaker* shall be able to deny.

FIRST THEN, I remember when I was *Quaker*, we now and then had an Epistle sent to our Quarterly Meetings in the Country, from the Second-Day Meeting in *London*, for a General Collection for the Service of Truth: This Epistle thus sent, I have Copied out, and have read it in our Meeting at *Milden-Hall*; I have both
given

From Quakerism *to* Christianity.

given to it, and took what our Meeting contributed, and have carried it to the Quarterly-Meeting, where I have taken all the Collections gathered quite thro' the Isle of *Ely*, if not the County of *Cambridge*, †to return to *London*, for the Publick Use: All this I know, and if need were, would depose it. I do not say, but the Yearly-Meeting, as in *Chap.* 7. sometimes do the like; as also, examine the Accounts, constitute and appoint Feoffees, and the like; and to which, the Second-Day Meeting is accountable: But, during the Intervals of their Yearly Convocation, the Second-Day Meeting hath both Power to receive and to dispose, as I shall shew hereafter.

† Which I do think, I also had to return to *London*.

Now, whereas for many Years together, the *Quaker* Teachers Bantered all other Ministers, for taking Money for their Subsistence; the National, for taking Tythes, and other Dues; the Dissenters, for taking the voluntary Gift of their Hearers; whilst the *Quakers* pretended to Teach freely, yea, to Write freely, and to do the Lord's Business freely; when alas! this was all a Cheat, as in the Story of *Bell* and the *Dragon:* For they had not only their Charges for themselves, and Horses free, Cloaths, Hats, Linnen and Woollen oft times free, but now and then a good Watch free also; besides, out of the Bank, they had their frequent Salleries and Stipends, 10, † 20, and 30 *l.* at a time; yea, I have been told, That T. G. had once 100 *l.* at a time, and *J. Parke* 20 *l. per Annum*: Yet, when told of this Hypocrisie, they have Answer'd, They did not Preach for Money, tho' their Teachers did take Money: And might not all other Ministers say so too, That Money was not the end for which they Preached, but the good of Souls; only what they had, was to maintain them in that Station to which they were call'd and set apart?

But *W. Rogers* wrote a Scourge for *G. Whitehead, Anno* 1685. where he hath these Words.

† Witness S. *Cater* and *John Songhurst*, of whom I have a pretty Story. When *W. Mead* was Purser, *i. e. Songhurst* pretending want of Money, *G. Fox* sent him to *W. M. W. Mead* deposited 12 *l.* and enter'd it in his Book. This did not please *Songhurst*; he goes to *G. Fox*, and acquaints him with it. *Fox* told him, that was *W. Mead's* way. Well, *Songhurst* did not like to stand on Record, a taker of Money, who had so many Years pretended to Preach freely; away goes he to *W. M.* with his Money in his Sack's Mouth; *W. Mead* takes it, and enters it on the contrary Page, Receiv'd of *Songhurst* 12 *l.* This made it worse; for, now he had not the Money, yet still stands Recorded, &c.

For *G. Whitehead* an Apostate Quaker, in a Poem, Printed 1685.

See a few Words out of W. Roger's Second Scourge.

But, bless'd be God, *Rome's* Sister hath a Wound,
And 'tis not *Whitehead's* Craft, can heal it sound;
The Church, her Practice, which he oft defends,
Is most like *Rome's*, so far as Power attends:
And yet, when She, *Rome's* Sister, is but call'd,
She Winces, like toucht Horses that are gall'd.
Confusion Her attends, next follows WOE,
For thus She whirls, but God knows where She'll go:

The Pilgrim's Progreſs,

When *Fox* had fram'd i'th' Church a Government,
Preachers approv'd by Man, Beyond-Seas went;
Who, when they wanted Monies to proceed,
The Church Her Caſh then did ſupply their need:
And therefore, when her Caſh was empty'd, SHE
Crav'd Money for to ſerve the MINISTRY.
At length, her Papers like to Briefs, did Cry

† *This Scourge ſmarted, and made poor Ellwood confeſs all, as yon'll hear a-non.*

For MONEY, MONEY, for the MINISTRY †:
And when that Practice was diſlik'd by ſome,
She frown'd like one, who's Downfal's near to come;
Elſe, Why muſt each one with his Key appear
Where Caſh is kept, to ſhew what Money's there?
This Church will fall, Her Load will be her Guile,
If you, O Flock! keep Purſe Strings faſt a while;
And Woes may long attend ſuch prating Preachers,
As for Preferment, turn deceitful Teachers.
Some wonder (*Whitehead*) keeps ſo long in Favour,
Since *Fox* is more deſpis'd, thro' *Whitehead*'s Labour;
Fox is term'd Head, yet *Whitehead* ſtear'd the Courſe,
Till both were ſcorn'd, and they grew worſe and worſe.

Thus Reader, I have given you *W. Roger*'s Sence, firſt, That *Rome*'s Siſter hath got a Wound, yea, almoſt a deadly Wound; that the *Quakers* Church are the moſt like *Rome*; and this is true in Fact: Next, Their Preachers take Money for Preaching, and for Preferment turn deceitful Teachers; all true as Goſpel. Next, That they have a Fund, which is moſt dangerous: Next, That their Papers and Epiſtles for Money, did fly amongſt us like ſo many Briefs, craving Money, Money, for the Miniſtry; Money, Money, to aſſiſt us in our Confederacy, or we are not able to ſupplant Chriſtianity. I will next give you a recital of a Letter ſent me, written about *John Clemence, &c.* bearing Date 26th of the Eleventh Month, 1684.

Dear Friend, &c.

'I underſtand, that there is a new Controverſie lately riſen, about
'the Money thou once told me, was gathered amongſt Friends, for
'the relief of *J. C.* ---- Friends here † are much concerned about it,

† *At Cambridge.*

'knowing right well, that all honeſt Friends in that Day, gave it
'freely, expecting nothing again; ſome are dead; I ſuppoſe, they
'did not make the COMMON BANKERS their Executors; the

† *But Fox, Whitehead, &c. never liked thoſe Friends.*

'Donets Will muſt be fulfilled in all things, and not the COMMON
'PURSE-MONGERS † at this Day; that being contrary to true Re-
'ligion, to take thought for to morrow. I have been examined by
'the *LAW PROFESSORS*, Whether we had a COMMON
PURSE,

From Quakerism to Christianity.

'PURSE or BANK? I answered, we had NONE.
' † This gave so much satisfaction, that Friends in
' this Town * have been quiet EVER SINCE. †
' The Magistrates look upon COMMON BANK-
' ERS, to be as bad as those that hoard up Arms
' and Ammunition, and not [*said She,*] without
' reason; for Money answers all things. If Friends
' would put away this DAGON, and take MO-
' NEY only for their present Necessities, things
' would soon be better with them; God will not
' bless those that break his Commands, with
' HOARDING up COMMON BANKS, and
' Quarrelling with those that will not bring in MO-
' NEY fast enough to them: I have observed, it
' hath been frequent with some, to reckon those that
' brought in most Money into their COMMON
' BANK, to be the best Christians, * &c.
  Ann Docwra.

† A great Lie, and with a design to Deceive, next to Perjury.
* Cambridge.
. † Thus have the well-meaning Magistrates been all along deceived by the Quakers Lies; for all may see, she knew as well of their COMMON BANK, COMMON PURSE, their DAGON, as I did; only to blind the Magistrates and get Liberty, she thus deceiv'd 'em.

* A sign she cannot plead Ignorance of their Fund, if she had so long made that Observation; and therefore, her Lie looks the more designed; Quaker-like, who stick at nothing that may advance the New Catholick Cause.

Thus Reader, I have shewed by a recital of Mrs. *Docwra*'s Letter, what sence she had of their Common Fund, *i. e.* that it was as bad as Hoarding up Arms and Ammunition; and she is so far in the right on't. You see also, what Testimonies hath been given out, both Publick and Private, against these private Purse-mongers, and their raising Common Banks, as that which is so pernicious to the Civil Government, that it is as bad as Arms and Ammunition; for Money answers all things: For, having this private Fund, they can pay their Ministers, and enable them to range the World over, pretending to Teach freely, to forsake their Fathers Country, Riches and Honours, (as you have heard,) and all, to come and spend themselves, their Strength and Years, for the good of Souls; and all this freely, without Money, and without Price: And you see, your Teachers, they must have their Tythes, their Gleabe-Lands, their Easter-Reckonings, and their Midsummer-Dues; by which you may see, they are followers of *Balaam*, the Son of *Bozer*, who loved the Wages of Unrighteousness: Now by our Fruit, and the Fruit of the World's Teachers, you may try us, and prove us. Thus poor Hearts, the very same People that give to these Collections, † know nothing of their Teachers taking Money; nay, many of them will dispute strenuously against you, on their Teachers behalf; That they take no Money, that they Teach freely, as above told. And thus are these silly Sheep carried away with the Wiles of their Teachers, and follow them as the *Israelites* did Rebellious *Absalom*, in the simplicity of their Hearts.

† *I mean innocent middle sort, who are not admitted into the Knowledge of these things.*

2 Sam. 15. 11.

But Reader, this Scourge did so torment this well-favour'd Harlot, it did so sting and nettel her, that poor *Whitehead*'s dull Pen was not able to bear up: Then came in *Tho. Ellwood*, and tho' he wrote as much to the Point as his Craft could invent, yet *W. Roger*'s Stroaks entered so deep, and made such a VVound, as that he, *i. e. Ellwood*, was forc'd, poor Man, (full ill against his will,) to confess, their Ministers did take Money, and their Clerks were paid out of their Fund; which they had not only for Forty Years pretended to the contrary, but by Ten thousand Sermons solemnly declared, that they neither take Silver, Gold nor Apparel, but freely they had received, and freely delivered to the People. O the horrible deceit of this People ! However, let it suffice, that *W. Rogers* have whipt them into a better Temper, who now confess the Fact, and plead the Apostles Practice. But I deny, that ever the Apostles pretended to take neither Silver, Gold nor Apparel; and yet, contrary to his pretension, took all he could lay his Hands on: No; this is the Practice only of the Quakers; no Man questioning the lawfulness of the Ministers Maintainance, save the Quakers only, who yet take with both Hands; their Fruit hath made them manifest. VVell, lets hear T. *Ellwood, viz.*

<small>Rogero Mastix, p. 18.</small>

But that Christ's Ministers should be supply'd
VVith Necessaries, by the Church's Bride,
Is such a known and certain Truth, as none
Perhaps hath e're oppos'd, but thou alone :
That 'tis the Church's Duty to supply
The needful VVants of all her Ministry;
And truth it is, too plain to be deny'd,

<small>† No, *Thomas*, 'tis Quakers Plea, tho' for self-ends, they now plead it.</small>

Christ's Church should for Christ's Ministers provide.
VVhat carps thou at then, *William*? VVould thy Muse
Plead, that St. *Paul* did not this Priviledge use †?
That what was lacking to him privately,
The *Macedonian* Brethren did supply.

<small>*Their Clerk, who had 50 *l.* per *An.* as much contrary to their Pretences, as for their Teachers to take Money; but now both confest. † 'Tis confest, you have Hirelings in your Herd.</small>

Thus it appears, the Apostle did partake
Of that Provision which the Church did make;
Pretend thou canst not, that the Stock is given
To such as have no need thereof, but even
Thy flurt at *Richardson,* * for taking Pay;
For what? As Clerk, he writes; does much bewray
Thy Folly and Injustice. Is't not fit,
VVho works for others, should be paid for it,
And that by them, who him to work desire?
The Labourer is worthy of his Hire †.

Observe Reader, the Charge is confest: First, That they have
a Stock,

From Quakerism *to* Christianity. 61

a Stock, by which they supply the wants of their Teachers, *i. e.* pay them; yea, and well too: Witness their Increase in Wealth. 2dly, That their Clerks take Money for Writing, and that they are Hirelings; this I and others knew well enough, but *Whitehead* had so denied the same, that there was thousands of Quakers would not believe a word of it: But now, *W. Roger*'s Scourge hath so lash'd this painted Harlot, that she by her dear Son *Ellwood*, hath confess'd it, and spake more Truth in this matter, than *Whitehead*, and twenty more of their Apostate Scribes have been ever made to do; and I am willing to do him right herein; for according to the Proverb, *I am willing to give the Devil his due.* I need not quote Book and Page, to prove their Preachers pretences to Preach freely, without Money, &c. Their Books are full of Proof, and their Sermons from *Dan* to *Beersheba*: But I have said, they pretended to write freely; and this I ought to prove; which I shall do, from their Great Apostle and Second *Moses*, namely G. *Fox*, † *viz.*

† See their Book stiled, Concerning Marriages, &c. p. 4,5,6. Printed 1659. G. *Fox.*

'If any Friends go together in the Power of the Lord, or find a
'necessity thereunto, that after the thing hath been made known be-
'tween themselves, before any thing be concluded, it be declared to
'Friends, who are able * to see and feel into it; and if they see the
'thing in the Light and Power to stand, it may be declared to Friends
'in the Meeting, as they are moved; or, as they are moved, they
'may declare it in the mid-time of the Market, on the Market-Day,
'in the next MarketTown as they are moved, or they may not, as their
'freedom is: Then, after a convenient time, and the thing be seen
'and felt, and had Unity with, then an Assembly of about 12 Friends
'met together, they may speak their Testimony as they are moved,
'how the Lord hath joined them together in Marriage; and then a
'Certificate by Friends then present, may be given, of the Day,
'Month and Year, that it may be Recorded; and as they are mo-
'ved, they may declare it to the Magistrate, and they will, † or they
'may not; AND THAT NOTHING MAY BE RECORDED
'FOR MONEY IN THESE THINGS, BUT FREELY, A FREE
'PEOPLE, AND IN LOVE SERVE ONE ANOTHER; and
'that is it, that you should feel the Thing in the Power, &c.
                                               George Fox.

* *Viz.* Their Teachers which Practise, came afterwards to be abhor'd.

† G. *Fox* was Infallible sence or non-sence, *tot quot & omnes.*

Now let me subjoin a Second Testimony of *George Fox*'s, against taking of Money, &c.

'† Friends, you are to do the Nations Business freely, and that is
'the way to get into the Hearts of People, &c.

† Several Papers given forth *per* G. *Fox, An.* 1659.

I remember there is in one of the Quakers Declarations, a Reserve left for Fighting afterwards: We YET, (say they,) cannot believe, he will make use of the Sword by us, but for the PRESENT, we are given up to Bear and Suffer, &c. So had G. *Fox* said, that as YET
                                                          let

let nothing be RECORDED for MONEY, but for the PRESENT, *i. e.* till you have a fair Opportunity, do things freely, &c. Then there had been a fair Plea; † then AS YET, might by *G. Whitehead*, have been rendered *Adhuc*, and not *Tamen*; for 'tis manifest, that their early pretence to Teach, Preach, write Certificates, &c. freely, was but to get into the Affections of the People, until a more fair opportunity; and then *Experientia docet*, they can take 50 *l. per Annum*, for writing Certificates, &c. Thirty Pounds for writing five or six Sheets, call'd a *Primmer*, to teach Children; 10 *l.* at a time for Preaching, &c. But *G. W.* by his Book, stiled *The Contentious Apostate*. &c. p. 22. he seems to deny *G. Fox*'s Order for Marriage, where it's said, nothing is to be Recorded for Money, &c. as above-cited: But *G. W.* I have it, and you may soon see it in the Library of Christ's Church Colledge in *Oxford*, where that and many others of your Books, which you would be glad were extinct, will remain for Ages to see, and be able thereby to detect your Fallacies. And now follows part of the recited DECLARATION, *viz.*

† As there is now for Whipping, Fining, Imprisoning and Fighting, &c.

See New *Rome* Unmask'd, &c. p. 58. to 63. where I have enlarged hereon from the Quakers Books.

† To the present distracted Nation of *England*, &c. Printed 1659. p. 8.

* No, stay a little longer.
† Ay, be patient a little longer.

'† We have chosen the Son of God to be our King, and he hath
' chosen us to be his People; and he might command Thousands and
' Ten thousands of his Servants at this Day, to Fight in his Cause; he
' might lead them forth, and bring them in, and give them Victory
' over all their Enemies, and turn his Hand upon their Persecutors;
' but yet his Kingdom is not of this World, neither is his Warfare
' of carnal Weapons, neither hath he chosen us for that end, neither
' can we YET believe * that he will make use of us in that way, tho'
' it be his only Right to Rule in Nations, and our Heirship to pos-
' sess the utmost parts of the Earth; but for THE PRESENT † we
' are given up to bear, and suffer all things for his Names-sake, &c.

But Reader, if you look back to *Fox*'s Order for Marriage, you may observe, that he points to have the Matter laid before their Ministers;
' and thereupon, I shall shew you a brief Testimony of one of their
' Female Preachers, a Woman of Note amongst them, in a Letter
' I have by me; part of that against their Hoarding up Money,
' which is as bad as Hoarding up Arms and Amunition, *viz.*

* *Ann Docwra*'s Letter, dated *Feb.* 26. 1684.

† Not since Popery, till Quakerism came in its Room.

' --- * I have heard something concerning this Controversie now on
' foot, which I perceive arises from a Personal Quarrel, about a
' Maid that was chusing a Husband for her self; and also, 'tis expect-
' ed she should give up her concern in that Business, to some of our
' PREACHERS, which was never practised until of late, † amongst
' any that profess'd true Religion; it is that which hath made the
' *JESUITES* to be *ABHOR'D* amongst some of the wisest and ho-
' nestest of the Papists themselves; so that they would not let them
' come within their Houses. If the Maid be a wise Woman, and of
' Age to dispose of her self, she will not let any of our Preachers
' meddle

From Quakerism *to* Christianity.

'meddle with her Concerns † of chusing a Husband for her; they
'should only meddle with their own Business, and let honest Friends
'make their Choice themselves, &c.   *A. D.* look back.

† Why, G. Fox advised to it, &c.

Reader, The main thing I recite part of this Letter, is, to shew the sense some still amongst them have of their own Teacher's Jesuitical Practice, either in making or breaking of Matches, according as they are pleased or displeased: I could write a Book by it self, only to shew the baseness of their Teachers Practice, not only in making Matches, but in making Mischief in Families, in setting Men and their Wives at variance.

And more particularly, *G. W.* my old Antagonist, as may be seen in the Books quoted, both relating to my self, *W. Mucklow, Tho. Crisp, &c.* setting aside *John Feild,* and others of his Stamp, that I believe, the very boldest of the Jesuites never exceeded them. But having in my Book, *New Rome Unmask'd, &c.* p. 57, to 64. shewed the evil Tendency of this their Doctrine and Practice, I refer to that; but since that *G. W.* in his *Sober Expostulations,* p. 108. is driving on the same Trade: Of which, possibly more hereafter.

The Conten. Apostate, p. 5. *The Apostate Incend.* p. 8. *Judgment fixed,* &c. *p.*289.

But come *Thomas,* the chief Business in this Chapter, is to prove, That the Quakers have a Common Purse, that they have a Common Fund or Bank, that your Teachers are supply'd thereout, that your Clerks (as Hirelings) are paid their Yearly Salleries and Stipends, *&c.* This and more you have confess'd, which hundreds of your Teachers have deny'd, and sometimes gained the Good-will of Magistrates, and their own Quiet thereby. But I would not have the World so mistaken of thee neither, as to call thee *TOM-TELL-TROTH*; no, this I presume was done in a passion, even whilst the smart and anguish of *W. Roger's* Scourge was upon thee; for I dare say, *TOM TELL-TROTH* would be a Nick-name for any Quaker-Teacher; and when I view thy *Poem,* p. 26, to 29. I hope thou may'st find in this Book an Answer to it, where thou callest upon *W. Rogers* to name the Men, I have done it, if that will please thee; where thou pretendedst to forbear *John Story,* (yet like *Joab,* smite at his Name; which when living, was precious to many, and now dead, is not forgotten;) I am well satisfied, that he was a Man of a tender Spirit, and had more Christianity and Charity, than all the mercenary Sixty six Judges. I remember, that at the *Bull* and *Mouth* Meeting, *Anno* 1677. *W. Penn* came past eight or ten Persons sitting on the same Bench with me, to ask me to set my Hand to their Epistle of Condemnation. But glad am I, that I was made sensible of their evil intent; for, *Thomas,* there was thy self, *John Moone, Ezekiel Woolley, Samuel Cater,* and many of you concerned in that Paper, as wicked a Generation of Men, as void of Charity, or any thing that is truly Christian, as the *Newgate-Birds.* And what a sad thing is it, that such dissembling Hypocrites, and wicked Impostors, should

Witness Ann Decwra, who telling the Magistrates they had none, they were Quiet after, &c.

claim

The Pilgrim's Progreſs,

claim to themſelves the Name of the one only true Church of Chriſt. And ſo I ſhall adjourn this Head, until I come to the Chapter where the Cage is, where I ſhall make good my Charge, and name Particulars, as thou haſt deſired; only as a Word of Uſe and Application, I ſhall recite a few Verſes wrote by *Ann Doctwra, Anno* 1684. which, as I Printed at the end of *W. Roger's* Scourge, the Original Manuſcript is ſtill by me.

After ſo many ſtrange Miſhaps,
In purſuit of *John Story*, with all thy Traps,
I pity moſt thy † laſt Relapſe.
    Thy Weakneſs ſhews, thy Day is done,
    The Night o're-ſpreads thy Setting-Sun.

† G. Fox.

Cabaliſtick Art is out of Date,
Thy Myſterious Allegories came too late;
To ſay the Truth, it is thy Fate.
    None can avoid what God decrees,
    Thou'rt like a Drone amongſt the Bees.

Thy Strength declines, thy Power decay,
And thou ly'ſt hid this Trying-Day;
To ſave thy ſelf, is no new way.
    Remember now the time that's paſt,
    And how thou'ſt loſt thy Crown at laſt.

Thou did'ſt eſcape thy Enemies Pains,
With States-mens Arts, and Preachers Gains,
But *Dalilah's* Wiles has crack'd thy Brains.
    A Female Power ſurpriz'd thy Strength,
    Thy Honour's laid in the Duſt at length.

Such Women as did Aſſociate,
To help to Govern thy new State,
Who's Ambient Acts, time will relate.
    Theſe Women they did claim a right,
    To waſh the *Ethiopian* white;

To keep things ſweet and clean, ſay they:
But foul things came ſo in their way,
They work'd in vain both Night and Day.
    Profeſſion wipes off no ſuch Blots,
    The *Leopard* does not change his Spots.

To compass Sea and Land thou went,
To Proselite thy Will was bent,
So raised Storms of Discontent.
    Thus God does blast what Man devise,
    To infatuate the Worldly-wise.

This Stubble thou hast built upon,
Is for the Fire; the time comes on
To try the Work that thou hast done.
    The secret Hand of Providence
    Protecteth only Innocence.

These Verses she wrote concerning *G. Fox*; and tho' she (being but a Woman,) is turned to her old Vomit, yet I hope, when *W. Rogers*, *John Raunce*, and others, who had a hand in *W. Roger*'s Poem, and see, and behold the base Abuse of *Tho. Ellwood, &c.* in his *Rogero Mastix, &c.* will see cause to keep at an equal distance from such a deceitful Tribe, as were as cruel to that meek Man *John Story*, as *Doeg* the *Edomite* was to the Priests of the Lord, of whom *David* said, *Psal.* 140. 2, 3. *Which imagine Mischiefs in their Heart; continually are they gathered together for War; they have sharpned their Tongues like a Serpent; Adders Poyson is under their Lips.*

CHAP. X.

Treateth of the Quakers Six-Week Meeting *in* London, *and the pernicious Consequences thereof.*

FIRST, THis Six-Week Meeting of theirs, is chiefly to consult about, and defend their own Members throughout the Kingdom of *England*, and Dominion of *Wales*, from the Penalties of certain Laws, which they fore-know that they shall Transgress, or that hereafter they may Transgress, thro' their being faithful to the Laws and Commands of *G. Fox*, and the Government of the Quaker-Church.

SECONDLY, This Meeting of theirs, is one of their most ancient Meetings for Government, and is made up of chosen Men amongst them, expert in the Laws and Customs of the Nation, well skill'd in the Courts of *London* and *Westminster*, and other his Majesty's Courts of Record, and such as understand the way and manner of

Solliciting the Parliament; and to support them in all these things, they have the Common Bank to assist them; which as I have observed, is like Blood to their Veins, and Sinews to their Bones.

THIRDLY, That I may not seem to impose my single Judgment, that there is such a Meeting; that the Quakers thereto belonging, are thus Exercised, as well as Authorized, see their Aniversary Epistle.

† The Epistle to the Monthly and Quarterly Meetings of Friends in England and Wales, p. 3. Printed 1693.

'† This Meeting being acquainted, that Endeavours have been
'used, for Relief of Friends, in relation to Oaths, pursuant to the
'last Yearly Meetings Advice in that Case; and being sensible
'of the great care of the [Six-Week] Meeting for Sufferings, still
'leave it to the said Meeting for Sufferings, to continue their Care
'and Endeavours in that Case, &c. And also, it is agreed, That
'each Quarterly-Meeting take care, to advise the Correspondents
'for the Counties; and any others concerned, to write only to your
'Correspondents in London, about their Sufferings; and not to o-
'ther Persons, lest their Suffering-Case be delay'd, &c.

From whence it is plain, First, That they are a Meeting constituted, to take care of the Quakers Sufferings: And, 2dly, That this Meeting hold Correspondency with all the Monthly & Quarterly Meetings of the Quakers in England and Wales. 3dly, That the Solliciting the Parliament on the Quakers behalf, is their Business. 4thly, And that they have a Fund for the Service of their Truth, is undeniable from matter of Fact, in the last Chapter, as well as from the recited Epistle, which say, 'Friends appointed to view Accounts,

Epist. ibid. p. 3.

'report, That they find they are truly stated, and rightly kept, &c.

FOURTHLY, And therefore to point at the Quakers Practical Part

One Instance. herein, it is thus: If a Country Quaker be sued at the Exchequer, or other Courts, for the Nonpayment of Tythes, or for any other Act of Obedience to the Quakers Commandments, laid down by their second Moses, if he can but obtain a Certificate from the Quarterly Meeting, to which he belong; he then sends up the said Certificate with his Suffering-Case, to the Correspondents belonging to that Quarterly Meeting, and his Business is effectually taken Care of, to all Intents and Purposes; and this Six Week Meeting so manage the Matter, as either to baffle the Plantiff, be he Priest or Impropriator; [as I still remember—— *Smith*, Brother to *Robert Smith*, of *Whitle-seacoats*, did Councellor *Holeman*, of *Chaterice*, in the Isle of *Ely*, i. e. the Impropriator] or else to preserve their Friends, (they having a Salve for every Sore) as that he shall be a better Man when he ends his Contest, than when he begun.

For by the Management of this Confederacy, by such undue Methods, to prevent the Execution of the Law, as it carries off the Transgressor with flying Colours, so it tends to encourage every Litigious *Quaker* to stand it out with his Lawful Minister, and bid him

him do his worst, &c. So also has it been of very evil Consequence to the Ministers, who many of them have great Charges to maintain, and small Livings; and great part of that wrongfully detain'd, by means of the said Confederacy: I say, this has been, and in other Cases will be, very pernicious to the Publick Peace, and Possession of Liberty and Property, if it be not prevented.

FIFTHLY, The like may be said touching the Statute of 22 of C.II. For if in the Execution of that Act of Parliament, [or any other] the Justices or Constables made a wrong Step, if any *Quaker* get a Certificate from their Quarterly Meeting, signifying his Faithfulness to their Church Canon; in that Case made and provided, *viz.* That he neither have FORSAKEN, DECLINED, or REMOV'D, his Meeting, like the Worldly, Fearful, and Politick Professors; he shall either have his Cause so managed, as to ride Triumphant, or with *Sam. Cater*, be plentifully rewarded; who pretending he suffer'd 20 *l.* for preaching at *Phakenham*, in *Norfolk*, had 10 *l.* sent him out of the common Bank, or *London* Fund, by *John Peacock*, late of St. *Ives*, Woollen-Draper: Tho' after all, when *Cater*'s Business came to be examin'd, he did not suffer a Groat: Yet such is the Freeness of this *London* Fountain, that *Sam.* did but pretend he suffer'd 20 *l.* and he had 10 *l.* sent him, as an Encouragement to go on.

SIXTHLY, Those *Quakers* which sollicite the Parliament are Members of this Meetings, who derive their Authority and Licence so to do, from the Yearly Meeting, as above observ'd; who, when the Clergy-men are at home, minding their Cure, thinking themselves safe in their Callings, being by Law establish'd, then are the *Quakers* working like Moles under Ground; and solliciting sometimes against Tythes, sometimes against Colledges; yea, against the very Bells, as I shall shew from their ancient Testimony, to which they oft refer, and exhort others to keep up to it in all its parts: I say, that I may shew a Branch of their ancient Testimony; I shall recite part of the *Quakers* Petition against the Clergy, and their Maintenance, subscrib'd by above 7000 Persons, and deliver'd to the Parliament of *England* the 20th of *July*, 1659. † and all their Petitions since, to this day, have some Tincture of the Leven of this Petition, *viz.*

† Intituled, *Several Papers sent to th: Parliament*, &c. *Printed* 1695.

' We whose Hands are here underwritten, do testifie and declare
' against the Oppression of Tythes: The false Christians have set
' up a Law and Commandment to take Tythes; and so the Com-
' mands of Men must be disannull'd that take Tythes, and not to
' be obey'd by them that live in the Covenant of God:† And the
' unjust Power that held them up, and Priests, and Impropriators, and
' the Law, and Command, and the Author of it, not to be of God, nor
' of Christ.---We warn you, which to you is the Word of the Lord
' God, That all forced Maintenance of the Priests be taken away;

† Mark their ancient Testimony.

' for

The Pilgrim's Progress,

<small>† The Priests to Thresh, Dig, &c. and the *Quakers* to ride on good Horses, this would please wondrous well.
† ☞</small>

'for while such a thing is set up, it will spoil many idle Men, that 'will not thresh, nor plant, nor dig, nor make Vineyards, Plow 'nor Sow, *&c. P.* 58. WE WOULD HAVE YOU TO READ 'THESE THINGS, AND DO JUSTLY AS IT SPEAKS. †

'Let the Impropriators who bought or rent their Tythes of 'the Colledges, turn them up to the Colledges again, and let the 'Colledges be taken away, that make Ministers, *P.* 59. And you 'may sell all the Gleab Lands, Kings Rents, and his Houses; and 'the Bells to pay the Impropriators, who have bought the Tythes 'of Kings; let their Rents and Parks be sold to pay them again: 'And they that have bought them of Colledges, let the Gleab Lands 'be sold to pay them. *P.* 63. If you do not take off Oppression, 'how should the Lord stand by you, or the People of the Lord ei-'ther; if you query, how you should do with Impropriators?

Answ. 'Sell all the Gleab Lands, and the Bells, except one in a 'Town, or two in a City, to give Notice of a Fire: And all the 'late King's Parks, and his Rents, that had Tenths; and sold the 'Tythes; so let them, *i. e.* the King's Parks and Rents be sold, 'and the Colledges sold; and all the Tythes that belong to them 'thrown down. *P.* 65. You who are the Parliament of this Nati-'on, you should have thrown down Tythes, which Abundance of 'the sober People of the Nation hath petition'd you † to have taken 'them away; which your voting them up, hath voted your selves 'out of the sober Peoples Affection of the Nation, among the *Bruits*; 'you should have sold all the Gleab Lands, and sold all the Bells, 'saving one in a Town; and Colledges, and their Lands, and gi-'ven them all to the Poor of the Nation. *P.* 68. And the Priests 'cry to you Magistrates for Tythes, the Pope's Alms, and lie beg-'ging with their Petitions at your Doors: † And we would have 'you maintain these begging Priests some other way, than by the 'Pope's Alms. *P.* 69. AND EXCEPT YOU TAKE COUNSEL 'OF THE JUST, YOU SHALL NOT SIT. †

<small>† What Impudence is this! pretend to petition and beg, yet teach the Parliament, and tell them what they should do.
† It was highly necessary then, as well as 'tis now, for some to oppose Quakerism.
† ☞</small>

Reader, I have recited enough of the *Quakers* Petition against the Clergy, to shew the Nature of their ancient Testimony, and pointed with a Finger ☞ to two Sayings, which, with the rest, are full of Impudence: And when against the Clergy, I think I may take their Word; their whole Carriage and Deportment, both by Word and Writing, do confirm it: But when for themselves they have any Favour to obtain, DISTRUST THEM IN ALL THEY SAY, for they'll stick at no Promise; as in the Case of their Indulgence; witness their Acknowledging the Holy Scriptures of the Old and New Testament to be given forth by Divine Inspiration. That it is the Rules of Faith and Practice, *&c.* whilst they believe not one Word of what they themselves say; and as a Demonstration
thereof,

From Quakerism to Christianity.

thereof, I shall recite one of their Epistles, sent to the Monthly and Quarterly Meetings, shewing their Care of their own Books: Nay, them very Books, which teach, that the Scripture are Death, Dust, Beastly Ware, Serpents Food, &c. Therefore,

From the Meeting of Sufferings in London.†

Dear Friends,

'With our dear Love in the Truth unto you all, these are to let you understand, that our Friends have at several YEARLY MEET-
'INGS, had under their serious Consideration, how all those Books
'that are printed for the Service of Truth, and in the Unity of
'Friends, might MOST EFFECTUALLY be SPREAD for a ge-
'neral Service to Truth; and at the last YEARLY MEETING it
'was left unto this Meeting, who accordingly have taken Care
'and Pains therein, and settled as followeth.

'That those that print Friends Books, shall the first Opportu-
'nity after, printed, within one Month at most, send to one of the
'Correspondents in the Counties, *viz.*

'For your County, two Books of a sort for each Monthly Meet-
'ing in your County, if under Six Pence, and but one of a sort, if
'above Six Pence *per* Book, for these Reasons.

1st, For Friends to have general Notice what Book are printed.

2dly. That they may send for what other Quantities they see a Ser-
'vice for: And,

3dly. 'That the Printer may be encouraged in Printing for
'Friends.

4thly. 'That one Book at least of a sort that shall be printed,
'may be kept in each Monthly and Quarterly Meetings, for the Ser-
'vice of Truth and Friends, as there shall be occasion, for the fu-
'ture: And as 'twas agreed at the last YEARLY MEETING, 1692.
'in the Printed Epistle.

5thly. 'It is agreed, that for Encouragement, the Printer will al-
'low 2 *d.* in the Shilling for all such Books.

6thly. 'It's agreed, that some here shall be appointed, that two
'or three Weeks before each Quarter-day, to examine the Printer,
'to see that they sends no Books but what are approved by Friends,
'and no more than two of a sort, as aforesaid, except the Friends in
'the Country shall write for more, which it's hoped they will not
'fail in †, as they see a Service for them.

7thly, 'It's agreed or advised, that the Printers Accompts be ful-
'ly clear'd once a Year at least, by those Friends the Country shall
'send up to the Yearly Meeting.

8thly. 'It's agreed, that the Name of the Printer, imploy'd by
'Friends, should be sent with Directions how to write to him.

† Renewed Advice to the Monthly and Quarterly Meetings in *England* and *Wales*, for preserving and spreading FriendsBooks for Truths Service, Printed 1693.

For a Quaker Library.

† I have heard that they begin to fail, and send but slowly.

And

And dear *Friends and Brethren,*

> 'It's tenderly, and in Brotherly Love, advised and recommended
> 'unto you, that ye be careful and diligent in the SPREADING of
> 'ALL such Books that are printed for the Service of Truth, and are
> 'either written in DEFENCE of it, or Christian Doctrine, or Holy
> 'Profession, or by way of Epistle, Warning, Caution, Exhortation,
> 'or Prophesie; that so we may not be any way, or in any wise, Re-
> 'miss or Negligent, in promoting that Holy and Eternal Truth it hath
> 'pleased Almighty God to bless us with the Knowledge of, and hath
> 'raised us up to stand Witnesses for in our Age and Generation; nor
> 'nothing may be wanting on our parts, to promote it, and the spread-
> 'ing of it.

Not a word of the Bible.

Signed on the Behalf of the Meeting for Suf-
ferings in London, 18. 6. *Mo.* 1693.

By *Benj. Bealing.*

Postscript. 'And this Agreement and Account herein sent, we
'think it needful you should record it in your Quarterly Book; and
'sometimes read it for Remembrance, and general Notice.

Observations from hence.

Reader. From what hath been said, you may observe. *First,*
That there is such a Meeting as I have set forth; both from their
Yearly, and the recited Six Week Meeting, in case the *Quakers* deny it. *Secondly,* That their Business principally is to take care of
the Sufferings of their own Friends, and that how plentifully they reward such as are faithful to their Church-Canons; as in the instance
of *Sam. Cater,* who for pretending to suffer 20 *l.* tho' he suffered not
a Groat, yet had 10 *l.* sent him, as a Reward for meeting boldly,
contrary to the Law in that case made and provided. *Thirdly,*
That they have a Fund, or Common Bank, and that the Accounts
are examined by a Committee chosen out of the Yearly Meeting for
that purpose. *Fourthly,* That such as suffer for Non-payment of
Tythes, are to send to the Quarterly-Meetings Correspondents, lest
their Sufferings be delayed. *Fifthly,* You may also perceive, what
a Confederacy is held by the Quakers, and how they are inabled by
their Exchequer, to hold Suit with both Priest and Improprietor †.
Sixthly, You also may see, how the Quakers sollicite the Parliament
for Favours; as also, how they Petition against the Clergy, the
Churches, the Colledges, and Bells too: Yea, this is according to
their ancient Testimony, and they are not chang'd, they tell you so,
as I have herein before observed. And *Lastly,* You may by this recited Epistle, observe the Confederacy of their Yearly-Meeting, and
Six-Weeks Meeting, to spread their venemous Books, to infect both

† As in the instance of Mr. *Holeman,* who was a Justice of the Peace, a Counsellor at Law, yet tired.

Youth

From **Quakerism** *to* **Christianity.**

Youth and Aged, Male and Female, Old and Young, and all under the fine Notion of the Service of Truth, [meaning Quakerism:] For, if they meant the Truth of the Christian Doctrine, they would at one time or other, read a Chapter in their Meetings; at one time or other, recommend to their Monthly and Quarterly Meetings, the reading of some Portion of the Holy Scriptures: But not a word of this in their Epistles, not a Chapter read in their Meetings for forty Years together; but their own Epistles, their own Prophesies, their own Printed Exhortations: These they not only read in their private Meetings in their Families, but they must Record (you see,) this recited Epistle in their Quarterly-Book, and sometimes read it: Oh! 'tis a precious Epistle.

And now Christian Reader, I cannot but think my self unable to give a full and compleat Caution, against the spreading of the Gangrene of *Quakerism*: and therefore, give me leave in the Words of Mr. *Ralph Farmer*, a Minister, formerly of *Bristol*, to rehearse part of his Exhortation, *viz.*

'Now beloved, if thou be'st a Christian; What say'st thou? Is 'not here a Mystery of Ungodliness to the purpose? Where was it 'hatch'd, think'st thou? Could any less than all the Devils in Hell, 'keep a Conventicle, to Contrive and Plot this Black and Hellish 'Treason, against the Majesty of God, Jesus Christ, and the Holy 'Scriptures? Oh! ye Christian Magistrates, who rule for Christ, 'and to whom you shall one day give an account of your Govern-'ment, how you have ruled for him, and how tender you have been 'of his Honour: What is become of your Zeal for Christ, and his 'Glory? Good Sirs! if these wretched Souls have such Liberty of 'Conscience, to think thus contemptuously of our Blessed Lord Jesus 'Christ, and the Holy Gospel, let them not (upon pretence of Liber-'ty of Conscience,) be so audaciously Blasphemous, to write and 'speak thus: And, O ye Servants of the Lord, my Fathers and 'Brethren in the Ministry of our dear and ever Blessed Jesus, you 'that are the Pastor's of the Lord's Flock, and the Watchmen for the 'Sheep of his Pasture, lift up your Voices, and spare not; cry aloud 'to all your Congregations, and fore-warn them, that they be not a 'Prey to Satan's Devices; let the Wolves know, that you are not 'dumb Dogs, and cannot bark; and Idol-Shepherds, that can nei-'ther hear, nor see, nor understand any thing; and that at a time 'of need can say nothing; certainly, certainly, such as these may ill 'look for their Gain; from their Quarters they deserve it not; who, 'so they may be fed, care not (nor care to discover) what devouring 'Beast comes to destroy the Flock of Christ: But you, my dear 'Brethren, who are set over the Lord's Folds, and who watch for 'their Souls, as those that must give an account, and that have a de-'sire to do it with joy, and for the profit of your People; read and
'practise

In his Book, *i. e. The Myst. of Ungodliness,* &c.

'practise what St. *Paul* gives, in charge to the Pastors of the Church 'at *Ephesus*, † and let me give it thee here in his own Words. what 'he gave forth to his Son *Timothy* : *I charge thee before God, and* 'the Lord Jesus Christ, who shall judge the Quick and the Dead, at 'his Appearing and Kingdom, preach the Word, be instant in Sea-'son, out of Season, reprove, rebuke, exhort with all Long-suffer-'ing and Doctrine; for the time will come [and it is now] when they 'shall not endure sound Doctrine, but after their own Lusts shall they 'heap to themselves Teachers, having itching Ears; and they shall 'turn away their Ears from the Truth, and shall be turned unto Fa-'bles; but watch thou in all things; endure Afflictions; do the work 'of an Evangelist, (or Gospel Preacher;) make full Proof of thy 'Ministry, &c.*

† Acts 20. 28, 29, 30, 31.

CHAP. XI.

Shews the Quakers Second-Day Meetings, *and Hypocrisie thereof; with its ill Consequences, in order to Deceive.*

Reader,

I AM now come to their Second-Day Meeting, even to that Meeting where Satan dwells, and where he employs his arch-est Emissaries; I shall not wrong them, as believing I must one day give an account for my Actions, before the Man Christ Jesus, who shall judge both the Quick and Dead at the Great Day, where (I hope,) I shall not be afraid to meet G. *Whitehead* with this Testimony in my hand; so on the other hand, I shall not spare them, hide nor cover them, who have by their Wiles, by their Books of two sorts, deceived the Nations, deceived many of the Magistrates, many of the Clergy, nay, my self; for I could not have wrote thus fifteen Years ago †: I took them then, at least some Years before, to be Prophets, at least sincere, and to meet there, for the approving of what was Right, Sound and Orthodox, and for condemning the contrary: But behold, I have found the contrary, and that by sad Experience; yea, I have found, that their whole Business, is to deceive, and to carry on a Design; yea, a Confederacy, under the fine Notion of Unity and Concord: I have laboured many Years, under great Difficulties; I have spent my Estate, I have spent my Strength, I grow into Years; I have a Conscience to Discharge; I think I cannot do it, unless I compleat that Discovery which I have begun: Tho' I find it prejudicial to my Health, and other Business, I find my self conscientiously concerned in this weighty Affair: I do know, that the Reverend Author of the Book, Entituled, *The Snake*

† No, if I had not seen their deceitful Practices, and measur'd them by the Scriptures, I could not have known them rightly.

in

From Quakerism *to* Christianity.

in the Grass, † &c. have done exceeding well; he hath done beyond what I am able to do; 'tis a Learned Piece, and becomes a Learned Reader: But I am directing the greatest part of what I say, to the more unlearned; † to such (whether Quakers or others,) as sometimes must Spell as they read, and read over and over, before they can understand; this makes me sometimes write over and over the same thing, to inculcate, (if possible,) the Matter I am upon, into their Heads, that at last they may understand, as well as to lay a Foundation for Abler Pens. This then, I thought fit to premise by way of Introduction, &c.

† To whose Works I refer the Reader.
† *i. e.* The Common People, who are not so well School-Learn'd.

This Meeting of the Quakers is held every Second-Day of the Week, (which we call Monday,) throughout the Year in *London*; the Members of it are the Teachers of the Quakers reciding in and about *London*; whereof G. *Fox*, † (in his life time) was the Principal, and G. *Whitehead* now, as I am given to understand. The Meeting formerly was kept in *Ellis Hook*'s Chamber in *Lumbard-street*, now I presume in *Grace-Church-street*. This Meeting doth much resemble His Majesty's Privy Council: For the King, by and with the Advice of his Privy Council, can do many things; he can by Proclamation, put the Laws in Execution; I think, he can proclaim War, and make Peace: So can this Meeting; they can quicken the coming in of Money, granted by the Yearly Meeting; they can issue out their Proclamation for a War, against the Ministers of any Society; they can alter, and change any Message, stop any Prophesie, stifle any Revelation, silence the Voice uttered by the Spirit of the Lord, thro' their most eminent Prophets, in what respect they please, and make it speak louder and more shril, where they think there is most Service, or may be more conducive to their Design; they are like the Helm to the Ship, which turn it which way the Pilate please; they are the Wheel within the Wheel, which move all the whole Work, yet so invisibly, as few shall know how, and fewer know who; for they are Persons uncertain and accidental, and cannot be chargeable (by Name,) for any Errour, tho' guilty of every Errour in their Books, so far as Consent, Approbation and Recommendation can make them: For all Books Printed and Reprinted, pass thro' the fiery Tryal of their Infallible Examination; they Govern, they Rule, they steer the Vessel, but all INVISIBLY; they pay their Ministers, but their own People (many of them) that give to their Collections and Contributions, do not know it; nor, if you tell them of it, will they believe it: For none can tell, who pays, nor who receives, but now and then by chance, what some or other, as *Ellwood* blabb'd it out at unawares: But their principal Work is, to Approve and License their Books, Printed for the Service of the Truth, as they phrase it: But the last being their most principal Verb, I shall the more insist upon it, to shew their most horrible Deceit and Hypocrisie,

† For he seldom lived with his Wife, but kept at *London*.

L

Hypocrifie: For, suppose one of their People pretend he is moved of the Lord, by his Eternal Spirit, to write a Message or Warning to the Inhabitants of *Bristol*, with this Title; THIS IS THE WORD OF THE LORD, TO THEE, O *BRISTOL!* Well, this Book is sent up to their Second-Day Meeting, and there they take it into consideration; they then will Alter, and Change Words and Sentences; put in, and leave out, what they conceive suit best with the Times; and yet, let it go as THE WORD OF THE LORD. Thus do they sit in the Judgment-Seat, and like the Old Prophet, deceive; not only the Nations, but the poor young Prophet, that thought he had wrote from the Infallible Motion; when alas! 'tis now so alter'd, so added to, and diminish'd from, what it was, that it's meerly Calculated to the design of the Cabal, and yet shall go with the same Title, *i. e.* THIS IS THE WORD OF THE LORD, TO THEE, O *BRISTOL!* of this most horrible Deceit I could give a hundred Instances, and find Matter enough for to write a Book by it self; but I must consult Brevity, left my Pen out-run my Penny; and therefore, shall single out one Instance, which I hope, will give some satisfaction; it shall be out of a Book wrote by *Edward Burrough*, Entituled, *A Trumpet of the Lord sounded out of Sion, sounding forth the Controversie of the Lord of Hosts,* * &c.

* Printed in Quarto, 1656.

But before I go to the chief Matter intended, I shall recite the pretended Commission of this bold Prophet; and then it will appear, whether the Second-Day Meeting did well, in altering his Prophesie, by adding to, and taking from the same; for, either they did believe him to be a Prophet, that the Word of the Lord did come to him as expresly as to *Jeremiah, Ezekiel, Daniel,* and the rest of the Prophets, or they did not; if they did, how then dare they add and diminish and leave out, in the Reprint of his Works, what had gone for the Word of the Lord, from 1656 to 1672? If they did not believe him to be a Prophet divinely Inspir'd, but an Impostor, Why did they suffer the said Book to go as THE WORD OF THE LORD, from 1656 to 1672? So take it which way they will, and it will appear, that G. *Whitehead,* (whose Epistle of Recommendation is prefix'd and Printed to *Edw. Burrough's* Works,) and others of this Second-Day Meeting, are most horrible Cheats, and grand Deceivers: And therefore, now to the Commission which *Edw. Burroughs* received; which, to *G. W.* and others, that believed it, was both Authentick and Substantial, *viz.*

'By Order and Authority given unto me by the Spirit of the Li-
'ving God, King of Kings, and Lord of Lords, the 31st. Day of the
'Tenth Month, 1655. about the 4th. hour in the Morning, when
'my Meditations was of my God, upon my Bed, in the *Kilkenny*
'City; in the Nation of *Ireland*; at that time THE WORD OF
'THE

From Quakerism *to* Christianity.

'THE LORD CAME UNTO ME, saying, Write my Controver-
'sie with all the Inhabitants of the Earth, unto all sorts of People;
'as I will shew thee by this same Authority and Commission de-
'clared: This I send unto you the Tribes of the Earth, and this
'upon your Heads shall stand for ever, to be witnessed by the Light
'of Christ Jesus in all your Consciences, in the dreadful Day of
'Vengeance, which upon you, O Inhabitants of the Earth! is coming.
'Prepare, prepare, to meet the Lord. O Nations, Tongues and
'People! unto you all hereby a Warning is come; and a Visitation
'from the Presence of the Living God, which you are straitly requi-
'red to put in Practice, as at the terrible Day of dreadful Vengeance
'you will answer the contrary.

*Given under my Hand, and sealed by the Spirit of the Eternal God,
who lives for ever, thro' a Servant of the Lord,* E. Burrough.

Thus, Reader, you see the Commission which *Edw. Burrough* receiv'd; (whether counterfeit or not, is not my present Business,)
which was forthwith Printed in *Quarto*, and sent up and down the
Nation, as THE WORD OF THE LORD, and as such receiv'd
by thousands of us, and to be sure, approv'd of by the Second-Day
Meeting; yet when the Times chang'd, and the Second-Day Meeting came to Reprint the several Prophecies and Revelations of this
remarkable Prophet *Edw. Burrough*, amongst the rest, you will find
this Book, stiled, *The Trumpet of the Lord sounded, &c.* reprinted
in the Works of *Edw. Burrough* *. And,   * See E. B's.

First, To thee *Oliver Cromwel*, and his Council.   Works, p. 97.
2*dly*, To all Judges and Lawyers, and their Train.
3*dly*, To all Astrologers, Magicians, *&c.*
4*thly*, To all Generals, Collonels, Commanders, *&c.*

To all these four sorts, the Reprint has it with some little variati-
on; indeed, enough to spoil the Predictions; which, had they been
true, ought not to have been added to, nor taken from. And the Second-Day Meeting in 1672. pretended to believe them to be true, by
their Title in the Index, viz. *A Trumpet of the Lord sounded forth
of Sion, which containeth a Testimony from the Word of the Lord.*
But behold, and be astonished at the deceit of these Jugglers, *i. e.* the
Second-Day Meeters; for the fifth Prophesie, directed thus, *To all
you who are, and have been always Enemies to the very Appearance
of Righteousness, who are called Delinquents and Cavaliers*; I say,
this whole fifth Prophesie is left out in the Reprint, 'tho' as positive-
ly avowed to be the Word of the Lord as the other, as certainly sealed by the Spirit of the Eternal God as the other, and every way Authorized by as ample a Commission from the Spirit of the living God,
yea, the King of Kings, and Lord of Lords, as the other; and yet all
left out in the Reprint. And to make it appear so beyond all their
glossing, I shall recite it *verbatim*, as it follows the preceding Title
and Direction.   L 2   *To*

To the Delinquents and Cavaliers.

[margin: Pag. 9. in the Quarto Impression, printed 1656.]

'Thus saith the Lord, my Controversie is against you, even my
'Hand in Judgment, is upon you already; and you are become cursed
'in all your Hatchings and Endeavours, and from time to time my
'Hand hath been against you in Battel; and you have been, and are
'given up to be a Prey to your Enemies; for the purpose and intents
'of your Hearts, have been known always to be against the Form of
'Truth, and much more against my powerful Truth it self: And be-
'cause you attempted to take my Throne, (Conscience.) therefore I
'rose in my Fury against you, and will have War with all your Fol-
'lowers herein forever, who shall attempt to take my Throne, (Con-
'science;) and tho' my Hand hath been evidently against you, yet
'to this Day, you remain in Rebellion in your Minds, in hatching

[margin: Note, All this to the Delinquents, is left out in the Reprint, 1672.]

'Murder and Cruelty in your wicked Hearts: And tho' your Kings
'and Princes have been cut off in Wrath, and your cruel desperate
'Inventions, and Plots of Wickedness (conceived in your cursed
'Womb,) have been broken, and you cut short in your Desires;
'yet you repent not, nor will not see, how you are given up to be a
'Curse, and a Desolation, and a Prey, in Houses, and Lands, and Per-
'sons, to them whom I raised against you, and gave Power over you,
'yet you are hardned; and your Cruelty in Persecution against my Ser-
'vants, cannot be measured; where you have any Power, you smite
'with the Fist of Wickedness, and count it your Glory to despise my
'Name: In the Valleys of vain Hopes do you feed, and on the
'Mountains of foolish Expectations; and conceive in your cruel
'Womb of Tyranny, the overthrow of the Nations; but in the
'bringing forth, your selves are overthrown: And it is not for well-
'doing that you suffer, but my Hand is against you, and my Judg-

[margin: † Then some hopes left: Why then should not this have Been continued for their good?]

'ments are upon you; and, except you Repent,†shall continue upon
'Earth with you, and follow you, and pursue you to the Lake of
'Destruction, where there is no Repentance; and you, and your
'Kings, and Lordly Power, (by which you have thought to exercise
'Lordship over my Heritage.) shall be enslaved by the Devil, in the
'Pit of Darkness, in everlasting Bondage, where he [the Devil,]
'shall Reign your King and Lord for evermore.

From whence it is evident, That tho' this Prophesie was said to be
as true as any Chapter in the Bible; yea, that the Word of the Lord
came to *Burough* the 31*st*. of *December*, 1655. at the fourth hour
in the Morning, and sealed by the Spirit of the Eternal God; yet
this Second-Day Meeting hath, or claim to have a Power superiour,
and by Virtue thereof, can silence the Prophet, stifle his Prophesie,

[margin: It must be Real or Counterfeit.]

cancel his Revelation, and null and make void his Commission; for,
as I said, they either believed his Commission to be REAL, or
COUNTERFEIT; if REAL, as so they always pretended, then,
Is it not great Wickedness that it should be thus smothered up and
stifled, since, tho' the Delinquents and Cavaliers be very wicked,
yet

yet upon Repentance, there seems to be some hopes, which now this Prophesie cannot be instrumental in, since the Second-Day Meeting hath buried it in Oblivion, in that they did not Reprint it with the rest of the same Book in his Works, in *Folio*? † If COUNTERFEIT, What wicked Wretches were these Members of the Second-Day Meeting, in 1656. to Print it in *Quarto* as the Word of the Lord, and sealed by the Spirit of the Eternal God, and thereupon, and as such, sent it up and down to us, to deceive us, by recommending a COUNTERFEIT Commission for a REAL? Thus, let them take it which way they will, and it is wicked in the superlative Degree.

† *Printed* 1672

But this is not all; it shew'd their Cowardize and Temperizing; for this was wrote in O. *Cromwel*'s time, designed, I perceive, to curry Favour with him, and to shew himself and his Brethren, the Quakers are Enemies to Monarchy: But when it was Reprinted, it was done in K. *Charles* the Second's time; and then they wheel'd about, complain'd of O. *Cromwel*, and flatter'd the King, Cavaliers, and Court-Party; and then this Prophesie, sealed never so strong, revealed never so clear, the very Day, Month and Year specified, nay, the very Hour in the Morning, yet (as I have said,) it not suiting with the Design on foot, namely, To root out Christianity, and introduce Quakerism, it must be suspended, stifled and buried. Thus then it appears, how wickedly deceitful are these Second-Day Meeters, who can thus prevaricate and dissemble with God and Man; of which, I could give many Instances, but rather refer to *The Snake in the Grass, &c.* which doth most amply set forth their turning with the Times, and their facing about with every Wind that might seem to blow a prosperous Gale for the Advance of Quakerism, *&c.*

But to conclude, or rather confirm this Head, and to shew what Temporizers these Quakers have been, as well as knowingly Wicked, these Second-Day Meeters ever (from first to last) were; let me add one Citation more, as it lyes dispersed in a Book of *Edw. Burrough*'s, Printed in *Quarto*, 1659. containing several Letters written, and said to be delivered to *O. Cromwel, Anno* 1657. and some Letters said to be delivered to *R. Cromwel, Anno* 1658. then Protector: BUT I DISTRUST ALL THEY SAY †; for having compared this *Quarto* Book, I find many places which mentions the King, or the Kingly Government, left out in his Works in *Folio*; which Words so left out, you will find them in Capital Letters, which, as it shews their Temporizing, so it discovers their Wickedness to stifle Prophesies, if they believ'd them such to be; if not, still as wicked to let this *Burrough* in his Works, still go for a Prophet, and by *Whitehead, Coale, Howgill* and *Fox, &c.* recommended as such; I do say, it is such a depth of Hypocrisie, that I want Words to set it forth sufficiently.

† So cannot believe they did deliver them as Printed, since after Printed can thus alter them.

P. 15. 'And these things are not right in the sight of the Lord, 'that such who have been for many Years faithful in the Service, 'and in their Trust, and hazarded Life and Liberty for Conscience- 'sake,

Good Counsel and Advice rejected. Printed in *Quarto*, 1656. Reprinted in *Folio*, 1672.

The Pilgrim's Progress.

'fake, which they cannot now poffefs, becaufe of thee [Dear *Oliver*,]
'but are caft out for the exercife of their pure Confcience; confider
'of it, for this makes the Nation more unhappy, and lefs bleffed, when
'fuch who delight in true Juftice and Judgment, are caft out of their
'Places, † and fo deprived of giving their Judgment amongft Men;
'and abfolutely this will make thy Army lefs profperous, when fuch
'who fear the Lord, againft whom thou canft not juftly charge no
'Evil, are caft out and defpis'd, and this in time, thou may'ft fee
'to thy Sorrow; and as thy Friend, I lay this before thee, and do in
'plainnefs tell thee, If thou thus utterly deny the People of God in
'the Day of thy Profperity, and thou thus wholly caft them out of
'thy Service, they cannot ftand by thee, nor own thee in the Day of
'thy Trouble; † p. 16. when as fuch who feareth the Lord, are caft
'out of Judicatories in thy Government, and out of Defence in thy
'Armies: What, is this the end of that long Travel in Wars, and of
'fo many Promifes of Liberty of Confcience, that juft Men fhould
'thus be dealt withal, as one without Bowels of Compaffion, unto
'fuch who have truly ferved with thee in a faithful Service for the
'Common-Wealth, who many of them now are grievous Sufferers
'under thee? P. 17. Many Enemies thou haft which watch over
'thee, (*O. C.*) for Evil, and not for Good : —— Firft, There is a People
'fcattered thro' all thefe Nations, who is full of Wrath towards
'thee, EVEN OF THOSE KNOWN BY NAME MALIG-
'NANTS, † in whofe Hearts, to this day, there is continual Ha-
'tred againft thee, and all thy Off-fpring; — Daily Advantage they
'feek againft thee, by fecret Plottings of Malicioufnefs in their EVIL
'Hearts, feeking by all means, if it be poffible, how to be avenged,
'and to revenge themfelves, and THE CAUSE OF THEIR KING,
'with no better purpofe, than to deftroy thee; — Such is the Cruelty
'and Defperatenefs of fome of them, their own Lives are not dear
'unto them, to take away thine; I have felt the ftrength of their
'Rage againft thee, which carries them above Senfe or Fear, to fore-
'go any Danger, that they may fee their defired end of thee; their
'Malice towards thee, is fo feated in their wrathful Hearts, that it
'cannot eafily be quenched : I know the Lord hath CURSED them
'and their Endeavours to this day, and thou haft had Dominion and
'Power given thee of God, to break them in pieces; AND WHAT
'THOU HAST DONE TO THEIR KING, SHOULD NOT
'BE RECKONED AGAINST THEE BY THE LORD, † IF
'NOW THOU ART FAITHFUL TO WHAT HE REQUIRES
'OF THEE, *p.* 20. Tho' we the People of God, doth not envy thy
'Perfon nor Government, — yet Friend, the want of our Prayers to
'God for thee, is worfe to thee than the fecret Plotting of all wicked
'Men : And how can we mention thee in our Prayers to God for
'thee, except it be to be Deliver'd from thee.

† Oh! how the Quakers did flatter *O. Cromwel* to get into Offices, yea, Juftices forfooth.

† *Oliver* did not much value his new Saints, *i. e.* Quakers.

† Oh! how careful the Quakers were of their Dear Friend *O. C.*

† Murder acquitted, if *O. C.* would but ftand by the Quakers.

To

From Quakerism to Christianity.

To this agrees that Saying of *G. Fox* to Mr. *Camelfeild*, a Minister, in his Book, *i.e. Truths Defence, &c.* p. 15. 'No Prayers can 'we send to thee, but for thy Destruction, thou Man of Sin, and 'Enemy of Christ, *&c.* No, neither to *Oliver* their Governour, nor to the Priests; no, they cannot pray for their Enemies, unless they do Kindness for them, *i.e.* make them Justices or Commanders; no, no Penny, (or what's Equivolent,) no *Pater Noster* from the Quakers.) See the Margin †.

† Is that the Reason they'l not pray for K. *William* III.

P. 21. 'And this I have written to thee, out of perfect Love in 'the Fear of God: ---- And if thou could'st own them, (*i.e.* Qua- 'kers, they would own thee in the Face of all thy Enemies.

P. 35. to *Richard*. 'AS CONCERNING THY WAR, 'AND ARMIES ABROAD IN *SPAIN*, SOMETHING 'THERE IS IN IT * KNOWN TO THE LORD: ---- 'MAKE NO COVENANT WITH IDOLATERS, BUT 'TREAD DOWN THEIR IDOL GODS, WHICH 'THEY HAVE SET UP, AND HEW DOWN THEIR 'MOUNTAINS, IN WHICH THEIR CONFIDENCE 'STAND, AND PLOW UP THEIR GROUND, THAT 'THE SEED MAY BE SOWN AFTER THEE; IT'S 'HONOUR ENOUGH TO BE THE LORD'S PLOW- 'MAN. P. 44. And if thou walk with the Lord, and preserve his 'People (*i.e.* Quakers) that fear him, then shalt thou prosper, and 'thy Name shall be greater than was thy Fathers; and the number- 'less Number of this now distressed People, will be unto thee a 'Strength, and stand by thee in thy day of Trouble, and defend 'thee and thy just Government, † and their Hearts shall cleave unto 'thee, and thou shalt prosper for their sakes, and none of thy Ene- 'mies shall have Power over thee. P. 53. And as for thy Father, the 'late Protector, great things did the Lord do for him, in raising him 'up, and casting out his Enemies before him, and giving him Victo- 'ry, Renown and Power, † thro' Nations; and we know, the Lord 'shewed favour to him, and gave him Strength, Wisdom and Va- 'lour, and a right Spirit; and he was called of God, into that great 'Work, to subdue the grievous Tyrannies, once ruling over tender 'Consciences, and to break down the great Oppressions which had 'caused the Just to Groan; and the Lord was with him in Victory, 'and preserved him from great Dangers.

* Something ; yea, who knows not that, this is like a Gipsie-Prophesie.

† Then *Rich:* *Cromwel's* Government was just in the Quakers Account.

† O brave *Oliver!* the Quakers Champion.

Observations on the recited Quotation.

Reader, please to observe, First, That the Words in Capital Letters were Printed in the *Quarto* Book, 1659. and left out in the Reprint.

The Pilgrim's Progress,

print in *Folio*, 1672. which shews their Temporizing; and like Butter-flies, how they hide themselves, whilst the danger of the Storms are past. 2dly, Their wickedness in leaving out such Prophesies, if real; if counterfeit, then as bad to suffer them to go abroad so long, to deceive others. 3dly, How they pleaded their being in the Army, and their faithfulness to their Trust therein, as meritorious of their continuance in the Army for the defence of the Nation, as well as their desire of being in Offices in the Administration of Justice. † But hold! *Oliver*, as he did not believe their Prophesies, so he would not trust them in either Military or Civil Affairs. 4thly, You may see how they did cling to *O. Cromwel*, and next to *Richard*, justifying their Usurpation. 5thly, How they acquitted *O. Cromwel* in that horrible Murder of K. *Charles* I. saying, That if he would but stand by, cherish and support Quakerism, WHAT HE DID TO THE LATE KING, SHOULD NOT BE LAID TO HIS CHARGE BY THE LORD. 6thly, And, that if he would not do so, they could not pray for him, and that should be worse to him than all the Plottings of the wicked: And I take this to be the reason, why they refuse to pray for K. *William* III. for I have gone into several of their Meetings, and I have enquired of others that have done the like; I have likewise read divers of their Prayers in Print, as *Stev. Crisp*'s, and others, yet I could never hear, see, nor learn, that they ever prayed for K. *William* III. no, no more than for the Priests, or than for *Oliver*: But for this Omission, *Whitehead* hath a *Salvo* ready, *viz.* †
‘ But, where are all required by Christ or his Apostles, to pray for
‘ them (*i. e.* Kings, and all that are in Authority,) by Name, or
‘ charged as Offenders for not naming of Persons in our Prayers?
‘ May we not pray acceptably, † unless we tell God the Names of those
‘ we pray for? *&c.*

But, Reader, let me trace this Snake in the Grass, and hunt this Fox to his Burrow; and do not think it hard dealing: I know, there can be nothing said of them that grates, but they presently cry out of Persecution, of Malice, while they take the liberty to expose all sorts of People, how innocent soever, as at large I have set forth; * and shall shew one Instance more, before I enter upon my CHACE.

Viz. ‘ To all you that desire an Earthly King in *England*, — who
‘ profess your selves to be Christians, whether Presbyterians, or o-
‘ thers, — Do not the Priests, Presbyterians, and many of the Ru-
‘ lers, cry for an Earthly King? — And is not this the same Nature
‘ the *Jews* were in? And do they not in this Crucifie Jesus? — And
‘ are not all these Elders Christians, that will doat so much of an
‘ Earthly King, TRAYTORS against Christ? — Now Elders, if
‘ you say, *Peter* said, Honour the King, — this doth not hold forth,
‘ that *Peter* bid them set up an Earthly King over them; neither do
‘ you read, — that there were any Earthly Kings since the Days of
‘ the

---

† Oh! they'd gladly be Justices of the Peace.

† The Conten. Apost. *&c.* p. 27.

† And may you not? Who knows but you may mean another than the Rightful and Lawful King. * See the Pict. of Quakerism, *&c.* Part 2. p. 44. to 175.

G. *Fox*'s Judgment of Kingly Government, taken out of a Paper of his, written to the Presbyterians, *&c.* a little before the Restoration.

From Quakerism to Christianity. 81

'the Apostles, but among the Apostate Christians, †&c.

But no sooner did the King come in *Anno* 1660. but within a Month, G. *Fox*, and others, put forth a Declaration, saying, *p.* 4. 'We do therefore declare, to take off all Jealousies, Fears and Suspicions of our Truth and Fidelity to the King, and these present 'Governours, That our *INTENTIONS* and Endeavours are, and 'shall be, good, true, honest and peaceable towards them, and that 'we do love, own, and honour the King, and the present Governours '&c. It would require a Volume to set forth their Temporizing, and horrid Practices in this kind; but I shall only give a Taste, referring to *The Snake in the Grass*, &c. But 'tis comical to see this their early Turning with the Times: First, None more vigorous against Monarchy; and yet, none did sooner, nor yet more flatter, fawn, and creep to the same Government, than did the *Quakers*: But that which is most provoking, and for which I chiefly mention this, that upon every occasion, to ingratiate themselves into the Favour of the Government, they frequently charged the same Presbyterians, &c. with their being against the Government, of fighting Principles, yea, a People who would promote their Religion by the Power of the Sword. *Viz.* † 'How did the Presbyterians excite the Parliament in 'these very Terms: *Elijah* opposed Idolatry and Oppression, so do 'ye; down with *Baal's* Priests, (which is, saith *Penn*,) as much as to 'say, Away with your Arch-Bishops and Bishops, the whole Ministry, and Worship of the Church of *England*.

† See the *Quak. Unm. &c. p.* 1. for much more of this.

Yea, let their Words be never so contrary, they are not to be measured by their Words.

† See *W. Penn's* just Rebuke, to 21 Divines, &c. Printed 1674. p. 25.

Come smooth *George*, I have seen another of your Books, † where you say, *p.* 52. 'Some of the Presbyterian Non-conformists Preach'ers, are fled Beyond-Sea; others lurk in Corners here and there, 'and keep private Conventicles, where many times they preach Se'dition against their lawful Prince, by instigation of whom, that In'surrection hapned in 1666. Again, *p.* 53. And some of them have 'printed Books in Defence of the Lawfulness of making War against 'the Supream Magistrates, &c. Again, *p.* 23. And how many Gar'ments were rolled in Blood, by the instigation of the Presbyterian 'Teachers, the whole Nation was a witness; so that many thousands 'were made Widows and Fatherless, by that War they stirred up 'the People unto. P. 54. And in very Truth, the Presbyterian 'Church will never be able to purge her self, of the iniquity of kil'ling many Thousands in the three Nations, by the occasion of a most 'bloody War, raised up thro' the instigation of the Presbyterian 'Teachers, &c. And thus they continued bloody Enemies to the Presbyterians, notwithstanding G. *Fox* did so condemn them as Traytors, Antichrists, and Crucifiers of Jesus, for endeavouring the Restoration of K. *Charles* II. and that no People then on Earth, did more stir up, instigate, and encourage a bloody War against the King and Church of *England*, than the *Quakers* did: Witness their *Trumpet sounded*, † &c.

† The Way cast up, &c. p. 52, 53.

† See their Trumpet founded, &c. in the Eleventh Chapter.

M But

But, notwithstanding all this, and a hundred times as much, which might be shewed out of their Books, yet they continued villifying the Presbyterians, saying, † 'Knowing that ye look on it as a Duty, to 'fight by Military Weapons in defence of your Principle; yea, to 'promote *YOUR CAUSE* by the Power of the *SWORD*, in which 'you are Confirmed by some of *YOUR PREACHERS*, who are '*ALWAYS* labouring to persuade you to this, as one Evidence of 'your Zeal for God, and not to spare to hazard your Lives, Liber-'ties and Estates, in such a Glorious Cause, as you call it. — It were 'worth your serious Consideration, That if these (Presbyterian) '*PREACHERS* continue to *STIR* you *UP* to *RISE IN ARMS*, † 'they have not much of Self-interest in their Eye, they being now 'secluded from their Places, and that Power and Authority they and 'their Brethren had taken from them; Whether therefore they seek 'not to EMBROIL the NATIONS in NEW WARS, rather than 'still to be thus deprived? &c.

† A plain and peaceable Ad-vice to those called *Presby-terians* in *Scotland, &c.* Printed *Anno,* 1681. p. 1, 7.

† No, nor no-thing of it, but to stifle the Popish Plot, and throw it upon the Prote-stants.

Thus then it appears, that the Quakers to curry Favour with O. *Cromwell*, they complained fearfully of the Presbyterians, as Tray-tors, for joining with the Church of *England*, in the Happy Resto-ration of K. *Charles* II. So now from 1660 to 1681. they use all the Craft and Policy imaginable, to bring the *Odium* of that Reign upon the Presbyterians, and thereby to make way for the Papists, and to stifle all their wicked Plots and Conspiracies: And that it is not my single Judgment, I shall publish a Letter sent me.

SIR,

It being notoriously known, That since the discovery of the Po-pish Plot in England, *many Courses and Endeavours hath been used by the Papists and their Abettors, to stifle and hinder the Discovery and Punishment thereof.*

And particularly, by pretending a Presbyterian Plot against the King and his Government in England; *and in order thereto, it is evident, what Falsities, Scandals and Invectives against the Protestants in general, under the Name of Presbyterians, have weekly been Published in those Libels, Entituled,* Heraclitus, *the* Observator, *and others.*

And whereas, there hath been lately Printed for Benjamin Clarke *in* George-Yard, Lombard-street, London, * *this present Year,* 1681. *a certain Book, Entituled,* Advice to the Presbyterians in *Scotland, which appears to have been written two Years since; which Book doth very much reflect upon some Principles of the* Scotch Presbyterians; *whether rightly Suggest-*

* The Qua-kers Book-seller.

ed

ed or not, is not the intent of this Paper to examine; but twenty Years Experience of the Presbyterians in England, have prov'd their Practices in England, far different from the mention'd Reflections: Therefore, sundry well-meaning, Protestants of different Persuasions from the Presbyterians, for several Reasons, have thought the Publication of the said Book in Eng'and, * at this juncture of time, to be injurious to the Protestant Interest in general: And some of the said Protestants being informed, that Mr. Pennyman did intend to make a publick Protestation against the said Book this Day upon the Exchange, did think it their Duty to dissuade Mr. Pennyman from the doing thereof, as being probable to be the occasion of the greater Publication of the said Book, unto which he hath consented: And the same Persons do likewise desire and require you, as much as in you lyes, to hinder the Publication thereof, lest by your neglect, you strengthen the Hands of the Enemies of the Protestants, and Protestant Religion in general. *
28 July, 81.

* Of Alex. Skene, a Quaker-Teacher.

* Copy of this was sent to the Quakers.

Thus then it doth undeniably appear, how enviously Malicious, and of what a Persecuting Spirit the *Quakers* are; yet, poor Hearts, this in them is all Innocency, Meekness, and the Lamb's Spirit; but in others, so much as to tell them of it, it's Persecution. Pray, what was it in G. *Fox*, and others, to call the Clergy Witches, Devils, Blasphemers, false Prophets, Jesuits, Conjurers, Antichrists, and what not, that might render them odious to the People? This is no Persecution in the *Quakers*; no, they are innocent Souls, and as far from Persecution, as the Meat of an Oyster is from the Shell, when living in the Sea; for they for *the present*, are given up to suffer. Come G. *Whitehead*, what think you of your Brother *Smith*, who calls the Bishops Monsters, the Church of E*ngland* a corrupted Womb, and by him ript up? What do you think of his saying, the Common-Prayer Book receives its Strength from the Pope's Loins, and that the Pope gives Life to it? Oh that ye could but see your selves, and repent of your Wickedness! For, if the Government should believe you, that the Clergy are false Prophets, what remains but Death, and that according to the Law of God? But I challenge the *Quakers* to produce one single Clergy-man, that have Prophesied of a thing to come to pass, and it did not; as *Sol. Eccles*, a Quaker-Prophet did, who Prophesied, that *John Story* should die within a Year, who lived four Years after, as I else where have shewed.

Smith's Works, p. 175. A brief Discovery of a threefold Estate, &c. p. 7, 8. *Burrough's* Works. p. 30.

†† Good God! was ever the like Impudence known?

Again,

Again, If the Government believ'd the *Quakers*, whose Books affirm, that the Clergy are Witches and Devils, they ought not to suffer them to live, but presently say, ☞ There goes a Witch, † knock him on the Head : Again, ☞ There goes a Blasphemer, * stone him to Death : Again, ☞ There goes a false Prophet, let him die, †. Yea, (saith *W. Penn*,) * ' Whilst the idle gormandizing Priests of *England*, run away with above 150000 *l.* a Year, under pretence of ' being God's Ministers, —— and that no sort of People have been so ' versally, thro' Ages, the very Bane of Soul and Body, to the Universe, ' as that abominable Tribe ; for whom, the THEATRE of God's ' most dreadful Vengeance is reserv'd, to act their Eternal Tragedy ' upon, † &c.

† Exod 22. 18.
* Lev. 24. 16.
† Deut. 18 20.
* The Guide mistaken, &c. p. 18.

† Observe the Quakers Goliah of Gath, *W. P.*

Thus Reader, I have given thee a Relish of the Quakers Meekness, and Lamb-like Nature : And therefore, give me leave to Hunt this Fox ; Did I say, give me leave ? Nay, I am resolv'd, that if thou wilt not give me leave, I shall take it : What ! shall these *Rabshekà's* be perpetually Railing and Domineering over the Gospel Ministers without controul ? Shall these uncircumcised *Philistines* appear in Triumph forty Years together, and their *Goliah* vaunting himself, boasting of his Parts, Learning, and Interest at —— as the other did of his Strength and Stature, whose Staff of his Spear was like a Weavers Beam ; and who glorying therein, defied the Armies of *Israel*, as the Quakers do the Church of *England*, her Bishops and Clergy ? And as a fresh Motive to this my Chace, I saw two Letters from two worthy Clergy-men to their Acquaintance in the City, which complain'd of the Quakers Insolency. An Abstract thereof is as followeth, *viz.*

1 Sam. 17.

' I supply the Cure of —— I have with the Blessing of God upon ' my Pains, preserved the People in our Communion (except some ' few,) till now. But at this time, thro' the extraordinary Devices, ' Craft, and Subtilty of the Quakers, that Parish, and two or three ' more thereabouts, are in great danger of falling from the Church to ' Quakerism ; several of their new Converts go about to Houses, im- ' portuning Men and Women to go to hear their Speakers : They are ' so troublesom in this nature, as that I am persuaded, some have ' turned, and others must turn for a quiet Life. I have observed them ' to be much more hot and eager in making Proselytes since the Peace, ' than ever they were in the time of the War. They challenge us to ' meet them, and Dispute with them ; but, if we should accept their ' Challenge without our Bishops leave, I do not know how he would ' resent it ; besides, I am not hasty, lest the best Cause in the World ' should suffer thro' my Weakness : —— And the Advantage they ' would bring to their Cause hereby , is, to have it universally be- ' liev'd, that their Religion is so good, and so much favour'd by the ' Government, as that it neither can, nor dare be oppos'd by us. ——
' I

'I believe, the intent of the King and Parliament, in granting them
'an Indulgence, was not, that they should disturb the Professors of
'the Establish'd Religion by Law; but rather, that these legal Pro-
'fessors should not be capable of disturbing or molesting them: I
'pray God open the Eyes of our Governours, and cause them to take
'into consideration, this too much, and too deplorable, unlimited and
'unbounded Tolleration, (especially as the Quakers both claim and
'use it;) which, notwithstanding all the Care, and indefatigable La-
'bour and Pains of the Watchmen of *Israel*, will certainly (if not
'timely prevented,) be the overthrow of our Church, and Christia-
'nity it self, *&c.*

And to my own knowledge, they boast of having the Royal Ear, and such Friends at Court as give them great boldness, especially in Country Towns and Villages, where they ride Lord and Master, and begin to think themselves interested in the comprehension discoursed of: But if so, without first a general Retractation of the Errours by them broached, and of their scandalous Defamations of our Kings, our Parliaments, Bishops, Clergy, and Protestants in general, it will be no other than breeding a Viper in the Bowels of the Christian Churches, which God of his Mercy divert. Thus begging my Reader's pardon for this long Digression, I shall now take leave to renew my Chace, in Hunting the Fox; not so much to single out a single Person, (for that (God knows,) of every Society, there has been some Particulars under mistaken Notions, pursuing wrong Designs;) as to shew, that the Governing Party of the Quakers, who sit at their Helm, have been utterly against this present Government: For, as I told them Publickly, † *i. e.* ' This Government and the Protestant 'Interest are so linked together, that those which are not true to the 'one, cannot be true to the other, whatever they may pretend, *&c.* I say, not so much to single out of their Herd one particular Person, as to shew, that the Quakers in general, (who think themselves thus highly honoured, as the Merit of their Innocency,) have all along been averse to the Government, that so when they (like the Peacock,) behold their dark Parts, they may let fall their Plumes, and be humbled, and brought to a Confession, both of their Sins of Omission and Commission against God and Man: For,

†In my Printed Letter to the Quakers; Printed 1690. p. 2.

I having observed the Discourse of the Quakers, touching the late Happy Revolution, I found how their Pulse beat; and in the general, perceived a great Lukewarmness in them to the present Government: I also went sometimes to their Meetings, as I did to other Dissenters, to observe, whether they all pray'd for their Majesties; and to do the Dissenters right, both Presbyterians, Independants and Baptists, pray'd heartily for their Majesties, King *William* and Queen *Mary*; but not a word of such a Prayer amongst the *Quakers*: By which, I soon perceived, that their Peoples aversness to the Government,

The Pilgrim's Progress,

vernment, proceeded from the Doctrine and Example of their Teachers; upon which I Printed against this their Omission, saying, † 'Why do you not Pray for, and Address your selves to K. *William* 'and Q. *Mary*, as publickly and as heartily as you did to, and for 'the late K. *James* II. *viz.* as a Brave King? God and *Cæsar* (said '*Penn*,) are both of a mind; pray God bless the King and his Royal 'Family. These, and many more, were published thro' the Nati-'ons, (and from your Yearly Meetings too;) but no Salutation, no 'Message, no Prayer for, nor Address to K. *William* and Q. *Mary*; as 'if you were struck mute at the loss of your brave Popish King. 'What can you say for your selves? Are you like those, 1 *Sam.* 10. '27. *viz. The Children of* Beliel, *who said, How shall this Man* '*save us? And they despis'd him, and brought him no Presents,* (no 'Prayers, no Addresses;) *but the King held his Peace?* O ye unwor-'thy and ungrateful Persons! Hath not K. *William* granted you the 'Liberty of your Consciences? What! Have you nothing to say 'for K. *William?* Nay, you are so far from that, that you have 'acted quite contrary; for when K. *William* appointed a Fast for 'the Prosperity of his Arms, then you not only Preached against the 'Fast, but also to weaken the Hearts and Hands of his Friends, you 'vehemently cryed down all Wars and Fighting, † and the like. Is 'your Zeal for the Protestant Cause quite gone, or is it gone to '*Rome? &c.*

This Letter, I grant, put them into a Fume and Fret; but they soon found a *Salvo, viz.* * 'Where (said G. *Whitehead*,) are all re-'quired by Christ, or his Apostles, to pray for them, (*i. e.* Kings, 'and all that are in Authority,) by Name? *&c.* as before observed.

But I soon Printed a Reply to G. *Whitehead's* evasive Answer; where I gave instances of their Prayers and Addresses to the late K. *James* II. †

† In a Letter to the Quakers, 1690. p. 2.

I do not charge this as an Evil in it self, whilst our King; but to shew the Quakers Zeal to that, and Coldness to his present Majesty, whom God preserve.

† Mark this, with the juncture of time and occasion.
* The Conten. Apost. &c. p. 27.

† See New *Rome* Unm. p. 26, to 30.

The Humble Address of the People called *Quakers*, to King James II. June 1687.

'We cannot but with grateful Hearts, both admire and acknow-'ledge the Providence of God, that made the King's retiring into our 'Native Country, [*i. e. Scotland*, in 1679.] give a Happy turn to his 'Affairs, to the defeating and disappointing the Designs of his Ene-'mies: We do justly conceive OUR selves obliged by a special 'Tye, to praise God for his Goodness, in carrying the King thro', and 'over all his Troubles; since by the same Providence, and at the 'same time, by which the LORD began in that more observable man-'ner, to evidence his Care of him, he made him the happy Instru-'ment to deliver us from our Troubles; so that the Prosperity of his 'Affairs, and our peaceable Fruition of the Exercise of our Con-'sciences, bears the same Date, *&c.* *The*

From Quakerism to Christianity.

The Humble Address of the People call'd Quakers, to King James II. *from our Yearly Meeting,* 1688.

'We the King's loving and peaceable Subjects, from divers parts
'of his Dominions, being met together in this City, to inspect the
'AFFAIRS of our Christian Society, † THROUGHOUT THE
'WORLD, think it our DUTY humbly to Represent, &c. —
'Now since it hath pleased thee, O King! to renew to all thy Sub-
'jects, by thy last Declaration, thy GRACIOUS Assurance, to pur-
'sue the Establishment of this Christian Liberty, &c. WE think our
'selves deeply engaged, to renew OUR Assurances of Fidelity and
'Affection : —— And as we firmly believe, that God will never desert
'this just and righteous Cause of Liberty, NOR THE KING in
'maintaining of it ; So we hope, &c.

† Which by Interpretation is Infect.

Thus, Reader, you see here is nothing wanting but bended Knees ; here is in ALL Humility, in ALL Fidelity, with ALL Affection ; yea, ALL, ALL, ALL, all Prayers for him, for a long Life, for a prosperous Reign ; Laud and Praise in the highest, for HIS Deliverance, for the defeating his Enemies, [*i. e.* Protestants ;] besides, by a modest computation, Ten thousand Books spread up and down the Nation, in favour of his Government. †

† See my Sober Expost. with the Hearers of the Quakers, &c. p. 13.

But, since K. *William* came to the Crown, NO Salutation, NO Message, NO Prayers for, NO Address to him from their Yearly Meeting, † NO in all Humility, NO in all Fidelity, NO with all Affection, NO Publick Prayers for his long Life, for his prosperous Reign, NO Laud and Praise that his Enemies are Defeated. Here is all NO, NO, NO ; nor one Book wrote in favour of the Government, during this Reign.

† Unless this in 1698. now the War is ended, and no Hopes left them.

But, that my Reader may rightly understand, which side of the hedge the *Quakers* have to this day hid themselves, I will recite one *Query* to them anew, as in that Book of mine I did, † as I took it out of a *Jacobite Catechism,* p. 5. For, as I would not write one Sheet which hath not a tendency, to shew either their Errours, Hypocrisie, Covetousness, or Treachery to the Nation, so shall I take in all that concur thereto, tho' it be twenty Sheets. The *Query* is ;

†In my Book, New *Rome* Unm. &c. p. 31.

Query. 'What made the Quakers no more concern'd for the loss 'of those brave Patriots of our Country, *Essex, Russel,* (*Sidney, Cor-* '*nish, Bateman ?* &c.)

I could never get an Answer to this Query.

This was such an untoward, knotty Question, that all the Quakers were not able to Answer it, that ever I understood : No, no, instead of being sorry, G. *Whitehead,* Fr. *Camfeild, Gilbert Layty,* and *Alexander Parker,* deliver'd an Address to K. *Charles* II. at *Windsor,* about the time of the Execution of my Lord *Russel,* crying out extreamly against all HELLISH PLOTS, and all TRAYTEROUS CON-

This was the first Address they ever made to Authority.

CONSPIRACIES, and that they had nothing but Love and Good-will to him, and his Brother the Duke of *York*.

But to return to the Observation I have made on the *Quakers* Publick Prayers for, and their Yearly Meetings Address to the late K. *James* II. and their contrary Practice to K. *William* III. * I have something more to offer, as an Aggravation of their Ingratitude; for they made an ORDER for the calling in the Widow *Whitrow*'s Books, (she being formerly of their Society, and by her plain Dress some take her to be so still;) which was in favour of this Government. Now G. *Whitehead*, what Scripture had you for that? Or, by what Authority did you presume to give out this ORDER?

* No; for what they do at their Yearly Meeting, is done by the Body.

Now I shall transcribe the Widow *Whitrow*'s Paper, concerning the Quakers Order for calling in her Books; which is as followeth, *viz.*

† The very Titles of these Books, were sufficient for the Ruling Quakers to Censure the Books.
* *Sowle* was the Quakers Printer and Bookseller.
† This perplexed the *Foxonian* Quakers.

'*December*, 1689. The Widow *Whitrow* ordered *Andrew Sowle*
'to Print a Book for her, Entituled, *The Widow* Whitrow's *Humble Address to King* William III. And in *December*, 1690. or-
'dered him to Print another Book, Entituled, *For Queen* Mary, *the*
'*Humble Salutation and Faithful Greeting of the Widow* Whitrow,
'† *&c.* Both which, were well accepted; and which, *Andr. Sowle**
'sent into the Country to his Friends the Quakers; and many of the
'said People did buy them, and liked them well, † and sent for
'more: But the chief Quakers in *London*, at their Monthly Meet-
'ing at *Devonshire*-House, the 7th of *January* following, made an
'Order to have all those Books called in; and appointed *John Eth-*
'*ridge* and *William Ingram* to go to the Printer, and acquaint him

Too true, Sons of the *Foxonian* Quaker-Church.

'with the said ORDER; which accordingly they did: At which
'the Printers seem'd troubled, saying, They thought Friends would
'not have been against them, (*i. e.* such Books,) seeing they were
'mostly writ against the Pride and Wickedness of the Times: And
'asked, What it was they had against the Books? They Answered,

* Meaning their Monthly Meeting.
† *i. e.* Their brave King *James* II.

'They * had little against them, ONLY THAT THEY WERE
'WRIT IN FAVOUR OF THIS GOVERNMENT, and reflect-
'ed upon the former; † and that Friends had RESOLVED NOT
'TO MEDDLE WITH THE GOVERNMENT, *&c.* It is to
'be observed, That the first Book, called, *The Address, &c.* was
'Printed above a Year before, and sold by their Booksellers, and not
'any stop put to them, till some † were endeavouring the Overthrow
'of this Government; so that it is easily to be understood, what the
'meaning was of such an Order, at such a time and season, *&c.*

† *Viz.* The Lord *Preston*, W. P. *&c.*

* See New *Rome* Arraign'd, *&c.* p. 30.

This Account is still ready to be attested, if deny'd; and which I signify'd something of formerly, * but now I thought fit to recite it at large.

Well, this Order was made, where G. *Fox*, and the Chief Governing *Quakers* in *London*, were present, in *January*; but in *February* following

following, came out a Proclamation against one of their chief Men; who upon the News of it, and as a tacit confession of great Guilt, run up a Cock-loft, at least a Chamber four Story-high, to hide himself. Let now the *Quakers* remember their Book, where they say, 'Some of the Presbyterian Nonconforming-Preachers are 'fled Beyond-Sea, others lurk in Corners here and there, and keep 'private Conventicles, where many times they preach Sedition a-'gainst their lawful Prince, &c. as I before observed; and let Mr. *Penn* remember, and be humbled, and thankful for the Favours he has receiv'd, and the Forgiveness he has met with: And let him look again upon his Preface; † 'The PRIESTS like FOXES, see-'ing their KENNEL, — TUMULTUOUS, BLOOD-THIRSTY, 'COVENANT-BREAKING, GOVERNMENT-DESTROYING 'ANABAPTISTS, — keep their Old Haunt, of creeping into 'GARRETS, Cheese-lofts, Coal-holes, and such-like Mice 'Wales, *&c.

† Viz. To the *Christian Quaker, and his Divine Test.*

* Now *W. Penn* himself, was forced to hide, and upon a far worse occasion than those he mentions; as may be seen by Their Majesties Proclamation.

By the King and Queen, a Proclamation, for Discovering and Apprehending *William Penn*, and *James Grahme.*

MARIE R.

Whereas Their Majesties have received Information, That William Penn *Esq;* and James Grahme *Esq; with other Ill-affected Persons, have Designed and Endeavoured to Depose Their Majesties, and Subvert the Government of this Kingdom, by procuring an Invasion of the same by the* French, *and other Treasonable Practices, and have to that end held Correspondence, and Conspired with divers Enemies and Traitors, and particularly with Sir* Richard Grahme *Baronet, (Viscount* Preston, *in the Kingdom of* Scotland,*) and* John Ashton *Gent. lately Attainted of High Treason; For which Cause several Warrants for High Treason have been Issued out against them but they have withdrawn themselves from their usual Places of Abode, and are fled from Justice: Their Majesties therefore have thought fit, by and with the Advice of Their Privy Council, to Issue this Their Royal Proclamation; And Their Majesties do hereby Command and Require all their Loving Subjects to Discover, Take and Apprehend the said* William Penn *and* James Grahme, *where ever they may be found, and to carry them before the next Justice of the Peace, or Chief Magistrate, who is hereby Required to Commit them to the next Gaol, there to remain until they be thence Delivered by due Course of Law; And Their Majesties do hereby Re-*

N *quire*

quire the said *Justice* or other *Magistrate*, immediately to give no-Notice thereof to Them, or Their *Privy Council*. And Their Majesties do hereby *Publish* and *Declare* to all *Persons* that shall Conceal the *Persons* above-named, or any of them, or be Aiding or Assisting in the Concealing of them, or furthering their *Escape*, that they shall be proceeded against for such their *Offence* with the utmost *Severity*, according to *Law*.

    Given at Our Court at *Whitehall* the Fifth Day of *February*, 169¾. In the Second Year of Our Reign.

Whereupon (as I was credibly informed,) one Mr. *Pennyman* on the 22d. of that instant *February*, 1690. in abhorrence of this Traytorous Conspiracy, uttered these Words in their Meeting in *White-Hart Court*, in *Grace-Church-street*, *London*. Viz.

    'He that is a Traytor, or he that in the least goeth about to betray
    'this his Native Country, he is a Traytor to the Living God; and
    'he that is a Traytor to his Maker, is not, nor cannot be a Disciple
    'of Jesus, that Holy and Just One; and he that is guilty of such cur-
    'sed hellish Practices, must bear his Judgment, whoever he be.

But as an aggravation of this their Crime, they did not only make that ORDER for the suppressing the said Address to the King, which was writ (I believe) in Love and Good-will to him, &c. but suffered their Printer, *Andrew Sowle*, a Quaker, to Print several *Odious* and *Scandalous* Books and Papers of Mr. *Stafford's* against the Government; * and tho' they were friendly, and privately acquainted with it, with desire, that those scandalous Books, &c. might not be dipersed; yet they could not be prevailed withal to have them stopt. However, to do the Quakers all just Right, we must acknowledge, some of them (and indeed but some, and that of their Hearers too,) were for the Government; who, to give them their due, drew up a Paper against *W. Penn*, for being concerned in that horrible Plot, with the Lord *Preston*, &c. For they having seen his Letters (that he had writ on that Occasion,) in *Aaron Smith's* Custody, and were assured, that they were of his own Hand-writing: This Paper was signed by *W. Mead*, and a few more, * who would have had it made Publick; but the contrary Party being powerful, prevented it: Only when *W. Penn* (after his Skulking some Years,) appeared, (by our merciful King's Favour,) and Preached as formerly in the *Quakers* Meetings; then *W. Mead*, and some others, took him to task, telling him, That tho' the King had pass'd by his Offence, yet they knowing him Guilty, (as by the said Letters under his own Hand, was manifest;) they ought to have Satisfaction, as they were a Religious Society, before he Preach'd in their Assemblies: But he having the

* This is ready to be Attested on occasion.

* This was Nobly done, however.

the Teachers on his side, and the generality of the Hearers, he went on *nolens volens*; and if there had not been a Peace, 'tis to be still feared, that *W. Penn*, and his Confederates, (for some of 'em held it out to the very last, asserting it for a Truth, that there would be no Peace, unless, &c.) would have pursued their Design, which might have prov'd fatal to this Nation.

But still to shew, that the Quakers have rather merited the Displeasure of the Government, than the Favour and Countenance thereof, and of which they so often boast, *viz.* of their being Recognized Protestants, of their being Free-born *English*-men, and thereby of their Rights and Priviledges as such, I shall recite an Abstract of another Act of Parliament, and shew their Non-submission and Aversion thereunto; Entituled, *Anno Septimo & Octavo Gulielmi* III. *Regis*.

An Act for the better Security of His Majesties Royal Person and Government.

Whereas the Welfare and Safety of this Kingdom, and the Reformed Religion, do, next under God, intirely depend upon the Preservation of Your Majesty's Royal Person and Government; which, by the merciful Providence of God, of late, have been delivered from the Bloody and Barbarous Attempts of Traytors, and other Your Majesty's Enemies; who, there is just reason to believe, have been in great measure Encouraged, to undertake, and prosecute such their wicked Designs; partly by Your Majesty's great and undeserved Clemency * towards them; and partly, by the want of a sufficient Provision in the Law, for the securing Offices, and Places of Trust, to such as are Well-affected to Your Majesty's Government, and for the Repressing and Punishing such as are known to be Disaffected to the same. Be it Enacted, &c. No. 554 *Whereas, there has been a Horrid and Detestable Conspiracy, formed and carried on by* Papists, *and other Wicked and Trayterous Persons, for Assassinating His Ma-*

Numb. 551, 552.

* W. Penn, is not this true?

The Pilgrim's Progress,

Majesties Royal Person, in order to encourage an Invasion from France, to Subvert our Religion, Laws, and Liberty; We whose Names are hereunto Subscribed, do heartily, sincerely, and solemnly profess, testifie, and declare, That His present Majesty King William, *is* Rightful and Lawful * King *of these Realms* : And we do mutually promise and engage, to stand by, and assist each other, to the utmost of our Power, in the Support and Defence of His Majesty's most Sacred Person, and Government, against the late King James, and all his Adherents : * And in case His Majesty come to any violent or untimely Death, (which God forbid,) We do further, freely, and unanimously oblige our selves, to Unite, Associate, and stand by each other ; in revenging the same upon his Enemies, and their Adherents, and in Supporting and Defending the Succession of the *Crown,* &c.

* This was a bitter Pill to the Quakers Second-Day Meeting.

* Oh! this grated on our new Saints.

This Act of Parliament put the *Quakers* to a great consternation; and what to do, they could not tell; they having at the same time spent much Money, Time, and Pains, in procuring an Act of Parliament, that their Affirmation should be taken, instead of an Oath;. and it had gone thro' the House of Commons, and was under Consideration of the House of Lords: For, think they, if we do nothing,. our Act will not pass.

Well, at their Second-Day Meeting, *March* 23d. 169⅚. their Teachers Assembled together; and no doubt, great Consultings there were, and particularly about those Words, *Lawful* and *Rightful* King; * also, whether they should *join* with the *Protestants,* in their *Uniting* and *Associating* to *stand by each other* in *revenging* his *Blood,* in case he had come to a violent or untimely Death.&c. Well, these two Points were largely debated, and possibly, might hold many hours: However, it pass'd in the Negative ; but yet, left their Bill (for their Affirmation to be taken in lieu of an Oath,) should not pass, they agreed thus far, namely, to get a Paper printed; not mentioning what Meeting it was framed at, not Signed with any of their Names to it, nor the Name of King *William* once mentioned ; and, if this Paper [think they,] will but pass, it will not do us much hurt,

* For the *French* King had not yet owned him King of *Great Britain.*

From Quakerism to Christianity.

hurt, in case our Old Friend come again; for none of our Names are to the Paper, nor at what Meeting it was contrived at, nay, nor so much as the Name of what King we mean; and, in regard we have obtained the Repute of an innocent well-meaning People, it may do well enough: So, away they went trudging to the House of Lords, and presented divers of them. A Copy thereof is as followeth, *viz*.

The Ancient Testimony and Principle of the People call'd *Quakers*, renewed, with respect to the King and Government, and touching the present *Association*.

We the said People, do solemnly and sincerely declare, that it hath been our Judgment and Principle, from the first day We were called, to profess the Light of Christ Jesus manifested in our Consciences, unto this day, That the setting up, and putting down Kings and Governments, is God's peculiar Prerogative, for Causes best known to himself; and that it is not our work or business, to have any hand or contrivance therein, nor to be busie-bodies in Matters above our Station, much less to plot and contrive the Ruin or Over-turn of any of them, but to pray for the King, and for the Safety of our Nation, and Good of all Men, that we may live a peaceable and quiet life, in all Godliness and Honesty, under the Government which God is pleased to set over us: And according to this our ancient and innocent Principle, we often have given forth our Testimony, and now do, against all plotting Conspiracies, and contriving Insurrections, against the King or the Government, and against all Treacherous, Barbarous, and Murtherous Designs whatsoever, as Works of the Devil and Darkness: And we sincerely bless God, and are heartily thankful to the King and Government, for the Liberty and Priviledges we enjoy under them by Law, esteeming it our Duty to be true and faithful to them.

And whereas, we the said People, are required to Sign the said Association, We sincerely declare, That our refusing so to do, is not out of any Disaffection to the King or Government, nor in opposition to his being declared Rightful and Lawful King of these Realms; but purely, because we cannot for Conscience-sake, Fight, Kill or Revenge, either for our selves, or any Man else.

And we believe, that the timely Discovery and Prevention of the late barbarous Design, and Mischievous Plot, against the King and Government; and the sad Effects it might have had, is an

Eminent

The Pilgrim's Progreſs,

Eminent Mercy from Almighty God; for which, we and the whole Nation, have great cauſe to be humbly thankful to him, and to pray for the continuance of his Mercies to them and us.

From a Meeting of the ſaid People in *London*, the 23d. of the Firſt Month, called *March,* 169⅚.

Thus endeth their March *Ancient Teſtimony,* 169⅚.

Thus, Reader, I have given you a Copy *verbatim* of the Quakers Paper, preſented to the Houſe of Peers; and I being then in *London*, wrote a Reply thereunto, *March* 27. 1696. and preſented it to the Lord's Houſe, who immediately rejected the Quakers Paper, notwithſtanding all its fine and innocent Words, telling the *Quakers,* they muſt be plain, and tell them *what King* they mean: Secondly, Whether they believed he was both *Rightful* and *Lawful* King: Thirdly, That they muſt *Sign* their Paper. Now, theſe three things grated ſorely on their tender Conſciences; for they went home ſadly angry with *Francis Bugg,* for being inſtrumental in the Diſcovery of their deep Hypocriſie; for had that Paper paſs'd that no body Signed, no Kings Name to it; if the late King had returned, they had been Fiſh-whole ſtill, and as Loyal Subjects as ever they were before.

Thus, Reader, to prevent their Cavil, that I take but a piece of their Sentences, and wrong the Senſe, I have recited their whole Teſtimony *verbatim:* But, before I proceed to give you their *April* Ancient Teſtimony, let me give the reaſon, at leaſt one probable reaſon, why it was rejected, and would not paſs the Houſe of Lords, ſo as to effect their Deſign; as alſo, what Communication, I gueſs, they had about it, *&c.* For, I being at *London* the 24th. of the ſame Month, I went to the Houſe of Lords, where I had one of the recited Teſtimonies given me; I went to my Lodging, and perceiving their Prevailing, thro' their Pretences of ſeeming Sincerity and Innocency, *&c.* I wrote a Paper by way of Reply; and, the 27th. of *March* I gave away about 100 to the Lords, who accepted of them; and preſently one of the Peers came out, and call'd *G. Whitehead,* and told him, That their Paper would not do; for they had not ſo much as mention'd what King they mean'd, nor yet declar'd him Rightful and Lawful King of theſe Realms, nor yet Sign'd their Paper: And therefore, they muſt go home, and get another more Authentick, or their Bill for their Affirmation to paſs, in lieu of an Oath, would be rejected. Well, away they went very ſorrowful, and I conceive might have amongſt themſelves a Diſcourſe of this Nature, *viz. G. Whitehead,* 'Friends, our Paper is rejected; for yonder was our old An-
'tagoniſt *Fr. Bugg,* and he has deliver'd to the Peers a Paper, ſug-
'geſting, that we prevaricate; he has alſo delivered about a hundred
'of his Books to the Lords, Entituled, *The Quakers ſet in their*
'True

From Quakerism to Christianity.

'*True Light, &c.* and therefore, we must get another Ancient Te-
'stimony more full to the Matter, lest we lose the advantage of our
'Bill; but let us stay a while, for if we go presently, who knows
'but that Apostate may reply to our next Paper; for he is so Eagle-
'ey'd, that if he espy any thing that's defective, he may be instru-
'mental in throwing out our Bill: You cannot but remember, that
'we were fair for the same Bill to pass, in *Anno* 1693. but he then
'Printed a Sheet, and deliver'd to the House of Commons, and in
'three hours time our Bill was thrown out of the House. Indeed, we
'Printed a Sheet, stiled, *The Quakers Vindication, &c.* but he ha-
'ving printed a Thousand of those Sheets, and gave to the House a-
'bout 500, and sent to all the Coffee-Houses, from *Westminster* to
'*Bishopsgate*, about 400 more; he prevail'd against us: Nay, this
'was not all, but presently wrote a Book, Entituled, *Quakerism Wi-*
'*thering, and Christianity Reviving, &c.* and deliver'd between
'two or 300 of them to the House of Commons: We see our selves
'so baffled, that we saw it not meet to revive our Bill that Sessions
'of Parliament; and therefore let's be wise, let us stay until we think
'he is out of Town; for he has been here two or three Weeks alrea-
'dy; and, what with his Charge in Printing the Papers he gave to
'the Lords, and the Charge of giving in so many of *The Quakers*
'*set, &c.* together with his Charges of staying; one way or other,
'it cost him not so little as 6 or 7 *l.* and he having no Publick Fund
'to go to, it will make him weary, *&c.* I say, after this, they got
another Paper, and presented to the House of Lords; a Copy thereof
is as followeth.

> The Ancient Testimony and Principle of the People called Qua-
> kers, renewed, with respect to the King and Government, pre-
> sented to King *William* III.

*We the said People, do solemnly and sincerely declare, That
it hath been our Judgment and Principle, from the first day we
were called to profess the Light of Christ Jesus, manifested in our
Consciences, unto this day: That the setting up, and putting
down Kings and Governments, is God's peculiar Prerogative;
and that it is not our work or business, to have* any Hand, *or Contrivance therein, nor to be Busie-bodies above our Station, much
less to Plot, or contrive the Ruin or Over-turn of any of them, but
to pray for the King and Safety of the Nation, and good of all
Men,* * *that we may live a peaceable and quiet Life, in all Godliness and Honesty, under the Government, which God is pleased to
set over us: And, according to our Ancient and Innocent
Principle,*

* No; hold, not for the Priests nor Governours, unless they please you. *See p. 79.*

Principle, *we often have given forth our Testimony, and now freely and sincerely do the same, against all Plotting Conspiracies, and contriving Insurrections; and against all Treacherous, Barbarous, and Murderous Designs whatsoever, against the King, or the Government, as being Works of the Devil, and Darkness.*

And we believe, that the timely Discovery, and Prevention of the late Barbarous Design, and Mischievous Plot, against King William * *and the Government, and the sad Effects it might have had, is an eminent Mercy from Almighty God; for which, We, and the whole Nation, have great cause to be humbly thankful to him, and to pray for the continuance of his Mercies to Them and Us: And We sincerely bless God, and are heartily thankful to King William* * *and the Government, for the Liberty and Priviledges we enjoy under them, by Law. And further, We are really satisfied, that God by his special Providence, did bring in, and set up King William* * *over these Realms, and do own him Rightful and Lawful King;* † *and are obliged in good Conscience, to be true and faithful to Him, and the Government, as becomes obedient Followers of our Blessed Lord and Saviour Jesus Christ.*

* A forc'd put. First time.

* O brave! This is the second time.

* This is News indeed! Third time.
† But *George*, why did you not say so freely, without Whip or Spur?

At a Meeting of the said People in London, *the Third of* April, 1696.

Signed by many of Us, on behalf of our selves, and the rest of our Friends, and presented to the King, April 8. 1696.

Thus endeth their *April* Ancient Testimony.

Reader, before I come to make Observations upon these two, *March* and *April* Ancient Testimonies of the Quakers; there is one thing very remarkable, and worth your noticing, in the whole Conduct of Quakerism; and, that in two respects; the first is past, the second's still to come, and ought to be guarded against; and which makes me so long on this Head, and so plain with them in this Matter: And briefly thus:

That altho' no one People in *England*, did so flatter *Oliver Cromwel, Richard* his Son, the Rump and all the several Changes of Government, during the Usurpation, as the Quakers did, nor more oppose the Restauration of K. *Charles* II. Nay, not only so, but justifying *Oliver* in his Murthering K. *Charles* I. and in carrying on the War with all Vigour, against the Cavaliers and Delinquents: * But when

* See the 76, 77, 78 Pages of this Book, for a Sample.

From Quakerism *to* Christianity.

when the Times turned, Oh! how they laid all the blame of both the War and Usurpation upon the Presbyterians, Independants and Baptists; as if they themselves had all along, been as Innocent as New-born Babes. This puts me in mind of a pleasant Piece of News we had run thro' our whole Camp when I was a Quaker, *viz.*

Anno 1674. *W. Penn* put forth a Book, stil'd, *A just Rebuke to Twenty one Divines*, &c.

P. 25. 'Was it not a great reason of the Wars, that divided so 'many Families, shed so much Blood, and exhausted so great a 'Treasure? Did it not lay Episcopacy in the Dust, and excite the 'Parliament in these very Terms? *Elijah* opposed Idolatry and Op-'pression, so do ye; down with *Baal*'s Altars, down with *Baal*'s 'Priests; do not I beseech you, consent unto a Tolleration of *Baal*'s 'Worship in this Kingdom; which is as much as to say.[said *Penn*,] 'away with Arch-Bishops, Bishops, and the whole Ministry and 'Worship of the Church of *England*: Again, the Mouths of your 'Adversaries are opened against you, that so many *Delinquents*, that 'is to say (said *W. Penn*,) Royalists, are in Prison, and yet but few 'of them brought to Tryal: (Did he mean, said *W. Penn*, to release 'them?) With much more of this nature, *&c.*

Now, tho' I do think, that divers of these 21 Divines were as clear of what is suggested, as my self, if not all of them; yet, because they appeared in Print, against the Errours of the Quakers, they, to ingratiate themselves into the Favour of the then Government, expos'd these Men as Enemies to the *Delinquents, i. e.* Royalists. Well, the News we soon had amongst us, was, that the King and the Duke of *York* read this Book, with great Delight and Pleasure; and no doubt, but took the Quakers to be, not only their Informers, but a parcel of innocent Souls: * For it was soon observ'd, That the Dissenters Meetings were broken up, and the Quakers Meetings connived at: *A cunning Project.*

See p. 76, 77, 78. What Friends the Quakers were to the Delinquents, &c.

2*dly*, The second thing observable from hence, is, that in a little time, (for I see the Quakers begin to wheel about) no Man shall dare to appear in Print against them, but they will fall to their old Trade of Domineering and Insulting over them, as Enemies to the Government, whilst none more eminently against the present Government than themselves: For as then no People were more vigorous in Print, against the Restoration of K. *Charles* II. than the Quakers, yet, how did they complain of the Presbyterians, Independants and Baptists, as divers Instances are herein given, and more might be? Yet, such is their cunning and sly way of insinuation against others, thereby to ingratiate themselves, and to villifie and expose others, that it's hard to believe, and harder to detect them therein: For in one of their late Books, writing against the Reverend Author of *The* *Snake in the Grass, &c.* They call his Labours, * 'The Black At-'tempts

** Prim. Chris. continued, &c.* Pref. and p. 1, 11.*

'tempts of a Necessitous, Malicious Priest, an Expelled Clergy-man,
'makes a Trade for Bread, in part, to repair his Losses, which he
'charges the present Establishment to have brought upon him, * to
'divert his Cares and Fears, and to supply his Wants. Again, G.
Whitehead, in his Letter to G. *Keith*, sets forth his Fury against the
said Author, in these Words : † 'Especially, when the injurious Cir-
'cumstances of that venemous and obnoxious, creeping, sculking Ver-
'min, comes further to be exposed, &c. whilst no People have both
creeped up and down, sculked here and there, and fled from Justice,
more than the Quakers: Witness their Great *Goliah* for an instance;
nor no one People in *England*, held out to the very last, against the
present Government, more than the *Quakers*. But their deep Hypocrisie is both seen, felt, heard, and understood, far and near ; and therefore, as a further Demonstration of their wheeling-about, and late
temporizing with their two-fold Testimony; one presented in the
Month of *March*, the other (when that was rejected,) presented in
the Month of *April*, as at large above-recited, I shall now examine.

*'A direct Lie;
I never heard
him speak one
word of that
tendency;
tho' as some
others having
taken a form-
er Oath, can-
not satisfie his
Conscience.
† Observe the
Malice of
this merce-
nary Whitehead.*

*The Ancient Testimony and Principle of the People called Qua-
kers renewed, with respect to the King and Government.*

Answ. First, This I deny to be your Ancient Testimony; but
this which followeth, is your Ancient Testimony, viz.

First, Dreadful* is the Lord, and Powerful, who is coming
in his Power to execute true Judgment upon all you Judges, and to
change all your Laws ; ye Kings, all you Rulers, must down, and
cease ; and all you Underling-Officers, which has been as the
Arms of this great Tree, which the Fowls hath lodged under all
your Branches, must be cut down ; so you must be cut down with
the same Power, that cut down the King, * who Reigned over the
Nation, whose Family was a Nursery for Papists and Bishops :
Woe, woe is coming upon you all ; the same Teachers are standing
that was in the time of the King, and the time of the Bishops,
such as take Tythes ; you must both be tormented together, Beast
and False Prophet. * The Lord God will pour out his Plagues
upon you, the Lord of Hosts hath spoken it ; and except you Repent, † ye shall all likewise perish, and be consumed, as the King
was, and perish with the same Power : Sing all ye Saints, and rejoice, clap your Hands, and be glad, for the Lord Jehovah will
Reign, and the Government shall be taken from you, pretended
Rulers, Judges and Justices, Lawyers and Constables ; all this

* News com-
ing up out
of the *North*,
p. 18, 19, 20.

* Meaning an
Usurper's
Sword.

* Both Go-
vernment and
Church.

† i.e. Of ta-
king Tythes.

Tree,

From Quakerism to Christianity. 99

Tree *must be cut down, and Jesus Christ* [*in us,*] *will Rule alone. Sound the Trumpet, sound an Alarum, call up to the Battel, gather together for the Destruction, draw the Sword, hew down all fruitless Trees* * *which cumber the Ground, hew down all the Powers of the Earth, cleanse the Land from all Filthiness, purge forth the Dross, the Filth and Corruption, slay Baal, Balaam must be slain, all the Hirelings must be turned out of the Kingdom,* * *&c.*

* This was since they professed the Light.
* This is their Ancient Testimony.

Counsel and Advice, *&c.* p. 26, 27. *Oh Oliver! hadst thou been faithful, and thundered down Deceit, the* Hollanders *had been thy Subjects and Tributers, and* Germany *had given up to have done thy Will, and the* Spaniard *had quivered like a dry Leaf, ----- the King of* France *should have bowed under thee his Neck, the Pope should have withered as in Winter, the* Turk *in all his Fatness, should have smoak'd; thou shouldst not have stood trifling about small things; Sober Men, and True Hearts, took part with thee.* * *Oh! take heed, and do not slight such, lest thou weaken thy self, and not disown such as the Lord hath owned; thy Dread is not all gone, nor thy Amazement: Arise, and come out; for hadst thou been faithful,* * *thou shouldst have crumbled Nations to Dust, for that had been thy place: Now is thy Day of Tryal,* p. 36, 37. *thou shouldst have invited all the* Christians *upon Earth, in all Nations, to thee, that are against Popery, to come in, and join with thee* * *against Popery; for thou hast had Authority; stand to it, lose it not, nor abuse it; nor let any other take thy Crown, and do not stand cumbering thy self about* Dirty Priests. --- *And thou hast had Power over Nations, for Nations begins to be on heaps; and invite all them that profess against the* Pope *in all Nations, to join with thee against him; and do not lose thy Dominion nor Authority, nor the Wisdom of God, but with that thou may'st order all; and let thy Soldiers go forth with a free-willing Heart, that thou may'st rock Nations as a Cradle;* * *and keep thou in the Fear of the Lord, and all thy Soldiers, and them that are under thee. This is a Charge to thee in the presence of the Lord God.*

* i.e. Quakers, compare this with p. 76, 77.
* viz. Turned all the Priests out of the Kingdom.
* This their Ancient Testimony.
* This is their Ancient Testimony. See p. 76, 77.

I am a Lover of thy Soul, and Eternal Good,
an Establisher of Righteousness, G. F O X.

* *To thee, O* Oliver Cromwell! *thus saith the Lord, I had chosen thee among the Thousands in the Nations, to execute my Wrath upon my Enemies, and gave them to thy Sword, with which*

* The Righteousness of God, &c. p. 11.

These I affirm, were your Ancient Testimonies in Print, which deserves to be burnt on Tower-hill.

I Fought *for the Zeal of my own Name, and gave thee the Enemies of my own Seed to be a Curse, and a Reproach for ever, and made thee an Instrument against them.* ---- *And many have I cut down by my Sword in thy Hand, that my Wrath might be executed on them to the utmost.* G. Rofe.

SECONDLY, I must acknowledge, it is according to your Old Testimony, with respect to your Hypocrisie, *viz.* in pretending to pay your Acknowledgment to the King for his Kindness, and yet never mention by Name, what King you mean'd, when two Kings laid claim to the Crown; and for which your Paper was justly rejected, as a Fruit of your Hypocrisie; of which, your Second-Day Meeting is full.

THIRDLY, It was according to your Ancient Deceit, in not owning King *William* to be your *Rightful* and *Lawful* King; and yet, to tell the House of Lords, that your refusing to Sign the *Association*, was not in Opposition to his being declared *Rightful* and *Lawful* King of these Realms; which piece of Hypocrisie, the Lords soon perceived, and sent you packing with your Paper.

FOUTHLY, It was also according to your Ancient Testimony, in wheeling about, and Worshiping the Rising-Sun, to bring in your *April* Testimony, with the King's Name three times over, and to own him your Rightful and Lawful King, and YET to leave out your Promise of Signing the *Association*.

FIFTHLY, It was according to your Old Testimony of Deceit and Hypocrisie, to pretend in your said *April* Testimony, That you owned K. *William* III. to be Rightful and Lawful King; and yet, in your *March* Testimony, to pretend your Conscience would not allow you Liberty to Sign the *Association*, according to the Act of Parliament in that case made and provided, as above-recited, in regard you could not avenge your selves: But being told by my Paper, (which I presented to the Lords House, which was in Reply to yours,) That you told R. *Cromwell*, *You would be a Strength to him, and stand by him in the Day of his Trouble, and Defend him, and his just Government, &c.* Then in your next Paper, to wit, your *April* Ancient Testimony, you left out your refusing to Sign the *Association*, as well as the Cause, why you could not Sign it; * namely, because you pretended you cannot take Revenge: For, alas! in that my said Paper, I had shew'd the Lords, That you had Prosecuted a Man for killing a Quaker, gave 50 *l.* for the Discovery of him, got him, and procur'd him to be hang'd in Chains, and yet could not avenge the Blood of your Prince. † O tender Consciences! Thus you make *Conscience* your Stalking-Horse into all your Villanies; besides, your Inditing my self, and others, are Demonstrations that you can seek Revenge

See Burrough's Works p. 573.
* *O deep Deceit! 'Tis well for you that the Lords did not perceive this.*
† *They can revenge the Blood of a private Person, but cannot revenge the Blood of their Prince. Hopeful Subjects! They deserve Protection apace.*

venge for Personal Wrongs and Injuries; and yet you cannot for Conscience-sake, stand by, and defend K. *William*, as you promised you would *Richard Cromwell*, in his JUST GOVERNMENT, &c.

Some Inferences from the Eleventh Chapter.

IS it so then, that this Second-Days Meeting is as the Helm to the Ship, the Wheel within the Wheel, which set all going, and that they can leave out of their Reprints, such Prophesies as suit not with the Times? This shews them arrant Impostors. Is it so, that neither Second-Days Meeting, nor Yearly Meeting, have ever yet given out one Publick Address to K. *William* III. nor one Congratulatory Paper, to acknowledge him their *Rightful* and *Lawful* * King, and that they refused to Sign the *Association* with the rest of His Majesty's Subjects? What reason then have they, either grounded upon Reason or Merit, to expect such singular Favours from the Government, as they would seem to insinuate they have? And why boast they so much upon their Right of Priviledges, when they'll comply with nothing, but what suits with their Interest and Design? And where they are call'd to any Publick Test, either for their Fidelity to the Government, or to stand by, and defend the King, they then at every turn, plead their Conscience in excuse from their Duty? What, hath no body any Conscience but they? Is it so, that their Ancient Testimony is so utterly against Monarchy, against Parliaments and Magistrates, as to say, 'We stand Witnesses against 'Parliaments, Councils, Judges, Justices, who make, or execute 'Laws in their Wills, over the Consciences of Men, or punish for 'Conscience-sake; and to such Laws, Customs, Courts, or Arbitra-'ry Usurped Dominion, we cannot yield Obedience; — that the 'Parliament is the Beast, and the Church of *England* the Whore of '*Babylon*; that no King is to Rule but Jesus? * &c. And thereupon, they'll obey no Act of Parliament, which cross their Design. What reason is there for their so boasting at every turn of their being Recognized as Protestants, when their Principles are not only repugnant to all Christians, but their Practice to all Protestants the World over; and till they come to repent thereof, and retract their Errours, they are a scandal to Christianity, and a reproach to the Name of Protestant? I have by me the Address of the Honourable House of Commons, made in *February*, 1697. and His Majesty's Gracious Answer thereto; I have also His Majesty's Gracious Proclamation, which consists chiefly of Two Parts; the one against Vice, Immorality and Prophaneness; the other Part, against Writing, Printing, or Publishing pernicious Books and Pamphlets, containing impious Doctrines against the Holy Trinity, and other Fundamental Articles of the

* For their Ancient Testimony, *April* 3. 1696. and their late Paper presented to the King, *Feb.* 7. 1697. were both drawn up of a *Friday.*

* See *Bur.* Works, p. 203, 501, 524.

I have instanced three several Acts they'll not obey.

the Christian Faith, &c. I have also by me, a Copy of the Quakers Paper presented to His Majesty, dated the 7th of *Feb.* 1697. wherein they own him King, as the *Jewish* Captives did *Belshazzar, Dan.* 5. 21. and thereby themselves Captives; wherein they take some notice of the first particular, but not a Word of the latter: But this Chapter is extended beyond what at first I intended, so shall not at present, note the Quakers Hypocrisie in this Point, nor shew how far many of their Books, (and which I take to be the reason of their Silence,) are within the meaning of His Majesty's Royal Proclamation, which are not only express against the Blessed Trinity, but other Fundamentals of the Christian Religion. I pray God bless the King, and preserve his Royal Person, and inspire him with Holy Zeal, to go on with his Royal Resolution; and let all true Protestants and Good Christians say, *Amen.*

CHAP. XII.

By way of Introduction to the Thirteenth Chapter, wherein I shall shew several Reasons, why I so proceed.

Reader, let none marvel, why I proceed thus with these Men; for they say of themselves, * 'They are raised of the Lord, 'and Established by HIM, even contrary to all Men; and 'they have given their Power only to God, and they cannot give their 'Power to any Mortal Man, to stand or fall by any outward Autho-'rity, and to that they cannot SEEK, * &c. Now, as they confess, they were raised up, contrary to all Men; so have their Practice, Manners and Deportment, been contrary to all Men; and therefore, shall they be dealt with contrary to all Men. Bishop *Jewel*, and other Reformers, wrote smartly against the Papists; and for the Peoples sake, display'd their Errours, unmask'd their Leaders, and discover'd their Pious Frauds; yet protested, they were in Charity, and desired nothing more, than that they would have hearkened to them, and forsake their Errours: And I do solemnly say, I know of no one thing which this World affords, would please me better, than to see this People condemn what is Erroneous amongst them, and persevere in the Truth, and the Knowledge of our Lord Jesus Christ, true God, and perfect Man: But whilst they'll excuse, justifie, commend, and recommend such vile Errours, as no Protestant Society can endure, I shall proceed; and if I be blamed, better Men than I am, (as *Luther* for one,) was; who, when *John Eccius, Jacob Hochstrat,* wrote to him, he quickly reply'd, saying, * 'By how much the 'more they rage, so much the more I go on; I leave former things, 'that

* *Bur.* Works, p. 507.

* A grand Lie: Who seeks more?

* The Hist. of the Reform. &c. p. 34.

From Quakerism to Christianity.

'that they may bark at them, and go on to further things, that
'they may have some things more to bawl at. Also, consider the
Prophet *Elijah*, a Man both Sober, Serious, and Religious; yet,
when he beheld the Idolatry of the Priests of *Baal*, which did not
much exceed the Quakers, if at all, he could not but mock at them,
and have them in a Holy Division, in order to the more compleat
Discovery of them to the View of the Spectators: For it is writ-
ten, * *And it came to pass at Noon, that* Elijah *mocked them, and* *1 King.18.17
*said, Cry aloud, for he is a God; either he is Talking, or he is pur-
suing, or he is in a Journey, or peradventure, he Sleepeth, and must
be awaked*, &c.

Besides all this, here is more to be said; for as the Quakers were raised
contrary to all Men, as they confess themselves, so have they dealt by
others, as never any besides themselves ever did: And therefore, give
me leave to fill the same Cup to them again, which they so plentifully have filled to others; yea, good Measure, pressed down, and shaken together, and running over: For G. *Fox*, their great Apostle, Luke 6. 38.
and High Priest of their Profession, who was but a Journey-man Shoe-
maker, having heard some body say, That *Tu* was Latin for *Thou*,
the Second Person of the singular Number; and *Vos* was Latin
for *Ye*, the Second Person of the plural Number; nothing would
serve his Ambitious Brain, but he must make for the two *English* Universities, the Magistrates, Judges, Gentry, and Clergy of the Land,
a BATTLE-DOOR, to teach them the same, and that in thirty
Languages, of which he was not Master of one: And the present Quakers, in order to magnifie their Great Apostle *Fox*, have
Printed him the Author of the said BATTLE-DOOR, * which is *See the third
as great a Cheat put upon the present Quakers, as *Fox* put upon us in Index of
the Beginning, who made us believe, he had 24 Languages given Fox's Journal.
him by Divine Inspiration in one Night, as my self, and others (still
living,) did believe; for in the Introduction he said, † 'All Langua-
'ges are to me no more than Dust, who was before Languages were,
'and am come before Languages were, and am redeem'd out of Lan- See the Gen.
'guages into the Power, &c. For, tho' *Fox* was not the Author, Hist. of the
yet his Name is set to it nine or ten times, in order to confirm the Quakers, &c.
Cheat; for *John Stubbs*, and *Benjamin Furley*, had the chief hand p. 165.
in it: But in those early Days, the Government of the Fund, or Envy and
Common Bank, was wholly at the disposé of *Fox*, who like *Symon* ed, by way of
Magus, having a desire to be esteem'd some Great Man in Learning, Reply to Ro-
he hired some *Jews* to his Assistance, as I have been credibly inform- bert Bridgman,
ed, by those which heard the *Jews* say the same; yea, and since have &c. p. 8.
printed it in these Words, * 'We, for our own parts, went to the gon of the
'*Jews*, and spake with the *Jew* that received Eighty pounds in Quakers! as
'Mill'd Money, † paid by *Gerrard Roberts*, besides the Dozen Ann Docwra
'Bottles of Wine, given by M. F. (Widow to Judge *Fell*, who will not Mo-
' after- ney do?

'afterwards Marry'd *Fox*,) as he did affirm, for doing the chief
'part of the BATTLE-DOOR: And, what a Cheat was this to the
'Ignorant, to make them believe, as if it had been revealed to *G.*
'*Fox, &c.* And when *R. Bridgman*, to cover *Fox*, said, He (*George*
'*Fox*,) had some knowledge in *Hebrew*; my Author goes on, p. 20.
'*viz.* Some body paid enough for his Understanding in the *Hebrew*:
'Witness his 80 *l.* and dozen Bottles of Wine, *&c.* Oh monstrous!
'Oh horrible Cheat!

Now followeth the Form and Figure of a Penny Horn-Book for Children, to learn their *A, B, C.* as placed in that Book, Entituled, *A BATTLE-DOOR for Teachers and Professors, to learn Singular and Plural, &c.* as set at the beginning of most of the Languages in that Book, with a like Inscription, Signed on the Handle of the Horn-Book, as in this, *Geo. Fox*, which could have no other tendency, but to discover his great Presumption, to pretend to be Learned in thirty Languages, who was ignorant of his Mother-Tongue; neither did this Artifice only discover his Presumption, in pretending to be what he was not, *i.e.* a Learned Person; but it shewed also, his Pride and Contempt thereby designed; and Domineering over both Gentry and Clergy, as if they understood not the *English* of *Tu* and *Vos*, set in the said BATTLE-DOOR, and with this Inscription.

A
BATTLE-DOOR
For Teachers and Professors,

To Learn *Singular* and *Plural*; *Thou* to one, *You* to many; *Tu* Thou, *singular*; *Vos* You, *plural*.

That now, why the Teachers of the World, Scholars and School-Masters, teach People and Children, which will not have People nor Children to speak *Thou* to one, and *You* to many, is not Sense, nor good *Latin*, nor good *English*, nor good *Hebrew* : To you that stumble at the Word *Thou*, to a particular, because we do not say *You*, this is sent, *&c.*

GEO. FOX.

From Quakerism *to* Christianity.

The next thing I have to present the World with, is an Abstract of an Epistle of G. *Fox*'s, sent to be read in Churches : * Thus did the Pride, Arrogance, and Presumption of this People appear; which, as they confess, shewed, that they were raised contrary to all Men: As their Practice in a hundred things was contrary to all Men, so am I made willing to deal with them, as I would by no other Men: And since they have ordered a Liturgy for the Churches, giving forth an Epistle for them to read, why may not I form a few Words out of their own Books, and so far as I can make G. *Whitehead* to hold them forth ? And since the Quakers would make the Churches read their Nonsence, why may not I draw some natural Inferences from the Quakers, Doctrin since my end is nothing else, but to display their Errours, and make them appear in their Native Complexion, which by their Teachers, are more masked and obscured ? If any say, That by drawing a Scheme of their Meeting, and forming a Sermon for them to Preach, is to do such a thing as no Man ever did : Let them remember again, That no Man ever yet had the Impudence to write a BATTLE-DOOR for the Learned Gentry and Clergy of a Protestant and Learned Nation, as *England* is ; nor to form a Liturgy to be read in Churches, and especially, by a poor Journey-Man Shoe-maker, and an almost illiterate Man, that could neither write Sense, nor true *English*, and this may probably ballance the Wonder, especially, considering, that it is more than 20 Years since I wrote first against them ; and from first to last, could never prevail with them to retract one Errour, nor to condemn one of their Books, in which their vile and gross Errours are taught. An Abstract of their said Epistle to be read in Churches, is as followeth, *viz.*

* *London,*
Printed for
Matth. Simmons, 1657.

To all the People who meet in Steeple-houses in England, *and elsewhere.*

--- *So all you that have the Letter in* England, --- *therefore to you all, this is sent a Message from the Lord Jesus Christ in* England, *or elsewhere, into all the Steeple-houses, to be read ; for God is a Spirit ; and they that Worship him, must Worship him in Spirit, and in Truth ; and such were drove out of the Synagogues, drove out of the Idol's Temple, and drove together ; and so an Epistle was written to them ; and God is the same ; he is a Spirit, and his Spirit is drawing from all Steeple-houses :* --- *And these are them that witness,* Oxford *and* Cambridge *the two Mothers of Divinity, which now the Lord's Hand is against, and his Sword is drawn against ;* --- *they are in their* Witchcraft *and* Whoredom *;* --- *this is the Cage of unclean Birds, the professed Ministers :* --- *And therefore all* People *that are* here, *Christ is not in*

P *the*

the Letter, *nor the Life is not in the* Letter, *nor the Word is not in the* Letter ; *this mediate Stuff hath Reigned long in the* Cage * *of* unclean Birds, *this* Babylon : — *And the* Serpent *and* Dragon *which hath deceived the Nations,* --- *you get the* Letter *for the* Light, *a* Steeple-house *for a* Church ; Matthew, Mark, Luke *and* John, *for the* Gospel : * *The mighty Day of the Lord is coming, and is to be cried* in all *the Steeple-houses in* England, to be read, *and* cried ; --- *and it is that which you call your* Church, *the high places of* Idolatry ; *it takes away your Life, to cry against your Church, to take away your* High Place *of* Idolatry *there* ; --- *and this is to go abroad in* all Steeple-houses *in the* Nation, *and their* High Places, *and thro' the World, that they may come to God from them.*   G. FOX.

margin:
J. *Fx's* Journal, p. 227.

* This is their Ancient Testimony. See *News coming up, &c.* and his *Several Papers spread, &c.* All harp on this string, that *Matth. Mark, Luke* and *John,* are so far from being the Gospel, that they are Dust and Serpents Food.

Now Reader, I will challenge a Parallel to the Impudence of the Quakers. Amongst all the Hereticks that ever rose up since the Days of Christ, in *England, Scotland, Ireland, Holland,* or any Protestant Nation under the whole Heavens, to find me a Man unlearned, a poor Mechanick, to put forth a Book, Entituled, *A BATTLE-DOOR* for all Teachers, Scholars and School Masters, to learn them the *English* of *Tu* and *Vos,* with the Form and Figure of a Child's Penny Horn-Book, thereby to render them ridiculous and contemptible in the Eyes of the People, and with such horrid Cheats attending all the Circumstances, *i.e.* to pretend to Divine Inspiration, That he *(Fox,)* was before all Languages, and consequently, before the Building of *Babel,* where the Languages were divided ; and that he was, whilst living, come to the end of Languages, which remain now he is dead and gone. No, no, G. Fox was not the Author; it was *John Stubbs* and *Ben. Furley,* did the Learned Part, yet set their Hands only to the Title Page ; but G. Fox's Hand is set to the *Latin* BATTLE-DOOR, the *Italian* BATTLE-DOOR, the *Greek* BATTLE-DOOR, the *Hebrew* BATTLE-DOOR, the *Chaldee* BATTLE-DOOR, the *Syriack* BATTLE-DOOR; (besides, in three or four Places more,) and yet wholly ignorant in all those Languages, the *Jews* * for Money out of the Common Bank, did for him. O horrid ! O monstrous.   Next, I make the like Challenge to parallel the Quakers Impudence ; not only to go into Churches to disturb the Ministers, according to their Ancient Testimony, and which they cannot deny, since 'tis Recorded plentifully in their Second *Moses,* their great Exemplar's Journal ; but I mean, to send an Epistle to be read in the Churches, calling them at their Will and Pleasure, Steeple-Houses, high Places of Idolatry, where the Christians exercise their Witchcraft and Whoredom ; yea, a Cage of unclean Birds, Serpents and Dragons,

* For what *Ben. Furley* and *Ja. Stubbs* could not do.

Dragons, that take the Letter, *i. e.* the Scripture, for the Light, and *Matthew, Mark, Luke* and *John,* for the Gospel. Oh horrible! What Impudence is this! What *Luciferian* Pride is here, for a Dissenter, nay worse, for an Impostor thus to impose his Imposture upon a Christian Nation! Which being compared with what else in other Books I have observed out of the Quakers Writings, as that the Bishops, and Clergy, are Witches, Devils, Conjurers, Sodomites, Blood-hounds, Antichrists, the *Sir-Symons* of the Age, Jesuits, *&c.* yea, Monsters, and what not; and then let G. *Whitehead* tell me, first, What he thinks of the Quakers Meekness and Humility; and next, Whether this Epistle, BATTLE-DOOR, and great part of their Writings, be not Seditious in the nature of them; and such intollerable Scandals, as had they not had more patience than the Quakers, notwithstanding the loud Noise they make of Patience, Humility and Meekness, *&c.* they would never have lain under such Publick Scandals: And therefore, when in the next Chapter I come to touch their tender Part, as *Erasmus* once said to a Monk, I shall see how patient they'll be, when they are paid in their own Coin; nay, I hope far better, at least to a better Purpose.

CHAP. XIII.

The Quakers Convocation: George Whitehead's *Sermon, explaining their Ancient Testimony.*

Reader,

THink not the following Sermon a Romance, or Fiction; for the Design of it is good, and intended for their Conviction: Read the Books in the Margin, and you'll find it fully proved to be the Sum and Marrow of their Ancient Testimony; which, by their Contempt of the Scriptures, shews their Antichristian Principles, and how their Doctrine carries all Iniquity in the Womb of it, and opens the Flood-gates to all *Atheism, Deism, Socinianism, Arianism,* and all other vile Errours: And therefore, in hopes that this following Illustration of their Principles, may be of use to their Hearers, I proceed in this unusual Method. But with my Lord Bishop of *Lincoln,* I will say, * 'Not that this can be 'expected from the Leaders of that Party; they have Ends to serve 'in the Conduct of that deluded People, that will engage them, not-'withstanding Confutation and Conviction too.

* In his Advice to his Clergy. *Second Edit.* p. 25.

A SERMON for George Whitehead *to hold forth at their Convocation, or Yearly Meeting.*

FRIENDS, I beg your Attention to what shall be spoken this Day, upon this Solemn Occasion, being met to inspect the Affairs of our Society throughout the World: The chief Subject upon which I shall treat, is our Ancient Testimony, as you will find it written in our Gospel, *viz.* 'God is the same, Truth is the same, his People the same, and their Principles the same: * For our Principles 'are now no other, than what they were when we were first a People; † so we cannot but recommend unto you, the holding up the 'Holy Testimony of Truth, which had made us to be a People, —— 'and that in all the Parts of it; for Truth is one, and changes not,*&c.*

* The Quakers cleared, &c. p. 7.
† *Prim Chrif. contin.* p. 6.
* Their Yearly Epist. Printed 1696.

Beloved, in the opening the Words of my Text, I am to tell you,

First, That as God is the same, so are his People the same, and according to our Ancient Testimony, as unchangeable.

Secondly, That our Principles are now no other than they were in the Beginning, in all the Parts of our Ancient Testimony, whether relating to Monarchy, * Magistracy, the National Ministry, and all Points of Doctrine.

* News coming up, p. 18, 19, 20.

Thus having opened the Words of my Text, I shall now let you know the Doctrinal Parts I intend to Discourse of, and then proceed:

FIRST, The Scriptures, which the Christians profess to be their Rule; shewing their great mistake therein, and the uncertainty thereof.

SECONDLY, The Authority, Certainty, and Infallibility of our Friends Books and Sayings, and both Affirmatively.

THIRDLY, and *Lastly,* I shall apply the same by way of Use, and for your Consolation, Negatively: And these in their Order.

First then, As to the Christian's Mistake about the Scriptures, look into the Epistle General of our Great Apostle *Geo. Fox,* * *viz.* 'And therefore all People that are here, Christ is not in the Letter, 'nor the Life is not in the Letter, nor the Word is not in the Letter: 'This mediate Stuff has Reigned long in the Cage of unclean Birds; 'you get the Letter for the Light, a Steeple-house for the Church, '*Matthew, Mark, Luke* and *John,* for the Gospel, *&c.* Thus, Beloved, you see what great Mistakes are hapned to this People of *England,* who by following the Doctrine of their blind Guides, have taken *Matthew, Mark, Luke* and *John,* for the Gospel; that is, Glad-Tidings: No, no, 'tis Beastly Ware, yea, Dust and Serpents Meat; and this I can prove by two Books, wrote by our Apostle

* To all the People who meet in Steeple-houses, &c. p. 4, 5. Printed 1657.

Geo.

The QUAKERS SYNOD.
G: Whitehead
Call over ye List, Are none of Truths enemies here
are the doors shut
W: Bingly
yea the doors are lockt
B: Bealing, scribe
church canons
ye Journal of G. Fox
deputies
deputies
deputies
deputies

Geo. Fox, the one ſtiled, *News coming up*, &c. p. 14. the other, *Several Papers given forth for the ſpreading of Truth*, &c. p. 3, 4, 44, 45, 46. *viz.* 'So Duſt is the Serpents Meat; their Original 'is but Duſt, which is Death; ſo theſe Serpents feed upon Duſt; 'and their Goſpel is Duſt, *Matthew*, *Mark*, *Luke* and *John*, which 'is the Letter, &c. Thus, Friends, have I ſhewed you the great Ignorance of the World's Teachers, who firſt take *Matthew*, *Mark*, *Luke* and *John*, for the Goſpel; and now, ſee what they have got for their Rule: Who would think, they ſhould hear ſuch Teachers, as hold a Bible in his Hand, and tell People it's the Word of God, and bid them hear it, and obey the Doctrine of it, at their Peril; for it's the Law, (ſay they,) by which you ſhall be judged another Day: When, alas! my dearly Beloved, as I have more than once in Print affirmed, ſaying, 'That which is ſpoken from the Spi- 'rit of Truth in any, (meaning our ſelves.) is of as great Authority, 'as the Scriptures, or Chapters are, and greater, &c.   And I ſtill affirm the ſame, and do tell you, that it is according to our Ancient Teſtimony; and you know, we cannot change, nor alter, being as unchangeable as our *Light within*. Moreover, the Scriptures are ſo uncertain, that 'tis queſtionable, who was the firſt Pen-man thereof; whether *Moſes* or *Hermes*, yea, either or neither: How then can any Man depend upon them, as a Rule to walk by? Thus you ſee, how the Chriſtians are miſtaken: For have not I my ſelf told you, as well as my dear Brother *Chriſtopher Atkinſon*, 'That Friends do 'not call *Matthew*, *Mark*, *Luke* and *John*, the Goſpel and New Te- 'ſtament, as the Ignorant Prieſts do? * And is it not written in the Goſpel of my ſaid Brother *Chriſto. Atkinſon*, 'That for any to ſay, 'that Chriſt is God and Man in one Perſon, is a Lie? † What ground then hath any body to hold a Trinity of Perſons? Nay, my Brother *Penn* and I, hath jointly ſaid in our Apology, Dedicated to the King's Lieutenant General of *Ireland*, That we deny the Terms of three diſtinct Perſons in the Godhead; * whereby we do poſitively deny the Creeds, called the Apoſtles, *Athanaſian* and *Nicene* Creeds. If any Object, * Why we refuſe to acknowledge them in Words, not altogether of, tho' agreeing with the Scriptures, ſeeing we our ſelves uſe many Words not Scriptural; as thoſe of calling the Scriptures DEATH, DUST, BEASTLY WARE, SERPENTS MEAT, &c. thoſe of our calling the Clergy, MONSTERS, BLOOD-HOUNDS, GRINNING DOGS, SODOMITES, WITCHES, DEVILS, &c. thoſe of calling Chriſt, A GARMENT, A VESSEL? I Anſwer: The reaſon why we call them ſo, and Tranſlate the Words of Chriſt, *John* 5. 22, 27. from the Son of Man to the *Light within us*,*IS, becauſe we believe, there is no other Son of Man than the Light within us, which was in the Jews, Gentiles, &c. before his Incarnation, according to my Goſpel, and the Goſpel of my Brother *Jeffery Bullock*,

See G. W. Truth defending the Quakers, &c. p. 7. Printed 1657.
A Ser. Apol. p. 49.

* *David's* Enemies diſcov. &c. p. 7.
† The Sword of the Lord drawn, &c. p. 5.

* A Ser. Apol. p. 20.

* The Sandy Foundation ſhaken, p. 5. to 65.

* The Quakers Reaſon for denying the Bleſſed Trinity.

where

where we say, THEREFORE THE MAN CHRIST JESUS WAS, BEFORE HE CAME IN THE BODY, OR FLESH. * For to be plain with you, according to our Ancient Testimony, we own no other Trinity, nor God, than is within us; for the Light is God, the Light is the Son of Man, the Light is the Holy Ghost; and we having obtained the Repute to be a well-meaning People; and tell the Priests, in Answer to their Demand, *Do you own the Trinity? Do you own the Sacraments, &c.* We tell them, we deny their unscriptural Terms: Where is the Words *Trinity* and *Sacrament* in the Scriptures? Tho' we are not such Fools, but we know, the Word *Trinity* came from the Latin Word *Trinitas*, and *Sacrament* from *Sacra* or *Sacramentum*, a Holy Institution or Sacrament; yet to hide our selves from the dint of their Arguments, we tell them, They are not Scripture Terms: Nay, even this Sessions of Parliament, when the House of Commons were preparing a Bill against such as denied the Trinity, we soon perceived what might follow, and we gave in a Paper, *saying, 'Whereas the Bill Enacts, That if any Person or Persons, &c. shall deny any of the Persons in the Holy Trinity to be 'God, and make it punishable by the same Bill, were it not more 'safe and plain, to put it in Scripture Terms, as, instead of, *Deny any* 'one of the Persons to be God, to incert, *If any one shall deny any of* '*the Three that bear Record in Heaven, the Father, the Word*, or '*the Holy Ghost, to be God*, 1 John 5. 7. Now, if we can keep the Parliament to these Words, we shall hide our selves, and retain our Ancient Testimony unshaken.

* Judgment filed, &c. p. 116, 336.

* Entituled, Some Considerations upon the Bill, for the more effectual Suppressing of Blasphemy and Prophaneness, Humbly offer'd.

Again, if any of you should yet Object, that notwithstanding we, (according to our Ancient Testimony,) call the Scriptures *Death, Dust, Beastly Ware, Serpents Meat,* †&c. and say, that *whoever Preach out of them, are Conjurers,* * &c. Yet notwithstanding all this, we profess, *to prefer the Holy Scriptures above all other Books extant in the World.* † To this I Answer, That you must observe the Context, as well as the Text; and then you shall see, we do not interfere; for in the same Book, *p.* 72. *viz.* 'I may see cause 'otherwise to word the Matter, and yet our Intentions be the same.

† *News coming up out of the North,* &c. P. 14. A Brief Discovery of a three-fold State, &c. p. 9. * Saul's Errand to Damascus, &c. p. 7. † The Counterfeit Convert, &c. p. 26, 27.

Besides, Beloved, I would have none mistake me; for tho' I am the Man that did say, we prefer the Scriptures above all other Books extant in the World, * which in one sense is true, yet not in another: *First,* I hope, you do not understand it of its Intrinsick Value, of its real Authority, so as to be a Rule of Faith and Practice; and that the Commands therein are Obligatory upon US; if you do, you are greatly mistaken, and that for these Reasons following: And,

* The Count. Conv. &c. p. 26.

First, 'That which is spoken from the Spirit of Truth in any, is 'of as great Authority as the Scriptures or Chapters are, and greater. *

* *Truth Defending the Quakers,* &c. p. 7.

Secondly, 'That is no Command from God to me, what he com-
'mands

From Quakerism to Christianity.

'mands to another: Neither did any of the Saints which we read of *Burrough's*
'in Scriptures, act by the Command which was to another, not Works, &c.
'having the Command to themselves? &c.

Thirdly, 'No Command in the Scriptures, is any further obliging
'upon any Man, than as he finds a Conviction upon his Conscience;
'otherwise Men should be engaged without, if not against Convicti- * *Quakerism a*
'on; a thing unreasonable in a Man. * New Nick-

Fourthly, To this triple treble Cord, which I think is not easily name, &c.
broken, let me add our constant Practice ever since we have been a p. 71.
People, and it will not only confirm these Proofs, but shew our sincerity to our Ancient Testimony; I say, as a Proof that we do not prefer the Scriptures above our own Books; let it suffice, That this forty eight Years, never an Apostate that ever went from us, can prove, nay, not once say, if they'll do us Justice, * that ever we read any * *George*, what one Chapter in the Bible, or any one Epistle of the Apostles in our you say is Meetings, whilst it hath been our frequent Practice to read our own true; I am a Epistles: And surely, if we deemed the Scriptures best, most cer- thy sincerity tain, and more edifying for us, respecting our Ancient Testimony, herein. you may depend on't, that we would read the Scriptures in our Meetings; nay, we challenge all our Adversaries, to shew us one Book of our Friends in the Unity, that ever so much as recommended the reading any one Chapter, or any one Epistle of the Apostles in our Meetings. Thus much in Answer to one part of the Objection, with respect to the Truth, Certainty, Value and Worth of the Scriptures: But still I say, they are occasionally good; and in one sense, I do prefer the Scriptures above our own Books, and then you may lay your Lives on't, above all Books in the World; for sometimes the * *The Gen.* Scriptures, as the Case may stand, are like the Philosopher's Stone; Hist. of the what they touch, they turn into Gold: And in that sense, our Con- Quakers, fession to the Parliament, with the Consequences, are a Demonstration, p. 112. *viz.* * 'I believe with my Heart, and confess with my Mouth, the † *Sacred*, an 'Sacred † Scriptures to be Divine, left us by Men inspired of God, unscriptural 'as an exact Rule of our Faith and Behaviour; and I profess to be- now will 'lieve in One Only God, who is the Father, and in Jesus Christ his down with 'Eternal Son, very God, and very Man, and in the Holy Spirit, one these new 'and the same God with the Father and Son, Blessed for evermore. Saints to serve a turn,

Now, my Friends, tho' this Confession be as contrary to our An- &c. cient Testimony, as Light is contrary to Darkness, as by our Books quoted you may see; yet we kept our meaning to our selves, mean'd at the same time, *The Scriptures to be Dust, Death, and Serpents Meat*; * *That to say, Christ is God and Man in one Person, is* * *News coming a Lie*: † But, as I said, *We may* (sometimes) *see cause*, (yea, and up, &c. p. 14. great cause too,) *otherwise to word the matter*; (yea, contrary to our † *The Sword of* Ancient Testimony,) *and yet mean the same thing*, * &c. that is to theLord drawn, say, mean not a word we say: And now to the consequence, and for * *The Counter.* which we prefer the Bible. . For, Convert, &c. p. 72.

For, Friends, we no sooner Signed this Confession, but we had our Liberty; and we no sooner had our Liberty, but all our *London* Preachers spread themselves, like Locusts, all over *England* and *Wales*; * some went *East*, some *West*, yea, *North* and *South*; and being generally Trades men, We not only got our Quarters free, our Horses free, and well maintain'd in our Travels; a Silver Watch here, a Beaver there, a piece of Hair Camblet, and sometimes other Gifts: Moreover, by our Liberty obtained, by the recited Confession, we got into great Trades; and by spreading our selves in the Country, into great Acquaintance, and thereby received Orders, (of the best of the Country Trades men,) for Parcels, whilst the Protestant Tradesmen in *London*, * who had not this Advantage, stood still, and in their Shops had little to do, whilst we fill'd our Coffers. Witness *Tho. Greene* for one instance, whose Wife would scarce suffer him at home; she being willing (according to the Proverb,) to make Hay whilst the Sun shines; insomuch that in a little time, he raised his small Beginning to many Thousands: All which shew, that the Scriptures are accidentally good, &c. And this leads me to the second Proposition, namely,

Like Mice uncall'd for, and like Flies unsent for, and fall upon their Provision.

* Londoners, look about you, for none like the Quakers, but Jews and Jesuites, as time will farther shew.

The Authority of our Friends Books and Sayings, &c.

First, I shall shew you, that as 'tis Blasphemy to call the Scriptures the Word of God; * so I shall shew you, that our Scriptures, (for as I told you, in my *Serious Apol. p. 48*. Writings signifie Scripture,) are the Word of God, and this you will find written in the Epistle of our Second *Moses*, in these Words, † 'Friends, to you all, *this is the Word of the Lord*, take heed of judging one another; *this is the Word of the Lord, unto you*: I charge you in the Presence of the Lord God, to send this (Epistle,) among all Friends and Brethren, every where to be *read in all Meetings*, to you all, *This is the Word of God*. Again, that I may corroborate and strengthen your Faith in the Exercise of our Ancient Testimony: * Read in the Gospel of our Great Apostle and High Priest of our Profession, G. *Fox*, where you'll find these Words, *viz*. 'You may '(said G. F. to the Priests,) as well condemn the Scriptures to the 'Fire, as our Writings; for our giving forth Papers and Printed 'Books, it is from the IMMEDIATE ETERNAL SPIRIT of 'God; † upon which, our Dear Brother *Tho. Ellwood* saith, That 'none can squirt any Filth on the Epistles of Friends, but it will tend 'to bespatter the Apostles: * And in confidence thereof, our Brother *Robert Barclay* hath these Words, That as the true Principles 'of the Gospel, by their (*i. e.* Quakers) Testimony, are restored; 'so is also the ANCIENT Apostolick Order of the Church of Christ 're-established amongst them, (*i. e.* Quakers,) and settled upon it's 'right Basis and Foundation; —— that as thro' our faithful Testimony

* To all that would know the way to the Kingdom, &c. p. 4. Mene Tekel, &c. p. 22.
† Several Papers given forth, for spreading Truth, &c. p. 60, 61, 62.

* G. W. keeps to his Text.

† Truths Defence, &c. p. 2. 102.
* An Antidote against, &c. p. 1, 44, 57, 125.

'in

From Quakerism to Christianity.

'in the Hand of the Lord, that *Antichristian* and *Apostatized* Ge-
'neration, *the National Ministry*, hath received a deadly Blow, by
'our discovering and witnessing against their Forced Maintainance
'and Tythes; so that their Kingdom, in the Hearts of Thousands, [* Let all Law-yers, Tradesmen, Clergy, and Magistrates, guard against the prevalency of Quakerism, for they are all highly concerned.]
'begin to Totter, and lose its Strength, and shall assuredly fall to
'the Ground: So on the other hand, do we weaken the Strength of
'their Kingdom, who judge for Reward. The Nation shall come
'to be disburdened of that deceitful Tribe of Lawyers, as well as
'Priests. * I never knew any that left us, prove steady to those to
'whom they go. I find, other Professors make but small Boasts of
'any Proselytes they get out from us; I hear little of their proving
'Champions, for the Principles of others against us. †

Thus, Friends, you see, that upon confidence of the Truth of our [† *The Anarchy*, &c. p. 1, 16, 42.]
Elder Brother, *Geo. Fox*'s Ancient Testimony, *viz.* That it was Blasphemy to call the Scriptures the Word of God, (and yet laudable to
call his Papers, sent up and down to be read in Meetings, *The Word
of God, the Word of the Lord God*;) I say, you see how stoutly our
Brother *Ellwood* avouched, that none could squirt any Filth on the
Epistles of Friends, but it must inevitably fall upon the Epistles of
St. *Paul*; and he was in the right on't, * and likewise *R. Barclay*, [* G. W. is no Changling, he keeps to his Text.]
in confidence of the Truth of *G. Fox*'s Testimony, *viz.* That to call
the Scriptures *The Word of God*, was no less than *Blasphemy*; whilst
his own Writings sent up and down to spread Truth, and in order to
it, to be read in Meetings, was *The Word of the Lord*; and as such
to be read, and as such to be receiv'd: You may see, I say, how he
built his Hopes of our Restoration, and the Downfal both of the Clergy and Lawyers, insomuch that he did not once think, any should
ever go from us, to prove Champions for the Principles of others against us: And therefore, I exhort you this Day, to stand Faithful
to your Ancient Testimony, which is, to throw down the Scriptures,
and exalt our own Books; and so will the Work of your Light prosper in your Hands.

Besides, for your Encouragement, (and that you may see my Sincerity and Seriousness, which is the sign of my Writing in every
of my Epistles,) look into one of my Gospels, and you shall find these
Words: *That which is spoken from the Spirit of Truth in any, is
of as great Authority, as the Scriptures and Chapters are, and greater,* * &c.

Wherefore, ye dear Lambs, be ye encouraged, and go on boldly; [* *Truth Defending the Quakers*, &c. p. 7.]
and if any Apostate write against us, besure you warn all our Friends
in the Country not to read a Page thereof; but tell them, all are Lies, [* True; for never were a People held more Captive; but the Blind lead the Blind.]
all is Malice, &c. and they are bound to believe you, * according
to my Doctrine, in these Words: 'It was for your sakes, and
'the Truth's, that I was pressed in Spirit, thus to appear against this
'deceitful Worker, which hath shewn his Enmity against the Truth.

Q 'and

The Pilgrim's Progress,

'and Us the Church of Christ, and Elect People of God, called Qua-
'kers. And, p. 16. I affirm, That the true Church (as above de-
'scribed,) is in the true Faith, that is in God: And we must believe
'thus, as the true Church believes; or else, it were but both a Fol-
'ly and Hypocrisie, to profess our selves Members thereof, * &c.

* *The Apost. In-*
cendiary, &c.
p. 3, 16.

So that, my tender Lambs, you see, first, That we are the true
Church of Christ; next, That you are to believe as the Church believes; and there lyes *G. Fox*'s Journal on the Table, which you
have in all Quarterly Meetings, and ought to have it in all Schools,
* yea, in private Families; for as our Brother *Mead* hath well express'd himself, it is the best Book in the World, for our keeping
up our Ancient Testimony, yea, better than the Bible, said he. And
now to conclude this Head, look into the Book of Canons, † which
lyes before you on the Table, and turn to those Church Canons,
which were made *Anno* 1675. at a Yearly Meeting, or a Convocation; where (in order to corroborate all that hath been said on this
Head,) it is thus Written:

* *They have*
got it in some
Schools alrea-
dy, where their
Youth read a
Portion of it
every day, &c.
† *Look into the*
Book of Church-
Cannons, made
Anno 1675.

'It is the Sense, Advice, Admonition and Judgment, in the Fear of
'God, and the Authority of his Power and Spirit to Friends and Bre-
'thren, in their several Meetings, That no such slight and contemp-
'tible Names and Expressions, as calling Men's and Women's Meet-
'ings, Courts, Sessions, or Synods; that they are Popish Impositi-
'ons, useless and burdensom; that Faithful Friend's Papers which
'*WE TESTIFIE*, have been given forth by the *Spirit* and *Power*
'of God, are Men's Edicts, or Canons; or Imbracing them, Bowing
'to Men, Elders in the Service of the Church, Popes and Bishops, with
'such scornful Sayings, be permitted among them; but let God's
'Power be set upon the top of that Unsavoury Spirit that uses them.

Subscribed by us,

W. Penn,	Jo. Burnyeat,
Ste. Crisp,	G. Whitehead,
Tho. Salthouse,	Alex. Parker, &c.

Thirdly *and* Lastly, *Let me Apply what has been said.*

FRIENDS, I am now come to the last thing proposed, to speak
to, on this Solemn Occasion; and it shall be by way of Use and Application, for your Comfort and Consolation, and that by way of Inference drawn from the foregoing Two Heads: And,

FIRST, Respecting Confession of Sin; shewing your Exaltation above the Patriarchs, Prophets, Apostles, Primitive Christians,
Saints and Martyrs, and all the Christian Churches, to this Day.

* *Edward Bur-*
rough's Works.
p. 47.
Quakerism a
new Nick-
name, &c.
p. 71.

SECONDLY, Respecting the Observation of the Ten Commandments; which are not binding to you, unless you receive them
anew, as the Inspired Prophets and Apostles did. *

THIRD-

From **Quakerism** *to* **Christianity.** 115

THIRDLY, Respecting the Ordinances of Baptism, and the Lord's Supper. And,

FIRST, You being the true Ancient Apostolick Church of Christ, and as Quakers, elected thereto; and that the Quakers are in the Truth, and none but they, as our Brother *Sol. Eccles* from the Spirit of Truth hath written, * hath no need to make any Confession of Sin in our Prayers to God, as our Practice for near fifty Years do confirm; nay, nor all the Apostates that ever went from us; nor all the Priests, our Adversaries, cannot prove from any one of our Books, wrote by my self, *G. Fox, Ed. Burrough, Fr. Howgill,* Father *Penn, Sam. Fisher, W. Smith, W. Baily, Richard Hebberthorn,* and others of our Friends in the Unity, that ever we made Confession of Sins to God, and asked Pardon for Christ's sake; nor that ever we recommended such a Practice to our Disciples, notwithstanding our Books wrote by our Friends above-named, contain more than 5555555 of Pages, in *Folio, Quarto* and *Octavo.* Now Friends, What cause have we to Rejoyce, and to Magnifie our *Light within,* which hath led us to such a State of sinless Perfection? And therefore, I exhort you to keep up our Ancient Testimony, in all its Parts; of which, this is not the least: For let me tell you, that *Jacob,* that worthy and godly Patriarch, he was so sensible of his sinful Imperfections, that when he prayed to God, he acknowledged himself *unworthy of the least of God's Mercies:* † And *Isaiah* the Prophet said, *But we are all as an unclean thing, and all our Righteousness are as filthy Rags, and we all do fade as a Leaf, and our Iniquities like the Wind, have taken us away.* * And *Jeremiah* the Prophet cryed under a sense of his Sins, *We have Transgressed and Rebelled;* † yea, *Job,* that Man of God said, *I have sinned; What shall I do unto thee, O thou preserver of Men?* * Yea, *David,* a Man after God's own Heart, said, *For I will declare mine Iniquity; I will be sorry for my Sin: — Have mercy upon me, O God, according to thy Loving Kindness; according unto the multitude of thy tender Mercies, blot out my Transgressions; wash me thoroughly from mine Iniquity, and cleanse me from my Sin; for I acknowledge my Transgressions, and my Sin is ever before me; against thee, thee only, have I Sinned, and done this Evil in thy sight; that thou mightest be justified when thou speakest, and be clear when thou judgest; behold I was shapen in Iniquity, and in Sin did my Mother conceive me,* * &c.

* *See the Quakers Challenge, &c.* p. 1.

† Gen. 32. 10.

* Isa. 64. 6.

† Lam. 3. 41.

* Job 7. 20.

* Psal. 38, 18, and 51. 1, 2, 3, 4, 5.

Again, *Solomon* said, *For there is not a just Man upon Earth, that doth good, AND SINNETH NOT;* † adding by way of Interrogation, *Who can say, I have made my Heart clean, I am pure from my Sin?* * Yea, that good Man *Nehemiah,* Fasted, Prayed, and Wept before the Lord God of *Israel,* saying

† Eccles. 7. 20.
* Prov. 20. 9.
* Besides the *Quakers* and the *Gnosticks.*

Q 2

O Lord God of Heaven, the great and terrible God, that keepeth Covenant and Mercy, for them that love him, and observe his Commandments: * Let thine Ear now be attentive, and thine Eyes open, that thou mayest hear the Prayer of thy Servant, which I pray before thee now, Day and Night, for the Children of Israel, thy Servants; and confess, the Sins of the Children of Israel which we have sinned against thee; I and my Father's House have sinned: † Yea, Daniel, that Beloved of the Lord, he said, And I prayed unto the Lord my God, and made my Confession, and said, O Lord, the great and dreadful God, keeping the Covenant and Mercy to them that love him, and to them that keep his Commandments: WE have sinned, and committed Iniquity, and have done Wickedly, and have Rebelled, even by Departing from thy Precepts, and from thy Judgments; and whilst I was Speaking, and Praying, and Confessing my Sins, and the Sins of my People Israel, and presenting my Supplication before the Lord my God, * &c. Yea, John the Evangelist said, If we say, that we have no Sin, we deceive our selves, and the Truth is not in us. * Moreover, St. Paul himself cryed out of a Body of Sin; saying, For the good that I would do, I do not; but the Evil which I would not, that I do: I find then a Law, that when I would do Good, Evil is present with me: O wretched Man that I am, who shall deliver me from the Body of this Death? † This is a faithful Saying, and worthy of all Acceptation, That Christ Jesus came into the World, to save Sinners, of whom I am Chief: All which Practice, is according to Christ's Command and Precept, * who said, Whatsoever you shall ask the Father in my Name, he will give it you. † And when our Brethren, the Donatists and Pelagians, who professed a sinless Perfection, as we do, told the Ancient Christians, that a constant Practice of Confession, implied a constant course of Sinning: St. Augustine reply'd to them, saying, Confess always, for thou hast Matter always to confess. * Tho. Bilny confessed, that he was a miserable Sinner; And (said he,) therefore with all my Power, I teach, that all Men should first acknowledge their Sins. * Dr. Robert Barnes said, The whole Church prayeth, Lord forgive us our Sins: Wherefore, she hath Spots and Wrinkles; but by acknowledging them, (thro' the Merits of Christ,) her Wrinkles be scratched out. * Martin Luther saith, But thou wilt say,

the

From Quakerism to Christianity.

the Church is Holy; the Fathers are Holy; it is true, notwithstanding, albeit the Church is Holy, yet is she compelled to pray, Forgive us our Trespasses: So, tho' the Fathers are Holy, yet are they saved thro' the Forgiveness of Sins*. Next, hear what *Humble Bradford* said to his *London* Friends: John Bradford, *an Unworthy Servant of the Lord, be merciful to our Sins, for they are great.----Let us heartily bewail our Sins; repent us of our former Evil Life*, &c.

[margin: * See *Luther's* Commentary upon *Gal.* p. 36.]

Thus, my Well-beloved Friends and Brethren, I have shewed you many Instances, both of the Patriarchs, Prophets, Apostles, Primitive Christians, and Martyrs, who have all along confessed their Sins to God, and begg'd Pardon for Jesus Christ's sake; and go you but to the Windows or Doors of the Churches, and other Christian Assemblies, (but besure you go no further) and you may still hear them, *i. e.* Episcopal, Presbyterians, Independants, and Baptists, crying out of a Body of Sin; saying, *They have erred and strayed from the Ways of God* (from Seven to Seventy, as our Brother, Father *Penn*, has well observ'd) * *we have done Despite to the Spirit of Grace, we have broke thy Commandments, we have added to the Guilt of Original Sin, by our many and repeated Actual Sins; and therefore we prostrate our selves, and humbly beg thy Pardon, for the alone sake of thy dear Son, and our blessed Redeemer, Jesus Christ, our only Advocate, and Mediator; to whom, with thee, and thy blessed Spirit, be all Honour, Glory, and Dominion, for ever,* Amen.

[margin: *Fox's* Acts and *Mon.* p. 1167.]
[margin: * Truth exalted in a Short but Sure Testimony, &c. p. 9.]

Now Friends, What a happy thing is this, that you need not trouble your selves with any Confession of Sins, since you are not like other Men; nor like these *Publicans*; and therefore I exhort you to keep to your Ancient Testimony in all the Parts of it, make no Confession of Sins, nor besure you do not recommend the Practice of it, by Word or Writing, but keep to our Ancient Practice; nor is there any need for our Hearers to follow those Christian Precepts, *viz. And whatsoever you do in Word or Deed, do all in the NAME of the LORD JESUS;* giving Thanks to God the Father BY HIM; † whether *therefore yet EAT or DRINK, or whatsoever ye do, do all to the Glory of God:* First, because the Name Jesus belongs to every Believer, (I should say *Quaker*) as well as to him that suffer'd at *Jerusalem*, according to our Ancient Testimony:* Secondly, because you know that we our selves, to be seen of Men, do make a kind of a Prayer to our Light within, when we are at their Tables, when Company is present; but if alone, either at Home or Abroad, we seldom give Thanks for our Food,

[margin: † *Col.* 3. 17. 1 *Cor.* 10. 31. *Matth.* 15. 36.]
[margin: * A Question to Professors, &c. p. 20, 27. 33.]

Food, and seldomer with our Eyes towards Heaven, as Christ did, as *Stephen* did, or as the Martyrs did: No, you know we are of another, yea, of a different Faith and Practice from all the Ancient Patriarchs, Prophets, Apostles, Martyrs, and Holy Confessors, and all Christian Churches to this Day, being exalted above them; for we sit in Heavenly Places, singing the Songs of *Sion*, in the Beauty of Holiness, without Sin, or any Imperfection, which all the Recited were chargeable with, as imply'd by their Confessions, and their relying upon the Merits of another, to wit, The Man Christ Jesus, as believing they shall one Day appear before his Tribunal, and be judged by the Law of God, recorded in their Scriptures; but for our parts, we differ from them in all Respects, having our whole God within us, as safely, as the Papists have their Crucifixes in their Pockets. And thus much, to shew you the great Happiness and Excellency of our Dispensation; so no need of Confession, according to our ancient Testimony.

The Second Inference, i. e. The Ten Commandments.

And Friends, Whereas the Christians propose to us (sometimes) the Use of the Ten Commandments; whether we own them as a Rule to a Christian Life, look into one of my Gospels, and you will find it thus written: *Thou may'st as well ask, if the Moral Law (or Ten Commandments) be a Rule for Christ,* &c. *

Again, *Edw. Burrough*, one of our Prophets, said, *That is no Command from God to me, what he commands to another; neither did any of the Saints, which we read of in Scripture, act by the Command, which was to another, not having the Command to themselves: I challenge to find an Example for it; they obey'd every one their own Command.* †

And in Defence of this Position, hear what Father *Penn* says, i. e. *No Command in the Scripture is any further obliging upon any Man, than as he finds a Conviction upon his Conscience, otherwise Men should be engaged without, if not against Conviction, a thing unreasonable in a Man:* And now, that none of you may think that these Doctrines of ours, point to, or aim only at extraordinary Commands, as *Moses* going to *Pharoah*, with some other Temporary Commands, my very Doctrine shew it to be the Ten Commandments. *First*, By telling the Priest they might as well carry the Ten Commandments to Christ; the Consequence of which is, that Christ had as much need to learn them as we have. *Secondly*, in that we never Recommended the Ten Commandments to our Hearers, that they should teach them to their Children, and so from Age to Age, one Generation after another, as the Churches do, and ever did, both Jewish and Christian.

* Truth defending the Quakers, &c. p. 18.

† Burrough's Works, p. 47.

Quak. a new Nick-Name, &c. p. 71.

Thirdly,

Thirdly, because we never read them in our Meetings, nor in any one of our Books, Recommend them to be so read: This therefore may confirm you in our Ancient Testimony, which have been to lay them by, as a dead Letter, Dust, Death, Serpents Food, and Beastly Ware, *&c.* And I exhort you to be Bold, and Valiant, to Maintain our Ancient Testimonies; and this leads me to the third and last Inference, namely,

Touching Baptism, and the Lord's Supper.

Dear Friends, I am now come to give you the Arguments of the Christians for Baptism, and the Supper, which is founded upon the Letter, which our Apostle, *G. Fox*, said was Dust, and Death, *viz.* ' Their Sacrament is Carnal; their Communion is Carnal;
' a little Bread and Wine; so Dust is the Serpents Meat. Their
' Original is but Dust, which is but the Letter, which is Death;
' and their Gospel is Dust; *Matthew, Mark, Luke,* and *John,*
' which is the Letter. † Again, *p.* 35. ' A Word to all you Deceiv-
' ers, who deceive the People; and Blasphemers, who utter forth
' your Blasphemy and Hypocrisie; That tell People of a Sacra-
' ment; and tell them it is the Ordinance of God: Blush, blush,
' and tremble before the Lord God Almighty, for dreadful is he that
' will pour forth his Vengeance upon you:——You who live in the
' Witchery, and bewitch the People, *&c.*

† News coming up out of the *North, &c.* p. 14. 35.

Dear Lambs, I first told you, that the Authority the Christians make use of, for these Two Ordinances, is bottomed upon the Letter. I have now shewed you a greater Authority, for the disannulling them; namely, what is said by the Spirit of Truth, tho' our second *Moses:* And to prove it, read the Gospel wrote by me, 1659. *viz.* ' That which is spoken from the Spirit of Truth in any, ' (then to be sure in *Geo. Fox*) is of as Great Authority as the ' Scriptures or Chapters are, and Greater. † Thus, Friends, I first told you, what Authority the Christians pleaded for these two Institutions, of Baptism, and the Supper; namely, the Scriptures: I have likewise told you, by what Authority we have laid them aside; but lest all of you should not remember the Words the Christians quote, not being much used to Scripture, they are these.

† Truth defending the *Quakers, &c.* p. 7.

Go ye therefore, and teach all Nations, Baptizing them in the Name of the Father, and of the Son, and of the Holy Ghost, teaching them to observe all things whatsoever I have commanded you: And lo I am with you always, even to the end of the World. * Again, And he (Christ) took Bread, and gave Thanks, and brake it, and gave unto them, saying, This is my Body, which is given for you: THIS DO IN REMEMBRANCE OF

* Matth. 28. 19, 20.

OF ME. *Likewise, also the Cup, after Supper, saying, This*
† Luke 22. *Cup is the New-Testament in my Blood, which is shed for you.* †
19, 20. Again, *Matthew* hath it: *And as they were eating, Jesus took Bread, and blessed it, and brake it; and gave to the Disciples, and said, Take, eat, this is my Body: And he took the Cup, and gave thanks, and gave it to them, saying, Drink ye all of it, for this is my Blood of the New-Testament, which is shed for many for the*
* Matth. 26. *Remission of Sins.* * Again, *Paul* hath it: *For I received of the*
26, 27, 28. *Lord that which also I delivered unto you: That the Lord Jesus, the same Night in which he was betrayed, took Bread: And when he had given Thanks, he broke it, and said, Take, eat, this is my Body, which is broken for you;* THIS DO IN REMEMBRANCE OF ME. *After the same manner also, he took the Cup, when he had supped, saying, This Cup is the New-Testament in my Blood:* THIS DO YE, *as oft as ye drink it,*
† 1 Cor. 11. IN REMEMBRANCE OF ME†.
23, 24, 25.
    Beloved, I cannot but allow, that if the Letter, *viz.* the Scriptures, were of greater Authority than our Sayings, or that the Words of *Matthew, Luke* and *Paul*, were of greater Authority than are our Sayings, I should be of the Christian's side; for nothing in the World is plainer said, nor more possitively commanded: But
* By his Book Friends, in the beginning we were convinced by *G. Fox* *, that
News coming *Matthew, Mark, Luke* and *John* were Death, Dust, and Serpents
up, &c. p. 14. Meat; that the Scriptures were Beastly Ware; that all that preach-
35. Printed ed out of them were Conjurers; that the Letter of the Scripture is
1655. A brief
Discovery of Carnal, Death, and Killeth; that such as once told People of a
a three-fold Sacrament were Witches: And that therefore they ought not only
State, &c. p. to blush, but tremble; that such as preached Christ without, and
9. Printed
1653. *Saul's* bid People believe in him, as he is in Heaven above, were false
Errand to Da- Ministers †, Witches, Devils, &c. That it was Blasphemy to call
mascus, &c. p. the Scriptures the Word of God *, &c. And therefore I warn you
7. Printed
1654. all, to take heed of Apostatizing, from our Ancient Testimony, as you
† *Smith's* have it in my Text; for what we were convinced of, by our Light
Primmer, p.8. in the beginning, to be Evil, to be Death, Dust, Serpents Meat; 'tis
* *Fox's* Great so still; to be Beastly Ware, and Conjuration, 'tis so still; and there-
Myst. p. 240. fore keep up to your Ancient Testimony, my dear Lambs, in all the
Printed 1659. Parts of it; Ha, ha, ha; hme, hme, hme; silent.

After a little Silence, Will. Bingley, &c.

    Friends, Friends, I am filled, I am filled, as with new Wine, I am ready to burst at the joyful News I have heard to Day, respecting

From Quakerism *to* Christianity.

specting our Ancient Testimony: And Oh! magnified be our Light within, which hath thus exalted us above the Prophets, above the Apostles, above the Martyrs, and above all Christians, as our dear Brother, *G. W.* hath most excellently made it out: *First*, In opening his Text, and also in the two Branches proceeding from it, but more especially in the Use and Application, where he hath confirmed me, in not making Confession of Sin, nor regarding the Ten Commandments, nor those two Ordinances of Baptism and Supper, all which is ratified and confirmed by *G. Fox*'s Journal, laying there on the Table: But yet I have a short Testimony to bring in, touching the Priests, which I think our Friend *G. W.* left out unawares, for I take it to be as necessary an Ancient Testimony, to be kept up, as any other, only a little more Privately and Prudently; for they are as Great Enemies to our Design of Supplanting Christianity, as any the World afford; and my Proof for the Antiquity of my Testimony shall be out of *Edw. Burrough*'s Epist. *viz.*

(*a.*) 'And the Word of the Lord we founded, and did not spare, and
'caused the Deaf to Hear, and the Blind to see, and the Dread of the Lord
'went before us, and behind us, and Terror took hold on our Enemies.
'And *first* of all, our Mouths were *Opened,* (*b.*) and our Spirits *Filled*
'with *Indignation* against the *Priests* and *Teachers,* (*c.*) and with
'them, and against them, we *first* began to *War,* as being the Cau-
'sers of the People to err, and the Blind-Leaders, that carried the
'Blind into the Ditch; and against them, as the *Fountain* of
'all *Wickedness,* abounding in the Nations, and as being the *Issue* of
'*Prophaneness,* and against them we cried, shewing unto all these
'People, that they were not Lawful Ministers of Christ, but *De-*
'*ceivers* and *Antichrists*; and we spared not *Publickly,* (*d.*) and
'at all Seasons, to utter forth the *Judgments* of the Lord against
'them, and their Ways, and their *Churches,* and *Worships,* and
'*Practices*; and this was our *first Work* (*e.*) we enter'd upon, to
'*Thresh* down the *Deceivers,* and lay them open, that all People
'may see their Shame, and come and turn from them; neither
'can we pray for the Priests, but for their Destruction, *&c.* And
'this Testimony lay upon me to bear, which is in all Parts accord-
'ing to our Ancient Testimony. (*f.*)

Benjamin Bealing, Clerk. Let us sing an Hymn of Praise, and Self-Exaltation, and to the Confusion of our Adversaries; as you will find it written in the Epistle-General of that Son of Thunder, *Edw. Burrough,* prefixed to our Apostle, *George Fox*'s Great Mystery, Printed 1658.

(*a.*) *Edw. Burrough*'s Epistle to *G. F.*'s Great Mystery, Printed 1658.
(*b.*) Then the *Quakers* began.
(*c.*) True every Word.

(*d.*) Then why should you be spared?
(*e.*) So it was my first Work to thresh down the *Quaker Deceivers.*
(*f.*) *Truth's Defence, &c.* by *G. Fox,* and *Rich. Hubberthorn,* p. 15. Printed 1653.

The Waters have I seen dry'd up, the Seat of that great Whore,
Who hath made all Nations drunk with her inticing Power;
And caused the whole Earth, She hath, Her Fornication Cup to take,
Whereby Nations have long time err'd, on whom She long hath sate:

R

But now Her Miseries are seen, Her Witchcrafts are discover'd,
And She no more shall Men deceive, for Day Light is appear'd;
And the Bed woful I have seen, of Torments great prepar'd,
Whereon She must be cast, and Plagues must not be spared:
But Woe to Her, the Cup of Wrath is fill'd Her to receive,
And as to others She hath done, the same She shall now have;
And Drink She must of that full Cup, of God's fierce Indignation,
And then shall all Her Lovers mourn, and make great Lamentation:
For Fire in Her is kindled, which must Her all consume;
Behold Her Smoak ascendeth Day and Night up to Heaven:
The Antichrists, who hath put on, and cover'd with Sheeps cloathing,
And long rul'd King, on Nations Inwardly Ravening;
Who hath devour'd God's Heritage, and had a Kingdom great;
I have seen him made War against, and Truth give Him Defeat.
Behold the Whore, Her Flesh is burnt, Her Beauty doth now fall;
She that is all Harlots great Mother, whose Daughters are Whores all.

The Close of the Meeting, by Geo. Whitehead.

Friends, I have still one Word, of Exhortation, as you will find it in the Prophecy of our deceased Brother, *Samuel Fisher*, touching Magistracy and Government; which being according to our Ancient Testimony, I could not well omit, *viz.* * ' I will hold my Peace no longer, faith the Lord, as concerning this Evil, ' which they so prophanely commit, and do daily against my Chosen; but will utterly subvert and overturn them, and bring the ' Kingdoms and Dominions, and the Greatness of the Kingdom, ' under the whole Heaven, into the Hands of the Holy Ones † of ' the most High, and give unto my Son, and his Saints, to reign ' over all the Earth: And take ALL the RULE, and AUTHORI-' TY, and POWER, that shall stand up against my *Son in his* ' *Saints*; and put it down among all the rest, as one of his greatest ' Enemies, under his Feet, faith the Lord. For though the World ' take no Delight in them, yet I take Pleasure in my People, faith ' the Lord: And I will beautifie my Meek ones * with Salvation, ' and I will put my high Praise into their Mouths, and a *Two-edged Sword into their Hands* †; and they shall execute *Vengeance* upon the Heathen, and Punishments upon the People; and ' shall *bind* their *Kings* in Chains, and Nobles in Fetters of Iron, ' and execute upon them the Judgment that is written in my Eternal Decree, and Unchangeable Councel, faith the Lord. This ' Honour have all my Saints; this is the Heritage of my Servants, ' faith the Lord: And their Righteousness, and their Reign, their ' Salvation and Redemption, and all their *Dignity*, is of me only,

* *Sam. Fisher's Works, p. 19, 20. observ'd by Mr. Boothouse.*

† Meaning the *Quakers.*

* Meek *Quakers.*

†Mark, this is your Ancient Testimony as well as Prophesie, writ 1656.

and

From Quakerism *to* Christianity.

' and of me only, and not of themselves, shall they acknowledge it
' to be, SAITH THE LORD GOD ALMIGHTY, who is now
' doing all this his Holy Will and good Pleasure; and who is he
' that shall ever Disannul it.

Given forth under my Hand, as the Lord himself gave it into my Heart to see, and into my Mouth to speak, and unto my Hand, thus at large, to write it, the 25th. of the 7th. Month, 1656.

Samuel Fisher.

Friends, I am the longer in this Sermon, because my Text requires it; namely, To shew you our Ancient Testimony in all the Parts of it: And if any of the World's People at any time should understand this Discourse, for 'tis much if it do not come abroad, then tell them we mean all within, we are an Inward People: And whether we mention War and Fighting, Swords and Spears, Ox or Ass, Kill, Cut off, Destroy, take Vengeance of the Heathen, Subvert and Oturn Nations, Kingdoms, &c. all this we mean within, and this have; and this peradventure will satisfie them. And now, *Friends*, I shall instance but one Proof more, to evince what our Ancient Testimony was, and is in all its Parts, and then I shall with Prayer conclude; and it is in an Epistle, entituled, THIS IS ONLY TO GO AMONGST FRIENDS. † Which Epistle contains great part of our Ancient Testimony; for it answers to *George Fox*'s Title Page, *News coming up, &c.* and it answers to *Josiah Coal*'s Letter, where he saith, *Dear G. Fox, who art the Father of many Nations*; *whose Life hath reached through us thy Children; whose Being and Habitation is in the Power of the Highest, in which thou* [George] *Rulest and Governs in Righteousness: And* THY KINGDOM *is* ESTABLISHED *in* PEACE, *and the* INCREASE *thereof is* WITHOUT END.* It answers also our Brother *Solomon Eccles*, who said, *It might be said of G.* Fox, *as it was of Christ, that he was in the World, and the World was made by him; and yet the World knew him not* †: For if he was a King, and had a Kingdom, and such a Kingdom, as of the Increase thereof, there was never to be an end; then you may conclude, Friends, that he was the BRANCH, the 'STAR, the SON of RIGHTEOUSNESS, spoken of in Scriptures; but mark, THIS (*Epistle*) IT IS ONLY TO GO AMONGST FRIENDS,* *viz.*

' And O thou North of *England!* who art counted as Desolate,
' and Barren, and reckoned the least of the Nation; yet out of
thee

Pray is not this a Fifth-Monarchy Sermon? No, it's a Quaker Sermon, but it's all one Doctrine, and may become one Practice. P. 102. Ibid. i.e. *The Quakers are the truest Catholick Church in the World, &c.* If so, then your Saints are intended for this Holy War.

† Writ by Fr. *Howgill*, (whose Daughter is now in *Bridewell, London*) and *Edw. Burrough* in Dublin, Printed *Anno* 1656.
* *Josiah Coal*'s Letter from *Barbadoes*, recorded in the Book of Outlandish Letters, and by W. P. vindicated in *Judas, and the Jews, &c.* p. 44.
† The *Quakers* Challenge, *&c.* p. 6.
Indeed it was fit to go amongst none but *Quakers* and Fifth Monarchy-Men, so very well intituled.

* *Viz.* G. *Fox,* 'thee did the BRANCH * spring, and the STAR arise, which
which was 'gives Light unto all the Regions round about in THEE (*i. e.* the
prophesied of, '*North*) the Son of Righteousness appear'd with Wounding, and
and now is 'with Healing; and out of THEE the Terrors of the Lord proceed-
fulfilled, &c. 'ed, which makes the Earth to tremble, and be removed; out of
his *News out of* 'THEE † Kings, Priests and Prophets, did come forth, in the
the North, Title 'Name and Power of the most High, which uttered their Voices
Page, Printed 'as Thunders, and laid their Swords on the Neck of their Enemies*,
1655. 'and never return'd empty from the Slaughter.——Lift up your
† *i. e.* Out of 'Voice; blow the Trumpet; sound an Alarum out of the Holy
the *North* 'Mountain; proclaim the Acceptable Year, and the Day of Venge-
came G. *Fox,* 'ance of our God; gird on your Sword upon your Loyns, put on
Ja. Nayler, R. 'the Tryed Armour, and follow him for ever, who rides on the
Hubberthorn, G. 'white Horse, and is cloathed with the same, and makes War in
Whitehead, Ed. 'Righteousness. Ride on, ride on, my beloved Brethren, and Fel-
Burrough, &c. 'low Soldiers; make all plain before you; thresh on with the new
* *i. e.* When 'Threshing Instrument, which hath Teeth; beat the Mountains to
they were in 'Dust, and let the Breath of the Lord scatter it; make the Hea-
Oliver's Army 'then † tremble, and the Uncircumcised fall by the Sword; the
† *i. e.* All the 'Lord of Hosts is with us, and goes before us; spare none, neither
Christians. 'Ox nor Ass, neither Old nor Young*, Kill, Cut off, Destroy, bathe
* No, where 'your Sword in the Blood of *Amaleck* †††,
the *Quakers* 'and all the *Egyptians* and *Philistines*, and
have Power, 'all the Uncircumcised, and hew *Agag* to
expect no 'pieces, *⁎* break the Rocks in pieces,
Quarter. 'cut down the Cedars and strong Oaks,
'make the Devils subject, cast out the Un-
††† The *Quaker's* own Writings are 'clean Spirits, raise the Dead, shut up in
their best Construing Books, and will 'Prison, bring out of Prison, cast in your
best Interpret their Meaning who this 'Nets, launch into the Deep, divide the
Amaleck is, *viz.* Geo. *Bishop* in his *Warn-* 'Fish, bind the Tares in Bundles, cast them
ings of the Lord, p. 19 Printed 1660. *i. e.* 'into the Fire,——put on your Armour, and
he crys out to the Officers of the Ar- 'gird on your Sword, and lay hold on the
my, *Remember* Amaleck (says he) *the* 'Spear; and march into the Field, and pre-
Soul-Murdering, and Conscience-Binding 'pare your selves to Battel; for the Nati-
Clergy-man; blot out the Remembrance of 'ons doth defie our God, and faith in their
Amaleck *from under Heaven. News out of* 'Hearts, who is the God of the *Quakers* ?*
the North, &c. *p.* 27. proclaim thus; 'that we should fear him, and obey his
Slay Baal, Baalim *must be slain, and all* 'Voice. Arise, arise, and sound forth the
the Hirelings must be turned out of the King- 'Everlasting Word of War and Judgment in
dom, p. 18. 'the Ears of all the Nations, sound an Ala-
⁎ *Dreadful is the Lord, who is coming* 'rum, and make their Ears to tingle; our
to change all your Laws, ye Kings, p. 20. 'Enemies are whole Nations, and Multi-
The Government shall be taken from you Ru- 'tudes in number; a Rebellious People, that will not come under
lers; this Tree (of Government) *must be* 'OUR LAW †; which ariseth up against us, and will not have
cut down, and Jesus Christ (in us) *will* 'our King to Reign, * but tramples his Honour under Foot, and
Rule alone. 'despise
* A proper Question; for few (if
any) know.
† Meaning G. *Fox's* Ten Command-
ments, see *p.* 17.
* See *Sam. Fisher's* Prophecy.

From Quakerism to Christianity.   125

'despise his Law, and his Statutes, and accounteth his Subjects as
'Slaves and Bond-men; stand upon your Feet, and appear in your
'Terror, as an Army with Banners; and let the Nations know your
'Power, and the Stroke of your Hands; cut down on the Right
'Hand, and slay on the Left; and let not your Eye pity, nor your
'Hand spare, but wound the Lofty, and tread down the Honourable [*] *The first Reformers did so; and I am giving the little young Whore a double Cup.*
'of the Earth; and give unto the great Whore double, and give her
'no Rest, day nor night; but as she hath done, so let it be done un-
'to her; and give her double into her Bosom: * As she hath loved
'Blood, so give her Blood; and dash her Children against the Stones;
'and let none of the Heathen Nations, nor their Gods, escape out of [†] *† Hark! Are not these Fifth Monarchy-men.*
'your Hands, nor their Images, nor Idols; but lay waste Fenced Ci-
'ties, † and tread down the High Walls; for we have proclaimed [*] *This cannot be meant within. What Leaders and Captains within!*
'open War; your *CAPTAINS* are Mighty Men, and your *LEAD-*
'*ERS* are well-skill'd to handle the Sword; * and they are Riding
'on before you ----- against the Beast, and the false Prophet; and
'*CURSED* be every one, that riseth not up to the Help of the Lord [†] *† i.e. The King and Parliament.*
'against the Mighty: The Beast is Mighty, † and the false Propher
'is Great, * and they keep the Nation under their Power: But, [*] *i.e. The Clergy.*
O thou Beast, and thou false Prophet! you shall be Tormented
'together; thou Beast, upon which the false Prophet
'sits, * whom thou upholds by a Law, and defends [*] *You'd fain Ride too; but I hope, she'll throw you off, unless you retract these bloody Books, and horrid Principles.*
'by thy unrighteous Power; ----- and into the Pit
'and Lake, shall you be turned, to have your Resting-
'place: And thou false Prophet, which hath decei-
'ved the Nations, the Decree of our God is sealed [†] *† No marvel then they cannot pray for them, unless for their Destruction, as Fox said. See Truth's Defence, &c. p. 15.*
'against thee, † thy Smoke shall ascend for ever, and
'ever; and of thy Sin, there is *NO FORGIVENESS*;
'nor of thy Torment, no *REMISSION*; over you, do we, and shall
'for ever, rejoyce, and sing; and over your God, and your King; the
'Dragon, that Old Serpent, cursed be he, and his Memorial, for ever.

Written in *Ireland*, 1655. by *Edw. Burrough*, and *Fra. Howgill*; [*] *Note, This was to go only amongst the Friends.*
* and Printed in *Quarto*, with this Title, *This is only to go*
amongst Friends.

Thus, Friends, have I shewed you our Ancient Testimony in all
the Parts of it. First, Touching the World's Peoples Mistake in the
Scriptures, for a Rule to Walk by. Secondly, Of the certainty of our
own Papers and Epistles, which are the Word of God, and a certain
Rule to Walk by. Thirdly, And in the Application, I have shewed,
how our Light hath exalted you above the Patriarchs, Prophets, A-
postles, Martyrs, and Holy Confessors, and all Christian Churches,
to this Day. Fourthly, Our dear Brother *W. Bingly*, hath well re-
membered our Ancient Testimony, against the Hireling Priests; for
with

with them, and against them, we began to War, and that with Indignation too. Fifthly, *Ben. Bealing* hath found out a very suitable Hymn of Praise, even a melodious Song of Triumph; setting forth our Exaltation, and the Downfal of the Christian Churches, under the Notion of the false Church, the Mother of Harlots, Mystery of *Babylon*; in which, my Heart was, and still is refreshed, as with new Wine. Sixthly, I have also closed my Discourse with the Prophesie of *Sam. Fisher*, which you need not doubt, but will come to pass; it may be, sooner than you are aware of *; for he gave it forth as it came to him from the Lord, and no otherwise, the 25th Day of the Seventh Month, which the World's People call *Septemb. Anno* 1656. so that, it cannot, it cannot miss; only for the *present*, we must be content to stay, and patiently bear for the *present*; for as *yet*, we cannot think, we shall be made to handle the Sword; † but when the time does come, I have shewed you the Testimony of two of our Prophets, and early Champions, what we shall Do, how we shall Kill, Cut off, and Destroy, and bathe our Swords in the Blood of *Amaleck*, * and lay waste Fenced Cities, and tread down the Honourable of the Earth, and spare neither Old nor Young, Ox nor Ass, Male nor Female, that will not come under our Law, and VVorship our God.

And now I shall conclude with a Prayer, and that also, without any Confession of Sin; for all my Sins were pardoned * in *Oliver*'s time: 'For the Prince of this World was cast out of me, 1652. and 'Hell was Conquer'd, and Death and the Grave overcome, and the 'Kingdom that cannot be removed, was given ME; and this the 'Lord did do for ME, from his Fore-knowledge of ME; and the 'Lord then brought ME into *Sion*, which I then did VVitness. † 'Moreover, I was then moved, to VVitness against the Priests and 'Hirelings, Diviners and Deceivers, and to judge the VVhore, with 'her Enchantments; and to Torment the *Beast*, * and Plague the 'false Prophet, whose Judgment torment, and Misery was then be-'gun, and will never have end; which I VVitness, whom God hath 'set to root out, and pull down, &c. And thus much shall suffice at this time, to shew you our Ancient Testimony, in many Particulars, which you are exhorted to Maintain, Defend, and to Vindicate; and not at any time, to retract any one Syllable of it; for the Government of our Church, even Men and VVomens Meetings, were Ordained * by Christ within, *Geo. Fox*; as at large in my Book, *Judgment fixed, &c.* p. 317, 318. is made clearly out; and out of which Book, p. 354. I shall use this short Form of Prayer, because the Day is far spent, *viz.*

Let us Pray.

O God, I make my Appeal and Supplication against this Jealous, Dividing, and Rending Spirit, that hath appeared

in

---

* If the Six-Week Meeting mind their Business every Session of Parliament.
† Read p 62. herein.
* *Viz.* The Priests and Rulers, as in the large Marginal Note.

* See his Book, *Truth Defending the Quakers*, p. 8.
† *Jacob found in a Desart Land*, &c. p. 7, 8.

* *i.e.* The Governours.

* The Quaker's Ordinances, as in Sol. Eccles Prophesie.

in Strife and open Contention, against thy Servants: Thou knowest the Integrity of my Soul; * *Thou hast endued me with a Christian Spirit, with Faith, Patience and Rejoycing, under all my Sufferings; yet thou hast endued me also, with the Spirit of Righteous Judgment, Understanding and Zeal; and hast raised me up* †, *in Defence of thy Gospel: So I recommend all to thee, to manifest the end of all, and to plead and justifie my Cause; it being thy own Cause.* Amen, Amen, *faith my Soul.*

* Compare G.W's. Ser. Apol. p. 4, 5. with the Epistle, and Pag. 19. 317, 359. of his Jagment fixed, &c. and it will shew this Prayer not only Pharisaical, but deep Hypocrisie; especially, adding p. 72. of his Count. Conv. &c. where he tells you, He can see cause otherwise to word the Matter, and yet mean the same thing, &c.
† As he did Pharaoh.

Geo. Whitehead.

CHAP. XIV.

The Cage of Unclean Birds opened; the Idolatrous Practices, Blasphemous Principles, and Vicious Enormities of the Quakers, laid opened; which may be compar'd with Pope Leo X.

READER, by the foregoing Chapter, you have a View of the high Value the Quakers set upon themselves, and their Ancient Testimony; and how they Debase all Christian Churches, as the Whore, the false Church, the Mother of Harlots, even all: FIRST, All that Sprinkle Children, and tell People it is Baptism, and thereby an Ordinance of Christ *(a)*. SECONDLY, all that Preach Christ without, as he is in Heaven at God's Right Hand *(b)*. THIRDLY, All that do Study the Scriptures, and Preach out of them *(c)*. FOURTHLY, All that will not Fast with the Quakers, who are in the Truth, (faith *Solomon Eccles*;) and that none are in the Truth, but they *(d)*. FIFTHLY, All that pay, or receive Tythes *(e)*. SIXTHLY, All that take *Matthew, Mark, Luke* and *John*, for the Gospel, *viz.* Glad Tidings, and the Scriptures for their Rule *(f)*, &c.

Nay, *W. Penn* and *Whitehead* adds, 'That a Mountebank is an 'honest Man to a Parson; that such Wickedness (as Debauchery, 'Drunkenness and Whoredom,) more suiteth the Spirits of his '(*i. e.* Priests,) own Fraternity; the Priests, both Episcopal and 'Presbyterian, whose known Drunkenness and Whoredoms, &c. 'would fill Volumes to describe. Hear *W. Penn* again, *p.* 165. 'Had '*James Nayler's* Words been Ten thousand times more significant, 'earnest and sharp, against that cursed bitter Stock of Hirelings, they 'had been but enough, and I would then say not enough; but that
'the

(a) G. Fox's *Prim.* p. 48.
(b) Smith's *Primmer*, &c. p. 8.
(c) Saul's Errand, &c. p. 7.
(d) The Quakers Challenge, &c. p. 3, 6.
(e) An Antidote, &c. p. 78.
(f) G. Fox's Epistle, to be read in Steeple-houses, &c. p. 2, 3, 4, 5.

'the Reverence I bear to the Holy Spirit, would oblige me to acquiesce
'in whatever he should utter, thro' any Prophet or Servant of the
'Lord; * and we have nothing for them but Woes and Plagues, who
'have made drunk the Nations, and laid them to Sleep on the
'Downey-Beds of soft sin-pleasing Principles, whilst they have cut
'their Purses, and pick'd their Pockets; *Tophet's* prepared for them
'to act their Eternal Tragedy upon, whose Scenses will be renewed,
'direful anguishing Woes of an Eternal Irreconcilable Justice,* &c.

Again, saith the same *W. Penn*, in his Book. *The Guide Mistaken*,
&c. p. 18. 'And whilst the Idle, Gormandizing Priests of *England*,
'run away with above Fifteen hundred thousand Pounds a Year, un-
'der pretence of being God's Ministers; and, that no sort of Peo-
'ple, have been so universally, thro' Ages, the very Bane of Soul and
'Body, to the Universe, as that abominable Tribe; for whom,
'the Theatre of God's most Dreadful Vengeance wait, to act their
'Eternal Tragedy upon.*

Well, let us hear *W. Penn* once more, what he saith of the Teachers of the Presbyterians, Independants, Baptists, &c. *Quakerism a
new Nick-name*, &c. p. 165. viz. 'An Ill-bred, and Pedantick Crew
'the Bane of Reason, and Pest of the World; the old Incendiaries to
'Mischief, and the best to be spared of Mankind; against whom, the
'Boiling Vengance of an irritated God, is ready to be poured out,
'to the Destruction of such, if they repent not, * &c.

Reader, you see, here is nothing but Hell and Damnation. for the
Ministers of all Christian Societies: Pray let us hear their Opinion
of the Church of *England* in general, and that may give their sense
of all other Churches, since I see, they make little (if any) difference of their Teachers, viz. 'And as for the Purity of the Church of
'*England*, it's out of our sight; we can see a great deal of Impuri-
'ty, Corruption, and Soul-sickness in it: Indeed, they say enough
'of themselves, to cause all wholsom, sound, understanding Peo-
'ple, to shun them, and their Church and Worship, as Men shun
'a contagious Disease or Infection,* &c. To which, let me add but
one Passage more. (tho' I might One hundred) of Mr. *Penn's*, who
can express himself as well. and as much according to the Quakers
Ancient Testimony, as any Man amongst them: And briefly thus,
viz. 'Come tell me, ye of the Church of *England*, whence came
'your Forms of Prayer and Church-Government? Are they not the
'Off spring of that Idolatrous Popish Generation, * which is abo-
'minable to the God of Heaven? Are you not at, *Have mercy upon
'us, miserable Sinners?* There is no Health in us from Seven to
'Seventy. †

Reader, *W. Penn* tells his Reader, in his *Serious Apol.* &c. p. 79.
That his designed Method in his Answer, is not the common Road
of Printing his Adversaries Words at large, on all occasions; so I tell
thee,

thee, yet in many Cases I recite the whole: However, by this time, you have not only an account of the high Value the Quakers set upon themselves, as in the former Chapter, but of their debasing the Protestant Ministers and Churches, as a pack of Drunkards, Whoremongers, with an *etcætera*, worse than Mountebanks; a cursed bitter Stock of Hirelings, a Pedantick Crew, the best to be spared of Mankind; against whom, the Boyling Vengeance of God is reserved, *&c.* and who deserve nothing but Plagues and Woes, Hell and Damnation, yea, Pick-pockets, Cut-purses, *&c.* that the People ought to shun as a Pest-house, with too much of that Nature to be here inserted; especially, adding what in *The Picture of Quakerism, &c.* is set forth on this Head: And does it not amount to a just Provocation to any Child, to see such foul Aspersions, and horrible Slanders, cast upon his Mother, from whose Breasts of Consolation, he hath received great Consolation and Comfort, both to vindicate her, and to set forth what manner of Men they are, that thus scandalize his Mother-Church, not only privately in their Chimney-Corners, but in their Meetings, yea, in Print, in all Cities, Towns and Villages? *&c.* G. *Whitehead* said, That God laid a necessity upon him, to write his Book, *Judgment fixed, &c.* where he called me, and others, *Apostate Informers, Treacherous Hypocrites, False Brethren, Deceitful Workers, Betraying Judas's, Devils Incarnate, Dogs, Wolves, Raging Waves, &c.* And his God laying such a necessity upon him, thus to Write and Rail, in Vindication of Quakerism, he adds, *And in the discharging my Duty, I neither consult Events, nor fear Effects.* Now, in Answer, I cannot pretend to such an immediate Motion as the Quakers do; but I do really think my self in point of Duty and Conscience, to hear these Testimonies against the foul Aspersions of these Railing *Rabsheka*'s, and have both consulted and considered the Events that may ensue, and hope well of the Effects that may follow, even the Confutation of their Teachers, and Conviction of their Hearers; and I hope, the Conversion of the Sincere amongst them. And now to the Men, and what manner of Men they are, that thus undermine the Christian Religion, Ministry and Worship: And thus much by way of Introduction to the CAGE of UNCLEAN BIRDS.

Judgment Fixed, &c. Epist.

POSTSCRIPT.

Note, Reader, That *George Fox* (the First Bird in the CAGE,) did cause *John Fretwell, Chrisf. Gilborn, Ja. Nayler,* and others, to go down upon their Knees before him, publickly before Friends, (which is Idolatry;) and then and there, upon their Knees, to make their Confession, and own Judgment upon what he charged them with, before he would own them, or receive them into the Unity amongst Friends, *&c.* p. 6.

To all People professing the Eternal Truth, &c. p. 6. per John Harwood.

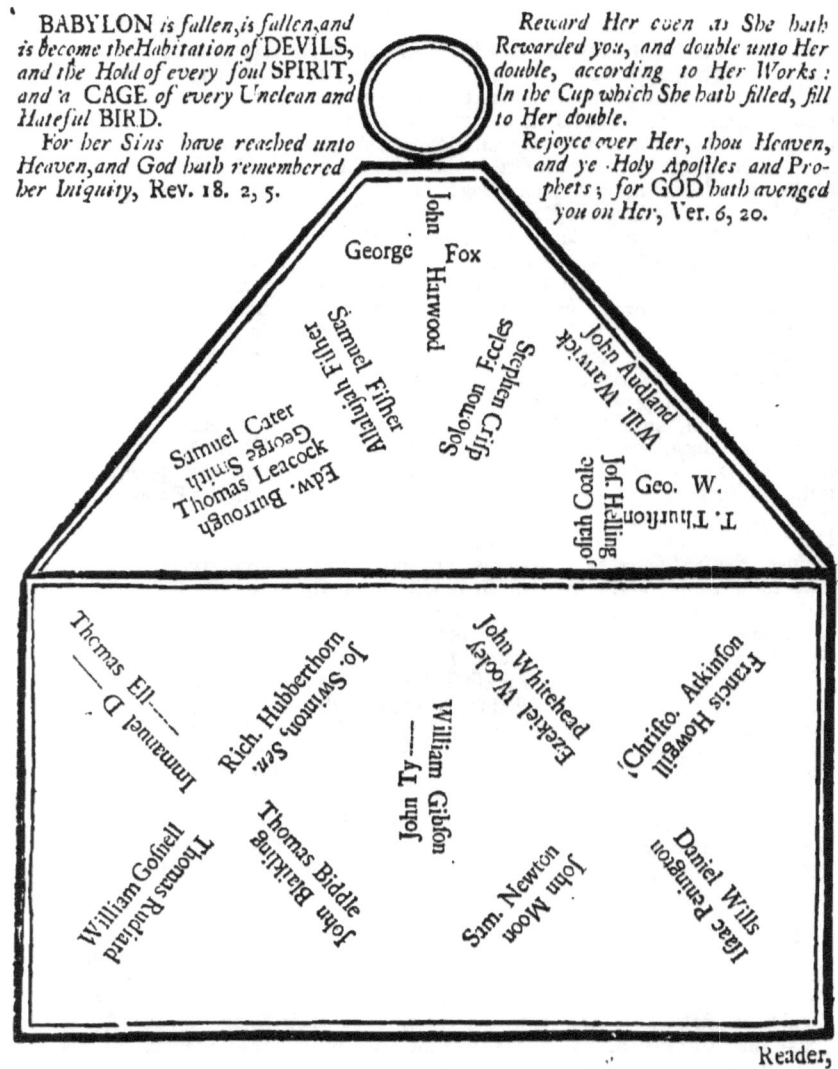

From Quakerism *to* Christianity.

Reader, I am now about opening the CAGE; and shall take out Twelve of the Birds, and open their Wings, and spread their Feathers; to the intent thou maist view them, and note their Features, and observe their Natures and Dispositions; and *Geo. Fox*, the CAGE-KEEPER, shall be over and above; with some little Observations upon him; and the rather, because G. *Whitehead* has denied, * That the Quakers call him their Branch, their Star, their Son of Righteousness, &c. I remember, that about the Year 1662. *Geo. Fox* came into the Isle of *Ely*, and at his Meetings, great part of his Discourse was about the CAGE of UNCLEAN BIRDS, saying, The Church of *England*, (*as in his Epistle to be read in Churches,*) and the Professors, were a CAGE of UNCLEAN BIRDS; and the Note he made them sing, was thus, Come Episcopals, How do you sing in the CAGE? *Answ.* No Perfection here, no Perfection here; well, come you Presbyterians, Independants, and Baptists; What say you? How do you sing? Let us hear your Note. *Answ.* No Perfection here, no Perfection here. Then said *George*, Come out of the CAGE, in a very Comical manner. Thus did he deride the Professors of Christianity, exalting themselves; a Figure of which, you have in *Geo. Whitehead's* Sermon in the Thirteenth Chapter: And now you shall hear, how his BIRDS Chirrup, and what Note they sing to his Lute. But to understand this rightly, I think it necessary, to give you a brief Description of *Geo. Fox*; that so, when you hear six of the Birds of one sort sing to his Tune, and dance after his Pipe, you may the better understand, whether they do not call him their Branch, &c.

* *In his Sober Expost. &c. p. 55, 58.*

FIRST, He (G. *Fox*,) a great Liar, like *Mahomet*, a great Seducer, like *Symon Magus*, a vain Boaster, like *Ignatius Loyola*, saying, 'That neither he nor his Name was known in the World *; when there was not ten Men in the whole Nation, more universally known.

* *Several Petitions Answered, &c. p. 60.*

SECONDLY, In that he taught 'That he that hath the same 'Spirit that raised up Jesus Christ, is equal with God; that he 'was before Languages were, and that he was come to the end of 'Languages. *

* *Saul's Errand, &c. p. 8. His Battle-door, the Introd. &c.*

'THIRDLY, In that he taught, 'That he was come to such a ful- 'ness of Glory, as that his Head and Ears was filled full of Glory, 'yea, that a Thundring Voice answered him, saying, I glorifie thee, 'and will glorifie thee again †; alluding to *John* 12. 28, 29.

† *The Examin. and Tryal of G. Fox, at Lancaster Assp. 21.*

FOURTHLY, In that he said, '*David's* Sepulcher was with the *size*, &c. 'Quakers, and that they had seen it *. An abominable Lie, like that of *Mahomet's* Journey up to Heaven, upon an Ass.

* *Truth's Defence, &c. p. 56.*

FIFTHLY, In saying, 'That if ever People own the Prophets 'and Apostles Writings, they will own the Writings of the Quakers; 'and that they may as well condemn the Scriptures to the Fire, as 'their Papers and Queries,* &c.

* *Several Petitions Answered, &c. p. 38. Truth's Defence, p. 2. 104.*

SIXTHLY,

SIXTHLY, In that he taught, *that he wrought Miracles* *; and yet never wrought a Miracle, in the Name of Jesus of *Nazareth* all his Days; (only some Lying Wonders forged out of his Luciferian Brain, without any Attestation, like *Symon Magus*.)

* Fox's *Journal*, the Third Index.

SEVENTHLY, In that he taught, That the Breach of the Eighth Commandment, *Thou shalt not Steal*, was no Sin, if moved thereto by *the Spirit of the Lord* †. In this, *Fox*, if not a Ranter, yet joined with them; and so are all that own his Doctrine.

† G. Fox's Great Mystery, &c. p. 77.

EIGHTHLY, In that he taught, 'That to call the Scriptures the 'Word of God, was Blasphemy; whilst that he, yea, even he, called his own Writings, the Word of God; and frequently, the 'Word of the Lord. *

* *Way to the Kingdom*, &c. p. 4. *Several Papers given out for spreading Truth*, &c.

NINTHLY, In teaching, 'That if Christ that's Crucified be not 'within, and that Christ that's Risen be not within, I say, that ye are 'Reprobates. —— Now, I say, that if there be any other Christ than 'he that's Crucified within, he is a false Christ; and he that hath 'not this Christ that was Risen and Crucified within, is a Reprobate. 'Tho' Devils and Reprobates make a talk of him without, God's 'Christ is not *DISTINCT* from his Saints, nor his Body (the Church;) 'for he is within them, not *DISTINCT* from their Spirits: And 'thou sayst, thou art saved by Christ without thee, and so hath re'corded thy self a Reprobate; and they that profess Christ without 'them, and another Christ within them, here is two Christs. *

* G. Fox's Gr. Myst. &c. p 206, 207, 250, 254.

And to confirm this false Doctrine, see *Edw. Burrough*'s Answer to a Question, and *William Smith*'s to his Child; which are as followeth.

Query, 'Is that very Man, (said the Minister to *Burrough*,) with 'that very Body, within you? Yea, or Nay.

Burrough Answers, 'The very Christ of God is within us; we dare 'not deny him. *

* *Burrough's Works*, p. 149.

Query, 'How may I know when Christ is truly Preached?

W. Smith's Answer. 'They that are false (Ministers,) Preach 'Christ without, and bid People believe in him, as he is in Heaven 'above: But they that are Christ's Ministers, Preach Christ with'in, * &c.

* *Smith's Primmer*, &c. p. 8.

Now, Reader, if this Doctrine be sound and Orthodox, then were all the Apostles, Martyrs, and all Christian Ministers, false Teachers and Deceivers; but, if this Doctrine be Heterodox, then the Quakers only are the false Teachers, Deceivers, and Antichrists. *W. Penn* also, is one with *Fox*, *Burrough* and *Smith*. See his *Christian Qua. and Div. Test.* p. 97, 98. and his *Sandy Foundation*, p. 21.

TENTHLY, *George Fox* speaking of his own Rise out of the *North*, gives his Book this Title, 'News coming up out of the '*North*, sounding towards the *South*; written (by *Fox*,) from the 'Mouth of the Lord, from one who is Naked, and stands Naked 'before the Lord, cloathed with Righteousness, whose Name is 'not

From Quakerism *to* Christianity.

'not known in the World, risen out of the *North,* which was pro-
'phesied of,† and now fulfilled.   † Query, by what Prophet?

Thus much briefly touching this Blasphemous Bird; which, being the Master of the Assembly, and first Founder of this Sect, he shall not be of the number of the Twelve intended, *viz.* Six of each sort, which now shall follow in their Order, the first Six being of the same Feather, witnessing to their Forerunner, and great Apostle; who, tho' he once said he had a Celestial Body*; that he had Power to bind and loose whom he pleased, yet his Body proved an Earthy one, and is dead and gone; and for some Years, whilst living amongst them, was like a Statue, or an Insensible Image, which could scarce see or understand, being grown Corpulent, and in bulk of two or three Men; and so dosed away his time with strong Liquors and Brandy, who left these Words for *W. Rogers, John Raunce, Anne Doctera*, and others, who had opposed his Tyranny and Usurpation, *viz. And as for this Spirit of Rebellion and Opposition that hath risen formerly and lately, it is out of the Kingdom of God, and Heavenly* Jerusalem, *and is for Judgment and Condemnation, with all its Books, Words and Works.* †   * Before two credible Witnesses, one being still alive.   † This was Printed in their Yearly Epistle, 1691. and Re-printed in *Fox*'s *Journal,* 1694. p. 616.

' Oh thou North of *England,* who art counted as Desolate and
' Barren, and reckoned the least of the Nations; yet out of thee
' did the Branch (*Fox*) spring, and the Star (*Fox*) arise, which
' gives Light unto all the Regions round about; in thee, the Son
' of Righteousness (*Fox*) appear'd; out of thee, Kings, Priests, and
' Prophets, did come forth, in the Name and Power of the most
' High (meaning *Hubberthorn, Howgil, Burrough, Farnsworth, Nay-*
' *ler, Atkinson, Whitehead,* &c.) which uttered their Voices as
' Thunders, *&c.*   *Burrough* the First Bird of the Blasphemous Six. See their Book, *This is only to go amongst Friends,* p.19.

Thus has *Burrough* ecchoed back, and confirmed *Fox* his Imposture, saying *Amen* to his Blasphemy, alluding to *Micah* 5. 2. to *Matth.* 2. 5, 6. as more largely handled in my Book, *New Rome Unmask'd,* &c. p. 79, to 88. and *New Rome Arraign'd,* &c. *p.* 5, 6, 7. And I marvel at *Whitehead*'s Impudency to deny it †; but to make it clear, and past his Exception, if possible, let's take out more Birds; but he that will deny *Burrough*'s Book to have this Title, *This is only to go amongst Friends,* which is the only, and all the Title; and which Book I have by me; what will not such a Fellow deny?   † In his Sober Expostulation, p. 57, 58.

Dear Geo. Fox, who art the Father of many Nations; whose Life hath reached through us thy Children, even to the Isles afar off, to the begetting many again to a lively Hope; for which, Generations to come shall call thee Blessed, whose Being and Habitation is in the Power of the Highest, in which thou (Geo. Fox) *Rulest.*   *Josiah Coale,* the Second Bird.

*Read Numb.
14, 17, 19.
Zech. 3. 8. cap.
6. v. 12. Malachi 4. 2.
Luke 1. 32, 33.
Isai. 9. 6, 7.

Sol. Eccles; the Third Bird.

† John 1. 10.
Several Petitions Answer'd, &c.
p. 60.
* See the first Instance of the ten, about Fox.

John Whitehead the Fourth Bird.

'Tis well Calculated; for about 1648. Fox first rose in the North, only did not spread forth his Branches till about 1650.

Rules and Governs in Righteousness: And THY KINGDOM is ESTABLISHED in PEACE; and the INCREASE THEREOF IS WITHOUT END.*

Thus then is it plain, That both *Burrough* and *Coale* call'd G. Fox, comparatively, the BRANCH, the SON of RIGHTEOUSNESS; yea, Christ. *

Stand up Muggleton, *thou Sorcerer; whose Mouth is full of Cursing, Lies and Blasphemy; who calls thy last Book a Looking-Glass for* Geo. Fox, *whose NAME thou art not worthy to take into thy Mouth; who is a Prophet indeed, and hath been faithful in the Lord's Business from the beginning: It was said of Christ, that he was in the World, and the World was made by him, and the World knew him not* †; *SO it may be said of this true Prophet, (*Geo. Fox*) whom* John *said he was not; but thou wilt feel this Prophet one Day as heavy as a Millstone upon thee; and altho' the World knows him not* *, *yet he is known*, &c. *The Quakers Challenge*, p. 6.

Thus do they all agree, that *Fox* is their *Star*, their *Branch*, &c. For if he be Christ, as *Eccles* saith; if he had a Kingdom established, of whose Encrease there never was to be an end, as *Coale* said; then he was Christ, and so the *Branch*, the *Star*, &c. as *Burrough* said; and indeed as they all mean, else they would condemn these Blasphemous Books; but instead thereof, this Letter of *Coale's* is vindicated in their Book, *Judas and the Jews*, p. 44. in all its parts. A small Treatise, wrote in *Alisbury* Prison, the 3d. Month, 1661. by *J. Whitehead*, where he saith, *In the Year* 1648. God, *who had Compassion on his People, did cause a BRANCH to spring forth of the Root of* David, *which was filled with Vertues, for the Covenant of Life, and Peace was in him: And he* (Fox) *spread, and shot forth many Branches, which did partake of the Fatness of the Root, and the Weary came to Rest under his* (Fox's) *Branches; and in him* (Fox) *was also the Word of Reconciliation, which turned the Hearts of the Fathers to the Children, and the Disobedient to the Wisdom of the Just. And in the Year* 1652. *I* (John Whitehead) *being a Branch of this Tree,* (Fox) *the Life of its Root caused me to Blossom, and bring forth Fruit for the Spirit, as a Key opened his* (Fox's) *Treasure, and shewed me* (for he was before Languages were) *that which was from the beginning*. Read p. 4, 5. of the same Treatise.

Thus

From **Quakerism** *to* **Christianity.**

Thus then has this *John Whitehead* put all out of Doubt, and quite confuted *Geo. Whitehead*, and overthrown all his Arguments, by confessing Matter of Fact. If I have made *Whitehead* oppose *Whitehead*, 'tis no more than in other Cases I have done; for the *Quakers* having no Bottom, no Solid Foundation; but all speaking as their Light move them, it's easie to see how they interfere and jarr; only *G. W.* has this Faculty; *he can otherwise word his matter, and yet mean the same:* A right Jesuit, a Doctrine first Coyn'd in their Mint, and only serve to their Ends; whose Work has been to sow Divisions, make Rents, and beget Schisms, *&c.* The next Bird shall be *John Audland*, in a Letter of his to *G. Fox*, from the West of *England*; an Abstract thereof is as follows, *viz.*

Dear and Precious one, in whom my Life is bound up, and my Strength in thee Stands; by thy Breathings I am nourished; by thee my Strength is renewed; Blessed art thou for evermore, and Blessed are all that enjoy thee: Life and Strength comes from thee, Holy One;——daily do I find thy Presence with me, which doth exceedingly preserve me, for I cannot reign but in thy Presence (Fox) *and Power: Pray for me, that I may stand in thy Dread* (Fox) *for evermore——I am thine,* (Fox) *Begotten and Nourished by thee; and in thy Power* (Fox) *am I preserv'd; Glory unto thee* (Fox) *Holy One for ever.*

John Audland, the Fifth Bird.

Reader, These are the Birds in the Cage; tell me, are they not all of a Feather? Do they not all agree in the main, That *G. Fox* was the *Quakers* BRANCH and STAR; yea, their All in All; the Bottom, and Corner, and Top-Stone of their Building? Pray spare me the Pains of a large Comment; I think there is no need; he that runs may read, and he that reads may understand the Foundation of *Quakerism*, no marvel then if it wither; no marvel if it fall like a Millstone into the bottom of the Sea, never more to rise. But let me add another Bird, since I have Plenty, *&c. p. 77.*

Here followeth the Testimony and Certificate of John Blaikling to the clearing of the Aspersions that William Rogers, &c. cast upon Geo. Fox,——that's blessed with Honour above many Brethren; and that thousands will stand by him in a Heavenly Record unto the Integrity of his Soul to Truth, that still lives with him: That his Life Reigns, and is Spotless, Innocent, and still retains his Integrity, whose ETERNAL HONOUR and BLESSED RENOWN shall remain; yea, his Presence, and the dropping of his Tender Words in the Lord's Love, was my Souls Nourishment, &c. †

John Blaikling, the Sixth Bird.

† The Christian Quak. disting. &c. 5th. Part, p. 77.

Come

The Pilgrim's Progress,

Come, *George Whitehead,* give me thy Hand &c. I'll take thee out of the Cage, and do thee this Honour, not to be a Partner with the last Six Blasphemous Birds, but as a Witness for them; that we may hear what thou canst say on their Behalf: But I'll put thee in again, and keep thee there, lest thou flyest up and down the Nation, and do more Mischief. Oh *George!* thou art a plump Bird; thou'rt grown fat, I find; well, what canst thou say.

I affirm, that G. Fox does deny the same (i. e. these Divine Attributes) *in reference to himself, as a particular Man or Person, whose Days and Years are limited; only the Truth of the Immortal Seed, Christ in him, he stands to maintain against all Opposers and Apostates:* * *And as to his* (Francis Bugg's) *Charge of Idolatry, if not Blasphemous Names and Titles given to* Geo. Fox *in certain Letters——how proves he* (Fran. Bugg) *that they gave and intended those Titles to the Person of* Geo. Fox, *and not to the Life of Christ in him?* †

* Judgment fixed, &c. p. 19.

† Innocency against Envy, &c. p. 18.

How, *George!* I'll tell thee how, because *Josiah Coale* said, Dear G.Fox,&c. by this I know they intended *Geo. Fox;* for if they had intended those Titles to the Life of Christ in him, they would have directed their Letters suitably; saying, *Dear Life of Christ in Geo. Fox, &c.* This I hope will satisfie thee, if Reason could take place; if not, I despair of giving thee or thy Friends Satisfaction. But *George,* for thy Comfort, if thou wilt mean as thou say'st, according to the Import of thy Words; and on that Foot, retract and condemn these thy Fallacious Covers and Excuses, and thy own Apparent Errors; and the Errors in thy Friends Books, which thou hast most impudently glossed over; with thy Hypocritical Paint, I will take thee out of the Cage; if not, there lye for ever, singing, *Here is Perfection, here is Perfection, &c.* Thus much shall serve, in answer to G. W's Book, * as well as to shew what manner of Birds are in the Cage, of this sort, namely, Blasphemers and Idolaters; and next, let me take out Six of the other sort, namely, of their Vicious Teachers, against whom G. *Whitehead* would not write a Book, for the World. No, seriously, I believe him, his Sincerity is so true to their Ancient Testimony; besides, if he should, there being so few of them clear, that here would be Hell broke loose; for if they should write one against another, all would come out, and then they'd appear a dark sort of *Quakers* indeed.

* A Sober Expostulation, &c. p. 54, 55, 56.

And *Christ. Atkinson* was G. *Whitehead's* Fellow-Traveller, Fellow-Sufferer, Fellow-Writer, and Fellow-Preacher: But so it was, that he got *Ursula,* the Maid-Servant of *Tho. Symonds,* with Child, when he was a Sufferer for their Ancient Testimony in *Norwich-Goal;* but this was not all, for he broke Prison, stole Goods, and run away; I have his Confession in print, Signed by *John Stubbs, William Cotton,* and *Thomas Symonds:* And its Worth noticing, to see what

Christopher Atkinson, the Seventh Bird, but the first of the last Six, before-mention'd.

From Quakerism *to* Christianity.

what Grief *Atkinson* was in, because it dishonour'd the Cause of *Quakerism*, in that it could not be kept private from the Knowledge of the World's People: But not a Word of Confession of Sin to God, nor asking his Pardon for Christ's sake. But to the second,

STEPHEN CRISP, in his Circuit, going to *Norwich*, by *Mendlesham*, in *Suffolk*, *Robert Duncon* advised him to carry it wisely at *Norwich*; for (said he) my Kinsman, *Samuel Duncon*, is a Man of a Timorous (or Brittle) Disposition. Well, away goes St. *Crisp* to *Norwich*, sets up his Horse at the Place allotted for their Teachers Horses, and then goes to *Samuel Duncon*'s House; but *Samuel* not being at home, *Stephen* takes up *Samuel's* Wife into the Chamber: Anon *Samuel* comes home, *where is my Wife?* (says he to the Maid) She's gone up the Chamber, (said she) with *Stephen Crisp*. Well, *Samuel* walks up and down the House; he rubs his Elbows, scratches his Head, and very melancholy he was; so between Nine and Ten of the Clock (as I was told by some *Quakers* that knew it) down came *Stephen* and *Sam*'s Wife: And this bred great Discontent between *Sam*. and his Wife,† but *Stephen* wanted no Boldness to carry it off. Many such Stories we had of him, knowing him to be very Light and Airy, and a great Lover of strong Wines and Waters of 8 *s.* a Pint, and many of us looked upon him little better than a Ranter, if not an Atheist; *W. C.* can enlarge on this Subject no doubt. If any question the Truth of this, let them go to *Joseph Carver*, *Tho. Budderyw*, if living, and other ancient *Quakers* in *Norwich*, and they can tell you more of this: As also of *Thomas Murford*, another of G. *Fox*'s Preachers, who used to lay Plaisters to some Parts of *Samuel*'s Wife, which ofttimes did Incommode her Husband. This is so well known at *Norwich*, that none but G. *W.* will have the Face to deny it: But if he do, I will set *W. I.* and *W. Mires* to talk with him, about that, and some other things.

Stephen Crisp, the Eighth Bird.

† She was a very handsom Woman, and 'twas thought too yeilding.

THO. LEACOCK lived at *Emny*, in *Norfolk*, two Miles distance from *Wisbech*, is the Bird I am now taking out of the Cage; his Fore part is like a Rook, but his Claws like a Kite, or some Bird of Prey; he was one of *Geo. Whitehead*'s great Assistants, both in Preaching and Disputing, and whom *George* mentions * as such. This *Leacock* was a notorious Drunkard, only (like some others of their Teachers, as well as Hearers, of the *Epicurean* sort) a private one: But to be short, so it fell out, that upon a time, being at a Neighbour's House, where Drink was free; he was so drunken, that going out to make Water, he stagger'd, and fell backward into a Cistern, made to catch Rain-Water; that had they not from within heard him fall like a Millstone, he had been drown'd in that little Sea; but from that he was by strong Hands saved, yet he broke his Bladder, and was forced to wear a Dish in his Breeches,

Tho. Leacock, the Ninth Bird.

* See his *Serious Apology*, *p.* 3.

to catch his Water, to his dying Day: And his Wife still continu'd the same Trade (if not dead within a Year,) who will sit and drink Brandy till she is so drunken, that she will p----ss as she sits. Let her then be hereby caution'd to take Warning by the Misfortune of her Sister *Quaker*-Woman in *London*, who, about three or four Months since, being drunken with Brandy, and alone, the Fire by Accident, if not in Judgment, took hold of her Cloaths, and (as I am credibly inform'd) was burnt alive in her drunken Fit: But let it be noted, that the said *Leacock* was a Man extream zealous against Ribbonds and Laces; in a word, for every Commandment of G. *Fox*. And moreover, as a Work of Super-errogation, he was excellent to convey away a Female Sister, if things fell out cross, that so Truth might not be dishonour'd, by the World's People knowing of it. I remember well, that about the Year 1662. there was a noted *Quaker* got his Maid with Child; and *Tho. Leacock* took her into *Norfolk*, and acted so wisely in it, that I do think it never was heard of by the World's People; and for which he has had many a hot butter'd Loaf: I will not say what else; Money answers all things.

John Moone, the Tenth Bird.   JOHN MOONE is the Tenth in number: He was an excellent Orator, a great Travelling Preacher, and of great Fame amongst the *Quakers*; of which I need not say much in this place; if the *Reader* be pleased to turn back to the Fourth Chapter, he shall see him amongst the Worthies, one of the Eleven Elders, Ten of them I have named, one half of them Cage Birds; pray observe from thence what Judges and Elders the *Quakers* Body is, to which the poor Hearers must submit; 'tis well worthy thy notice. However, after many Years Preaching, and suffering Imprisonment for G. *Fox*'s Cause in *England*, he went into *Pensilvania*, and was a great Preacher there, and a Justice of Peace forsooth under the Honourable *W. Penn:* But he could not leave his Vicious Habit; for he first got his Maid with Child, and so pursued that Course of Life, until he died of the foul Disease: I would have the *Quakers* look into *Geo. Whitehead*'s Sermon, and compare it with the Cage of their Unclean Birds, all Writers and Preachers, and I hope it will humble them, tho' my Verses did not, which yet were Intelligible to them; for I was loth to expose them, because I do believe, that amongst the Hearers, there are many honest-minded People; but I verily believe, that according to the number of the *Quaker* Teachers, compar'd with the Multitude of the Clergy, and other Protestant Teachers: I say, where there is one of the last mention'd chargeable with Vicious Immoralities, there is a Hundred of the *Quaker* Teachers; yet how Impudently have *W. Penn*, and the rest of that Gang, bespattered the Clergy, *Ut supra:* And particularly *W. Penn*, † *viz..* But to excuse this Brazen Impudence and Hypocrisie――his Hackney Mercenary

†See his Book, *The Guide mistaken, &c.* p. 28, 29, 53, 55.

From **Quakerism** *to* **Christianity.**

Mercenary Spirit——*He* (Jonathan Clapham) *boldly calls Christ his Redeemer, not observing how unsuitable his Life and Doctrine is with the Redeemed of the World: For whosoever is Redeemed by Christ, is perfectly so, in as much as all his Works are perfect: But as this Guide (Mr.* Claphams*) Conversation manifests the contrary, by his VERY GREAT MISCARRIAGES*——Nor is there any thing so much stumble Infidels, and brings a Reproach upon the Christian Religion, as Priests and People Writing, Talking, and Fighting hard for Christ, as Redeemer, whilst every Eye finds them as Polluted, and deeply Engaged in Dishonest and Immoral Practices, as those against whom they contend, &c.* Indeed I do not think the *Quaker* Teachers great Miscarriages are so visible to every Eye, as the Failings and Imperfections of Mr. *Clapham*'s, *&c.* were. But let the *Quakers* first pluck out the Beam out of their own Eye, and then they shall see the more clearly how to remove the Mote out of another's Eye: But to proceed to discover this Beam, let me take out another *Bird*; namely,

THOMAS THURSTON is the Eleventh *Bird*; was an Eminent Preacher up of *G. Fox*'s Orders, Laws and Commandments, and a great Favourite of *Fox*'s, who liv'd in *America*; who, in his Travels to spread their Truth, pretended to the Deputy-Governor's Wife, that he (*Tho. Thurston*) had a Motion from the Spirit to get her with Child†, she believing him, submits to a Tryal of Skill, and it proved so infallibly, the Woman's Husband being then in *Old-England*, where he stay'd about a Year or more; but at length he came home, and finding things bad, he examin'd his Wife strictly how it came to pass: She confest, that such a Friend (*Tho. Thurston*) told her, that he had a Motion from God to get her with Child, and she was overcome by him. Well, (*said her Husband*) if you will do one thing, I will forgive you; which is, To go to the *Quakers-Meeting*, and declare openly how you were deluded by this Preaching *Quaker*. She did so, and he forgave her; and as I am credibly informed, many of the *Quakers* thought his Motion was true, he was so eminent an Orator, and he still kept on some time a Preacher: And why might not *G. Fox* allow of the Breach of this Seventh Commandment, given forth by *Moses*, as well as he did of the Breach of the Eighth Commandments, *viz. And as for any being moved of the Lord, to take away your Hour-Glass from you, by the Eternal Power, it is owned**, &c. Such Influence had *Fox*'s Doctrine, as you may see in these two Cases, and a Hundred more I could mention; but enough of this *Bird.*

* A base Suggestion. I am told by many worthy and good Men, that Mr. *Clapham* was a Pious Man, and a good Liver.

Tho. Thurston, the Eleventh Bird.

† Come, *W. Penn,* was not this a great Miscarriage? Was it not visible to the Eye of the Deputy-Governour?

* *Geo. Fox*'s Great Myst. *&c.* p. 77.

T 2   Come

Come, *George*, What thinkeſt thou of thy Brother Preacher, *Tho. Thurſton?* He Preached amongſt the Infidels; and if he had been a Chriſtian Miniſter, I do agree, it might have ſtumbled them; but being a Quaker, and led thereto by the Spirit, it did confirm Quakeriſm. *George*, I could be more particular; I could tell you of ſeveral pretty Stories, and *W. Ingram* and *Walter Myres* ſhould evidence it. I could tell you of a *Cannon-ſtreet Story*; but you know that, and many others, I could tell you of a She-Preacher, who went from her Husband *Geo. Knight*, ſo long holding forth, that her Husband got a By-Child or two, and at laſt, marry'd another Wife: But ſince that, your She-Preachers keep more at home. I could tell you a Story of your Meeting, to cleanſe the Camp, about *John Swinton*, and others, and of *Rebecca Travers* her Teſtimony, which would make you look more like the Synagogue of Satan, than the Church of the Firſt-Born, as you boaſt; but I delight not in it, were it not to humble you: So that, I ſhall only mention one Bird more at preſent, he being a Favourite of yours, and your Brother *Cater*; who notwithſtanding his groſs Immoralities, yet you both wrote in favour of him, in theſe Words, *viz.* 'George Smith, a poor well-

Judgment fixed, &c. p. 207. The Lib. of an Apoſt. Conſc. &c. p. 18, 19.

'meaning Man, that hath been convinced about 13 or 14 Years; 'and ever ſince he came amongſt us, hath walked uprightly according 'to his Meaſure, and hath been of a blameleſs Converſation amongſt 'Men, from his Youth up, &c.

Come, G. *Whitehead*, this is high Commendation; but he was a Man for your turn, one ſtrict for *Fox*'s Commandments, and was not ungrateful to you for your high Praiſe and Commendation: For as one good Deed requires another, as the Proverb is, he in p. 29.

* *The Lib. of an Apoſtate, &c. p. 29.*

faith, * 'I have cauſe to believe better things of them all, (*i. e.* the 'Quakers;) and for *Sam. Cater*, whom thou (*Fra. Bugg*) ſo much 'abuſeſt, I know his Converſation hath been ſuch amongſt us, as be-

* *Thus they witneſs one for another, excuſe and juſtiſie each other.*

'comes a Man that fears God, that it is not thy Lies that can hurt 'him; for he hath a Witneſs in our Conſciences, * for his faithful 'ful Service, and upright Converſation amongſt us.

Come, *George*, here is hiding, here is excuſing, nay, juſtifying each other in your Abominations, like the two wicked Elders in the Story of *Suſanna*, ſaying, *Tuſh, God ſees us not, nor the World's People do not know it:* And G. *Smith* ſtanding Suit with the Mi-

As in the Year 1627. he did.

niſter of *Littleport*, about Tythes, he is faithful to G. *Fox*'s Commandments, and is a true Son of our Church, a well-meaning Man; one that hath lived uprightly ever ſince he came amongſt us, even from his Youth up. Oh, *George!* your Hypocriſie muſt come out; and therefore, and for that Reaſon only, I ſhall take out of the CAGE this your well-meaning, upright Bird, namely, *George Smith*, viz.

A *Nar-*

From Quakerism to Christianity. 141

A Narrative of Geo. Smith's *Uprightness,* contrarium ad Hominem.

GEORGE SMITH of *Littleport*, having a Wife of his own, (since Dead,) being a Bayly for a Gentleman of the same Town, (whose Wife was a handsom young Woman;) *G. Smith* in time, grew very kind to his Wife; the Gentleman falling Sick, gave his Wife warning of *G. Smith*: But he dying, there was room for him to accomplish his Design; and so it came to pass, that he got her with Child: And the time of her Delivery drawing near, *George* takes his Horse, and carries the Widow forth, designing such a Journey, as that her Child should not be heard to cry in *Littleport*, nor Tales thereof be told to the World's People. Well, away they road together lovingly, as if they had been Acquainted; but e'er they got two Miles, the good Woman had a Fit of the Belly-ake; and riding past a lone House, called *Wood-house,* standing between *Littleport* and *Ely*, *G. Smith* knocks at the Door, the 10th or 12th Day of *September*, 1684. upon which, out came the good Man, *i. e. William Pooley*, (still living:) What would you have, Neighbour *Smith?* says *Pooley*; I desire to come in, said *George,* my Friend behind me is not well. Upon which, out comes the good Woman of the House, saying, We are preparing our Cheese for *Sturbech* Fair; Oh! said *George*, Pray Neighbour *Pooley*, let us come in, I will give you any Content. Upon which the Man took down the Woman, who ask'd, saying, Have you not a private Room? Yes, said the good Woman of the House, a Parlour; none like it, thought the Sick-Woman. So in they went, the Sick Woman, Goody *Pooley*, and her Maid; and in half an Hour's time, was born to *G. Smith,* a Son; *George* praying Secrecy, * and he would pay them well. So away goes *G. Smith* home to his old Wife, and all things were Hush and Still, as Heart could wish; and about a Week or Ten Days after, home goes the Woman as sound as a Roach; and at the Months end, when the Babe had gotten a little strength, *G. Smith* comes again to Goodman *Pooley* and his Wife, and beggs heartily for their Assistance; and no doubt, with this Nod, *&* as their usual way is, ' I pray for Truth's sake, be private, left it get Air, for the ' Apostate Christians will make a mock at it. Well,*G. Smith* agrees to give them Five Pound to carry it 20 Miles, namely, to *Great Saxum,* within two Miles of *Bury* St. *Edmunds*, in *Suffolk*: Content, said they; so away they went by *Ely, Soham,* and so to *Deasnidg-Lodge*, where they staid one Night or two, whilst *G. Smith* went before to provide a Nurse; which he soon did, at *Saxum* aforesaid: For Money answers all things.

Well, the place being prepared, and notice of it, away goes *Pooley*

George Smith • *the Twelfth Bird.*

* *Pray mind the Quaker's Method; keep things private, and all is well.*

and

and his Wife, with the Child, and delivered it to the Wife of *John Chapman* of *Saxum* aforesaid, as the Act and Deed of *G. Smith*. But as soon as *Pooley* and his Wife had eat and drank, tho' wet and weary, *G. Smith* pack'd them away, left the Old and New Nurse should have a little Title-tattle together: But Good-man *Chapman* being not yet come from *Bury* with the Writings, which were made in the Name of one Mr. *Turner* of *Wretham*, in *Norfolk*, * as Father of the Child, who was called by *G. Smith*, *Robert Turner*; but said the New Nurse, Is the Child Baptized? Ay, ay, says *George*, all is done, all is done. So *G. Smith* himself staid; and having dispatch'd away *Pooley* and his Wife, he bought Nutts, and crack'd; and at last came Good-man *Chapman* with the said Writings; which upon his paying 40 *l*. * were sealed; and away goes *George* jogging home, as merry as a Cricket.

* *Forgery; for I went to both the Wrethams, and there is not a Man lives there of that Name.*
* *Tho' he fell short about 10 s. which he promised to send, but did not.*

This is *G. Whitehead*'s well-meaning Man, &c. Indeed, the said *G. Smith*'s Boy is with honest People; I saw him; he will be 14 Years old next *September*, and as like his Father, NOT *Turner*, BUT *Smith*, as you shall see a Lad; and is now called *Robert Smith*, and has been for some Years, since they understood things.

* *G. Smith's Second Child by the same Woman.*

And *Secondly*, Since all now is settled, and well, and private, that the World's People do not know of it, (for that with them, in all the like Cases, is the Principal *Verb*,) *George* and his Widow grew as loving as Pig and Lamb; they too't again afresh; she Conceives, and grew big again, (that's the worst on't:) However, the Woman would not venture out again, but rely'd on her Neighbour's Fidelity: The time of her Travel comes on; away goes *George*, helter-skelter, for *Eleanor Hall*, Wife of *Samuel Hall*, and another faithful Friend; and the time being come, to work they went; and in a little time, she was Delivered of a Daughter: And when the Child attain'd to the Age of about half an Hour, being a little drest up, *G. Smith* the Father, and *Eleanor Hall* the Midwife, carried the Child at the Age aforesaid, to a lone House, standing in the Field, called the *Brick-Kill-House*, a frequent Harbour for Beggars, since out of use; and in goes the Woman *Eleanor* with this Infant, under the faithful Promise of *George* to gratifie her, for all her Trouble, Care and Pains, and to send her and his Child, Sustenance: Ay, ay, that he would; having already sent out *G. Washington*, to provide a Nurse for it; and for whose return, the poor Woman *Eleanor Hall*, with the Child, waited in that Den two Days and Nights; in which place, she was sorely Affrighted: for in the Dead of the Night, something came and smote her on the Shoulder, that she was Lame of it many Weeks, (as she told me her self:) Moreover, she told me, she would not do the like again for 100 *l*.

Well,

From Quakerism *to* Christianity.

Well, at last G. *Washington* came, and with him his Housekeeper, *; and G. Smith gave him a Bagg of Money, *viz.* 5 *l.* for his own Care and Pains; and 40 *l.* to perform the Contract, which the said *Washington* had a few Days before made with Goodman *Owers* of *Burrow*, within about five Miles of *Bury*, aforesaid.

Well, this Female Child was born to *G. Smith*, by the Widow aforesaid, the 28th or 29th of *July*, 1688. being *Wednesday*; and by *Monday*, this *Washington*, and his Housekeeper, (whom he afterwards Marry'd,) carried this Child to the Sign of the *Harrow* in *Fordham*; and then away goes *Washington* to *Barrow*, with his 40 *l.* to Goodman *Owers*, (leaving the said Child and Housekeeper to Nurse it:) The next Day came Goodman *Owers* and his Wife, with *Washington*; and then there was nothing but Merriment, Brother and Sister at every word *: This Child was put out by the Order, and with the Money of *G. Smith*, in the Name of one Mr. *Scott*, a Linnen-Draper in *London* †, for 40 *l.* but I forget something which is remarkable; of this 40 *l.* there wanted 15 *s.* which *Washington* promised to send, as also to find it Linnen for a Year, or more; all which is forgot, as Good Wife *Owers* averrs; and she is a Woman of good Repute, and the Child lives well, and looks well; this Child was put to Goodman *Owers*, under the Name of *Mary Scott*; but they have Baptiz'd the Child, and call'd it *Mary Smith*; Goodman *Owers* is dead, but his Widow is alive, and lives at *Risby*, within three Miles of *Bury*, and six Miles of *Barton*-Mills, and two small Miles distance from Great *Saxum*, where the Boy lives; and this Boy and Girl often Visits each other: And if their Father had but that Grace to take care of them, it might mitigate his Crime; I am sure, it would have abated the Edge of my Pen; for he is my Kinsman: And were it not to Discover the Quakers Ways, I should not have been so large, and sent him a Letter to that purpose: A Copy of it followeth *.

* *This Washington Marry'd Ann his Housekeeper soon after, but is now dead; and Tho. Cook of Littleport, has marry'd her; and she is ready to Depose it, if need be.*

* *Viz. Between G. Washington, Goodman Owers and his Wife, to blind the People of the House, &c.*

† *Lying and Forgery meet in this Upright and Well-meaning Quaker; as G. Whitehead and S. Cater wrote of him.*

* *For I was advised by a Gentleman in Risby, to take some care about it, &c.*

COUSIN *GEORGE*,

I was requested by a Gentleman in our Country, to use some means, that your By-Children which are put out to Nurse in our Country, may have something settled upon them, for their future Maintainance; and pursuant thereunto, I do desire it of you, in regard it is but reasonable and just, that you should do it: Wherefore, I make Application to you in this private Way, as most suitable; and it may make some amends for your Crime, and extennate the heinousness of your Offence; for it seems to me a most horrible Crime, besides the Sin; and as an Aggravation thereof, to beget Children, and send them into the World as Vagrants, they being from under the Verge of the Law, and can be Heirs of nothing, but
the

The Pilgrim's Progreſs,

the *Shame of their Parents; which altho' they cannot help it, yet muſt they wear the Badge and Livery thereof, as long as they live. If you anſwer my Expectation in this Matter, as I have hitherto been ſparing of you, ſo I ſhall make no Complaint to any Juſtice of the Peace; if not, you may depend on it; if God give me length of Days, I ſhall do what I legally can, to have ſomething ſettled on them: And therefore, let me have your Anſwer.*

I am Your Friend and Kinſman, Francis Bugg, *Sen.*
Aug. 30. 1697.

But no Anſwer have I receiv'd ſince.

Come, *George Whitehead,* What think you of theſe Things? Where is your Seriouſneſs? Where is your Sincerity? You told me, that your God laid a Neceſſity upon you, to write againſt me, and others, wherein you call'd me, APOSTATE INFORMER, DEVIL INCARNATE, BEAST, DOG, WOLF, &c. But the before-mentioned, you ſooth up, as well-meaning and upright Lambs, and never write a Book againſt them, yet three Books againſt me in nine Months time: And, *George,* then you were Rampant; you neither ſtudied Events, nor feared Effects; you were reſolved to go on, come what will come; you were reſolved to Unchriſtian all that oppoſed you, and ſeparated from you; you were reſolved to ruin them, if poſſible, both in Name, Reputation, and Eſtate: I have felt the weight of your Hand, and the ſtrength of your Indignation, and implacable Malice; but, Bleſſed be the God, and Father of our Lord Jeſus Chriſt, that amongſt his manifold Mercies to me, that he hath vouchſafed to give me Time and Ability, to return your ſharp Arrows back into your own Boſoms; and I let them fly freely; I am not ſparing; for as *Jeremiah* ſaid, *The Lord hath opened his Armory, and hath brought forth the Weapons of his Indignation,* *. And, *George,* they will light on the Skirts of this Painted Harlot; and all thy Jeſuitical Craft cannot throw it off; for your Cauſe is drooping. I have given you the Key of the Cage; look into it, and you may ſee the Abominations of the Earth, even the Myſtery of Iniquity. Well, *George,* after it came into my Heart to write this Book, I ſaid, Shall I ſpare them any longer? Concluding, No: But give this Harlot a double Cup, and make her drink the very Dregs of it: And having laid faſt hold of the two main Pillars, upon which your Building ſtands, *viz.* INFALLIBILITY and PERFECTION, I did with all my Might ſhake*; and behold, it begins to tumble: For, *George,* the time is come, that one ſhall chaſe a Thouſand, and two ſhall put Ten Thouſand to Flight †: And art thou ſo blind, *George,* that thou canſt not ſee it? Doſt thou

Epiſtle to Judgment fixed.

* Jer. 50. 24.

* Judges 26. 29.
† Deut. 32. 30.

not

not see thy self, and thy Brethren, ready to fall upon your own Spears, for very Anguish and Vexation of Spirit? Art thou so ignorant, *George*, that thou canst not perceive thy self, calling to the Hills to hide thee, and the Mountains to cover and excuse thee *;* But, *George*, thou hast no more Answer than *Baal*'s Priests had, tho' you call from Morning to Evening, and thump your Breasts, and leap and jump from one end of your Wooden Pulpits to the other, stamping like the Friars; yet there is no Answer, there is none to Pity you, none to Mourn for you; no Advocate to Plead, for the stopping the Pens that are imployed against Quakerism; no, *Babylon* is falling, is falling, and great will be the Fall thereof, even like a Mill-stone into the Sea; so falls Quakerism, never more to rise again. *Amen. Amen. Alleluja.*

* *Sober Ex-post. 1ft. and 2d. Chap.*
1 Kings 18. 26.

CHAP. XV.

Sheweth the Enmity of the Quakers against me, for my Testimony against their Errours; and the Providence of God supporting me under my Sufferings.

IT is not unknown to many of the Quakers still alive, with what Zeal and Care, with what Sufferings by Fines and Imprisonments, with what Pains and Charge I was in divers Kinds exercised whilst I was a Quaker, and that for the carrying on the Cause of Quakerism; nothing seemed dear to me to part withal, or to spend, for the Advancement thereof: But, when I came to see them walk contrary to what they pretended, and that their seeming Sincerity was real Hypocrisie, I then began to look into things, that there might be a Reformation; and the first thing that gave me occasion, was, * That of forcing Apprentices to stand Bare-headed in their Houses and Shops, and yet at the same time pretended, they could not put off their Hats, in respect to Persons. This looked so bad, *i. e.* to receive, nay, exact Respect from our Inferiors, and not to give it to our Superiors, that I wrote a Letter to the Yearly Meeting *, as a Testimony against it, which gave great Offence.

* *See Innocency Vindicated, &c. p. 8.*
* *In May, 1675.*

The Next which gave Offence to me, and others, was our Teachers, who would exhort us to be bold, to give up all, telling us, The Fleece would grow again; who themselves at the same time, would give up nothing, nay, not set themselves in a like suffering Capacity with the Hearers, insomuch as that in the loss of 13550 *l.* our Teachers never lost 50 *l.* but the Hearers suffered for them, as also for themselves. And this I saw, and spake against, some Months before it fell to my turn, to be Fined for our Preachers: But at last,

See Paint. Harl. &c. P. 5.

I was Fined 15 *l.* for *Sam. Cater,* for that he did not declare his Name and Habitation, and thereby put himself in a like Suffering capacity with us the Hearers, as I shewed at large*, and how I prosecuted the Restitution of the said Fine of 15 *l.* and had it again, tho' with great loss, by Charges, Int. &c.

* See Reason *against Fall-* *ing,* &c. *p.* 73, to 80.

The Third thing which gave me Offence, was G. *Fox's* setting up a Female Government, by Women's Meeting Monthly, &c. This I opposed vigorously; and to be short, I do think I gave (by my Book) that Image a deadly Blow *: But by this time, G. *White-head, Samuel Cater, Robert Sandland,* and others, wrote several Books against me, wherein they called me, 'A Child of the Devil, ' Enemy of all Righteousness, an Apostate, a Betraying *Judas,* a ' Treacherous Hypocrite, a Dog, a Wolf, a Beast, an Informer, 18 or 20 times in one Book †, with abundance more such stuff. Well, upon this, I apply'd my self to our *Milden-Hall* Meeting, for a Certificate against these scandalous Detractions, (which they not only Printed, but sent up and down into all Counties where I dealt, particularly, into *Leicestershire,* in order to ruin my Reputation *.) Well, twenty-seven Members of this Meeting, gave me a Certificate, many of them still alive; and both then, and still the chief Men of the Meeting †. And this Certificate, with the several Books I wrote, so maul'd them, that *Sam. Cater,* and his Assistants, gave over: But G. *Whitehead,* he still goes on; he wrote sometimes three Books in less than a Year against me, calling me, 'Self-con-'demned Apostate, Counterfeit Convert, a Scandal to Christianity, 'a Fool, and Novice, &c.

* *De Christ. Lib.* &c. Part 2d.

† Judgment Fixed, &c. *The Lib. of an Apost. Conf.* &c. Righteous Judgment placed, &c.

* Which then was a most hateful Name amongst Tradesmen.

† See *New Rome Unmask'd,* &c. *Epist. to the Bereans and Introduct.* See *The Pict. of Quakerism,* &c. 2d. Part. p. 146. These Books they still sent into every County, which did me much hurt in my Trade.

And when this would not effect their manifest Design, then they sent Letters about against me, and raised all manner of Lies and Stories; and by Post, sent me not only Books wrote against *Francis Spira,* but Letters also. A relish of which is as followeth, *viz.*

Francis Bugg, Such as is thy Name, such thy Nature, the darkest of the Creeping Things in the whole Earth; they love the Night, feeding upon Filth, and Dung; Night is thy Habitation; the Earth has received thee; Night and Darkness is come upon thee: Thy Father is shut out of Heaven, and thou also; that makes ye Houl and Roar. Woe hastens, and the Eternal Night is come, and coming upon thee. Woe, and Alass! poor Night-Bugg, &c.

3d. 1st. *Month,* 1690.

This Letter sent me, without any Name to it, I sent a Copy of it the next Post to G. *Whitehead,* to know if he was the Author of it; but he sent me word he was not, nor did he know who was: Whether he said true or false therein, I cannot tell. But the 14th of the same

From Quakerism *to* Christianity.

same Month, I receiv'd another * from the same Man, tho' of a different Hand; but the last I know to be *Ste. Crisp*'s: And thus he wrote.

* Not of the same Hand-Writing, but the same Man, which was *Ste. Crisp*; for I know his Hand, and have shewed it to others that do.

Francis, *I am not* Geo. Whitehead: *Alas for Thee, and* Hogg, *and* Pennyman, *the Arrows from Heaven shall stick fast in your Consciences, when thou hast found me,* O Galilean! *And thou may hear more from me,* &c.

Then in Verse, thus:

Indeed, to Vaunt, and proudly Bragg,
Doth not become a feeble Night-Bugg.
I Prophesie, the Hour is near, O Bugg! *unclean,*
With wicked Julian *shalt cry, thou hast found me,* O Galilean!
As vile an Apostate as ever was wicked Julian;
A Wicked Pharisee, *no Penitent* Publican, &c.

Reader, here is enough to shew the Quakers Spirit; and besides, my knowledge of its being *Ste. Crisp*'s, by his Hand-Writing, it's to be observed, that (as above,) he said, *I might hear further from him*; for about three Months after, came out another Book, Entituled, *Innocency against Envy*, Signed by *G. W.* and *Ste. Crisp*; besides his usual Expression, *I Prophesie,* &c. by which, if *Whitehead* did not know of his first, yet he knew of his second Letter; and the Matter being the same in substance, I am satisfied it was his. I am likewise to let you know, that notwithstanding they pretended to the Parliament, that they cannot seek Revenge for themselves, and thereupon could not Sign the Association, yet they Indicted me for putting forth my Book against them, *New Rome Arraign'd,* &c. in the *Old-Baily, London*, which put me to great Charge; insomuch, as one way or other, by my attending this Controversie, by Writing and Printing; first, by opposing their Errours; next, by Vindicating my self from their repeated Abuses, both Publickly and Privately, both as a Man and Christian, I did come by great loss in my outward Estate; and when Men perceived it, they came so fast upon me, as that I could not bear up. I do not in all cases justifie my self, in the too much neglecting my Business, to attend the Motion of the Quakers, who are a compacted Corporation, and my self a single Person, there was too much odds: But I met with such Provocations, which would fill a Volume to relate; and thereupon I came to see my Fall by the Hand of *Saul*; for the Sons of *Zerviah* were too hard for me: For I had maintained the Contest without the help of the Clergy, from 1675 to the Year 1697. and in all that time, I never receiv'd of any one, or more of them, Ten Shillings, nor Ten Nights Lodgings: And whereas they now call me Mercenary,

See *The Pill. of Quakerism,* p. 79.

nary, because I have accepted of the Clergy's Kindness, which has been very Bountiful; let any *Quaker* of them all shew me that he have waged War at his own Charge and Cost, so long, and at so much Expence, Cost, Labour, Pains, Charge and Trouble, and I will not from henceforth call him Mercenary; but their Tongue is no Slander; and now I shall shew somewhat of the wonderful Providence of God, in my Preservation to this Day. For when I found how the Case stood with me, I waited Two or Three Months under some Heaviness and Concern, hearing from all Quarters how the *Quakers* glory'd over me: Notwithstanding they were the chief Cause of my Misfortune, not only with respect to the Controversie, but by Six or Eight of them breaking in my Debt: Upon which I went to visit Mr. *Erasmus Warren*, a Neighbouring Minister, and told him my Condition; and he spake comfortably to me, and bad me not be discouraged, for God was All-sufficient, and that the Earth was the Lord's, and the Fulness thereof, or to this purpose; and told me, that if I would write a Letter of Request to my Lord Bishop of *Norwich*, he, and some others, would Sign it: I did so, and it was Sign'd by himself, Mr. *Archer*, Mr. *Davis*, &c. So I went to *Norwich*, and did, with no little Heaviness, presume to go with it to my Lord Bishop, of whom I did rather expect some little chiding, (being sensible of my own Fault) than to be so kindly receiv'd: But when I came to him, he examined me about my Condition, and press'd me to be honest, and to pay as far as I was able. For *(said he)* our Religion teacheth us to do Right and Justly by all Men; and when you have done, rest upon God's Providence; it is not your Case alone; Times have been hard, and Disappointments many: And then asked me what I would have him do for me; I told him, that if his Lordship would please to give me a Certificate of his Thoughts of me; I was minded to make Application to my Lords, the Bishops of the Church of *England*, the two Universities, and to some particular Clergy-men. All which I no sooner asked, than he granted me; and it pleased God so to open the Hearts of my Lords, the Bishops, and Reverend Clergy, that I found Help in time of Need; and when it was in my Heart to write this Book, I asked one of my Lords, the Bishops, Leave, to give some Publick Acknowledgement of their Kindness; but he answer'd me, *No, go thy ways home, and be thankful, we desire no such thing:* But reading the Scriptures, and finding in St. *Mark's* Gospel*, that when Christ healed the Leper, he charged him, saying, *See thou say nothing to any Man*, &c. *But he* (the Leper, being cured) *went out, and began to publish it much, and to blaze abroad the Matter:* And I never read that Christ blamed the Man for his Gratitude; and I trust, no more will his Ministers and Servants, for this my Presumption: For, how can I receive such unexpected, and unmerited Favours,

* Mark 1, 44, 56.

and

From Quakerism to Christianity.

and not blaze it abroad? I, that for about Twenty Years Persecuted the Church, and drew Disciples after me †, into the Schism of *Quakerism*, and yet upon my Return met with no upbraiding, but rather, like the Returning Prodigal, am met half way, and loaden with Kindnesses. Surely, this is of the Lord's doing, (and it is marvellous in my Eye) to whom be the Praise of all his Mercies and Providences, now, and for ever. *Amen.*

† I know of no one Man drew more.

A Copy of my Lord Bishop of *Norwich's* Certificate is as followeth.

THese are to certifie, That I have known Francis Bugg some Years, and that he has appear'd to me a sober, honest, and industrious Man, and to have taken much Pains to undeceive and Convert the Quakers, by Publishing useful Books, and that not without Success; but by the Hardness of Times, several Losses, and the Charge of Printing the Books he writ, he is reduced to great Difficulties: Wherefore I apprehend him a real Object of Charity; and that he does truly deserve the Bounty of well-disposed Persons, unto whom I Recommend him.

Octob. 22. 1697.   John Norwich.

And having obtain'd this Favour, together with his Bounty, which was very considerable, I took my Leave of him with many Thanks for his Kindness and Liberality.

First, That I might take care, not only to do what was just to others, but to take care of my Family also; for he that does not is worse than an Infidel. *Secondly*, That I might not lye under the Contempts and Insultings of the *Quakers*; who, as they have for many Years sought my Ruin*, by all Ways and Methods they could devise, both in Person, Name, and Estate, so they have been observ'd like the *Philistines*,† to glory in my Misfortunes, as thinking they had accomplished their Ends: But notwithstanding all their Rejoycing, I had a secret Hope, that my Strength would be renewed, and that God would enable me to lay hold of their two main Pillars *, (*i.e.* Perfection and Infallibility) and putting thereto all my Might, I should yet be able to shake their Building, as at this Day, Blessed be God, the Father of our Lord Jesus Christ, who hath so wrought my Deliverance, as to bring things thus far to pass. *Thirdly*, That thereby I might be enabled to grapple with the *Quaker's Goliah*, that Uncircumcised *Philistine*, *Geo. Whitehead* by Name; who, together with his Brethren, have defied the Armies of *Israel*, even all the Professors of the Christian Faith, under every

* As they do all that oppose their Errors and Immoralities.
† *Judges* 16.
24, 25.
* Verse 29.

every Denomination: And not only so, but Excuse, Justifie, Vindicate, and Defend all the Idolatrous Practices, Blasphemous Principles, and Damnable Errors, Said, Wrote, and Printed, Broached, and Spread, by the *Quaker* Teachers, enough to Infect the Nations, if God had not put it into the Hearts of some Instruments, to discover the same; and thanks be to God, who from the beginning of my Discovery of their Errors, hath given me Strength, Ability and Courage, to go on, and not turn to the Right Hand, nor to the Left, in my Pursuit after *Sheba*, the Son of *Bichri*, that Man of *Belial* †, (*i. e. Geo. Whitehead*) until I have hem'd him in on every side, altho' I have been hard beset, and gone thro' many Difficulties and Streights *, and have been forced to climb up the Hill upon my Hands and Feet, like *Jonathan* †; yet as he slew Twenty upon the spot, so have I discomfited Twelve of their Principal Men, and maul'd *Doeg* the *Edomite*, alias *Jos. Wyeth**, that Pupil of *W. Penn*'s, who, as I am informed, was equally unbelieving with Mr. *Penn*, touching the late happy Peace, without a Restauration — such Hopes had they of extirpating the Protestant Interest, &c. for the time is come, that One shall chase a Thousand, and Two shall put Ten Thousand of them to flight; and thus doth God bring to pass his Acts, his strange Acts, by weak Instruments; to whom over all, be the Glory, together with the Son, and Blessed Spirit, Three Persons, and One God, now, henceforth, and for evermore. *Amen.*

† *2 Sam. 20. 21, 22.*
* Which few know but my self.
† *1 Sam. 14. 13.*
* See my Sober Expostulation with the Hearers of the Quakers against the Mercenary Teachers, &c. p. 1. to the 15.

And therefore, in the Words of *David* I will praise the Lord, saying, *O Lord, with my whole Heart I will shew forth all thy marvellous Works: I will be glad, and rejoyce in thee: I will sing Praise to thy Name, O thou most High, for thou hast maintained my Right, and my Cause; thou sittest on the Throne, judging Right. The Lord also will be a Refuge for the Oppressed, a Refuge in times of Trouble; and they that know thy Name will put their Trust in thee: for thou, Lord, hast not forsaken them that seek thee. Sing Praises to the Lord which dwelleth in* Sion; *declare among the People his Doings. The Heathen* † *are sunk down in the Pit that they made: in the Net which they hid, is their own Foot taken* *, &c.

† *i. e.* The Quakers, who denieth Jesus of *Nazareth.*
* *Psal 9.1,2,3. 9, 11.*

But, to proceed, having the recited Certificate of my Lord Bishop of *Norwich*, I presented it to several of my Lords, the Bishops, both the Universities, as well as to divers Particulars of the Clergy of the Church of *England*; and I humbly thank them, they were very kind to me, notwithstanding all the Endeavours of the *Quakers*, to represent me unworthy of their Notice; particularly at *Cambridge*, where they carry'd to the Colledges Books against me, which I had Answer'd and Refuted Ten or Fifteen Years since; insomuch, that some of the Heads of the Colledges took special Notice of the *Quaker*'s Malice, and thereupon, I do believe, were the more kind. Thus doth God bring Good out of Evil; nay,

should

From **Quakerism** *to* **Christianity.**

should I relate all the particular Methods the *Quakers* used in all Places where I came, to prevent me of their Kindness, and the Aboundings of the Favours I received, it would seem almost incredible, I being but a single Person, and known but to a few; the *Quakers* numerous, and (like the Followers of *Corah, Dathan,* and *Abiram* †) Men of Fame in some Cases. But so it was, they did not prevail; but God in his Providence made way for my Deliverance, beyond my Expectation, and in him do I trust, who taketh Care of the Sparrows *; and this puts me in Mind of the Widow, recorded in the Holy Scriptures †, whose Husband died, and left her in Debt. and not Effects to answer, insomuch, that the Creditor was come to take away her two Sons. This poor Woman was no doubt in Distress enough; but yet she neither exclaimed of her Husband, nor yet murmur'd at the Dispensation of Providence, which befel; neither did she sit still, and use no Means: But hearing that *Elisha* the Prophet was come to Town, she resolves to make Application to him; he could but deny her; she knew the worst, and hoped the best; and therefore in Faith, and full Assurance of the Mercy of God to them that trust in him; and not doubting but the Inspired Prophet knew her Inside, even the Sincerity of her Heart; and that notwithstanding this Calamity, she could appeal to him, that her Husband was an honest Man; a Man that feared God, and served him in Uprightness; and thereupon she puts on Courage, and goes to him, saying, ' Thy Servant, my ' Husband, is dead, and thou knowest that thy Servant did fear the ' Lord, and the Creditor is come to take unto him my two Sons ' to be Bondsmen.

† *Numb.* 16. 2.
* *Matth.* 10. 29, 30, 31.
† 2 *Kings* 4.

This was sorrowful News (no doubt) to the Prophet, to hear that one of the Sons of the Prophets, that professed Faith in the God of *Israel*, should so fail, as not to be able to pay his Debts. Well, the Prophet quickly understood the Widow, and as quickly reply'd, saying, *What shall I do for thee? tell me: What hast thou in the House?* Here is two notable Questions, and so quickly proposed, that he did not give the Widow leave to answer to the first, but added, *What hast thou in the House?* As if he should have said, *Why should I ask this humble Petitioner, what she would have me to do?* 'Tis plain, she would willingly be enabled to pay her Debts, rescue her two Sons, and have something to live on; she then reply'd, saying, *Thine Handmaid hath nothing at home, save a Pitcher of Oyl.* Upon which, the Prophet (as God would have it) wrought a Miracle, saying; ' Go borrow the Vessels of all thy Neighbours, even empty ' Vessels; borrow not a few; and when thou art come into thy ' House, shut the Door upon thee, and upon thy Sons, and pour out ' into all these Vessels, and set aside that which is full. She did so, and was thereby enabled to pay her Debts, redeem her Sons, and had.

left

The Pilgrim's Progress,

left wherewithal to live upon. O the wonderful Works of God! who thus instructs His to depend upon his Providence; for the Scriptures are written for our Learning; and truly, when I consider my own Case, I think it falls not much short of this Miracle; I am sure I have met with a wonderful Providence, in my Deliverance, considering I had no such Inspired Prophet to appeal to, nor such an Evidence to vouch on my part: I had nothing but Reason and Demonstration to offer, having prayed to God to Incline the Hearts of his Servants, to a Charitable Consideration of Things past, present, and to come: Nay, my Case seem'd worse than the Widows; for I do not read that she had any Enemies to Interpose, but I had many. The *Quakers* no sooner understood that the Clergy took my Case into their Pious Consideration, but they sent their Emissaries with Books after me, both to the Colledges, and particular Persons; wherein I was represented an Enemy of all Righteousness, a Child of the Devil; yea, a Devil Incarnate, a Wolf, a Dog, a Beast †, &c. And when this would not prevail against me, they then made Personal Complaints, that I was a Counterfeit Convert *; and to make this out, they told some of the Reverend Clergy in *Norfolk*, that though *Francis Bugg* pretended to be a Member of the Church of *England*, yet he never receiv'd the Communion with you. See what a Convert you have; what Reason is there then for you to assist and support him so as you do? Upon which, this Minister writes to Mr. *Archer* our Minister, to know the Truth of it; he sends him an Answer, by Letter, assuring him, that in *Anno* 1688. I receiv'd the Sacrament, and (if at home) ever since at the usual times. But when this would not do, they'd try another Project; for *John Hubbard*, of *Stoak* †, told Mr. *Meriton*, Minister of *Oxborow*, near him, that I was drunk the last time I was in *London* *; who sent me a Letter thereof, which providentially came into my Son's Hand, in my Absence: An Abstract of it is as followeth.

† Judgment fixed, &c. by G. W.
* As G. W. had Printed me to be. See his Book, *A Counterfeit Convert, a Scandal to Christianity*, &c.

† An eminent Quaker in *Norfolk*; and one of the twelve, mention'd in my Sober Expostulation, p. 1. Printed 1698.
* In March 1698.

SIR,

I gave your Book the other Day to John Hubbard, *who receiv'd it with a Scornful Smile; I discoursed with him upon the Subject of it, which he heard with much Impatience, yet at last he promised to read it; he could not forbear Invectives against the Author of it: The usual Courtship of that sort of People to every one that would convince them of their Errors, 'tis the Sibboleth of the Party; indeed they may very well challenge to themselves the sole Priviledge of exercising the Black Art of Railing, because they are the only Men that I know of, that can rail by Inspiration: One Mouthful of Dirt I remember he squirted upon you, yon*, i. e. *He said you were drunk the last time you were in* London. *Sir, I doubt not in the least your Innocency, but they must Calumniate still, or how shall they prove themselves right-bred Children of the Accuser of the Brethren: God Almighty assist and strengthen you to break the Brood of that Viperous Generation, that hath so poyson'd our Nation; that at last you may triumph over that old Serpent, that hath commenced so Bloody a War against them that keep the Testimony of Jesus; you must expect he will be fill'd with great Wrath; that he will both Hiss, and Sting, and pour out Water as a Flood after you, his time being short,* &c.

April 11. 1698.   Hen. Meriton.

Upon my receiving this Letter I went to *Stoake*, and asked *John Hubbard* what Ground he had to raise this false Accusation; I told him, that I did not remember that I spent a Groat at a time all the time I was in *London*†: He told me he heard so: Pray tell me your Author; at last he told me *Tho. Belch**, at the Ship in *Cheap-side, Linnen-Draper*. When I came to *London*, I got Mr. *Lawrence*, of St. *Gregory*'s Parish, to go with me to him, to whom I said, *Sir, do you know me?* No, said *Tho. Belch*: I told him that my Name was *Fran. Bugg*, and that I understood he had raised a Report of me, *viz*. That I was drunk in *London, March* last: I heard so, said *Belch*, if that be thy Name: *Who is your Author?* said I: He is not in Town, said he: I reply'd, *What is his Name?* and insisted on it a good while, but could not prevail with him to tell me: To the Truth of this Mr. *Lawrence* subscribed his Name,
                               John Lawrence.

† Which was more than a Month.
* A *Quaker* in *London*.

Reader, When I saw my self thus attack'd from all Quarters, by Books, by Letters, by Reports; sometimes, that I was a Drunkard, as you have heard; sometimes, that I was distracted, and so discomposed, as not able to rest Night nor Day, occasion'd by writing against the *Quakers*; sometimes, that I left my Wife and Son in their Society, to introduce me again into their Community, and Twenty Lies more, I went to the *Quakers-Meeting* in *Milden-Hall*, on *Sunday* the First of *May* last, as the most probable Raisers of these, or some of these Stories, and spake to them after this manner.

Friends. This is the 15th. Year since I came to this Meeting for a Certificate on my Behalf against the Suggestions of *S. Cater* and *G. Whitehead, &c.* which were, That I was an Informer; which at that time, was a hateful Name to a Tradesman, and very Prejudicial to my Reputation, as well as divers other False and Scandalous Detractions in their Books: And this Meeting (at least the major part of it, Twenty-seven in number) gave me ONE * with great Courage and Freedom, which at that time was very useful; and I now come to you for a Testification against my self, and ask no Favour at your Hands, touching several Reports raised on me, *Ut supra*; and upon your signing it with your Names, I promise to print it, and what I cannot justly deny, I will fairly confess.

* As in the Picture of Quakerism, Part 2. p. 146.

But several answer'd me, (and not opposed by the rest, or any of them) That they never heard any such Report, nor knew any cause why there should be such Reports.

But for the further clearing the Matter, and removing Stumbling-Blocks out of the way, I shall recite the Substance of several Certificates, which I took FROM my Son (who, tho' one of them, yet I hope he is sincere; for I have heard him say, and that before some *Quakers*, Come, what is Wrong is Wrong, whether it be in *Geo. Fox* or my Father, and I will no more stand by what is Wrong in the one, than I will in the other.) FROM *Philip Cranifs*, who was my Servant near 20 Years *, and as familiarly concern'd in all my Concerns in Trade, both Buying and Selling; having taken in and deliver'd out many Thousand Pounds worth of Goods, and is still living, and of known Reputation. FROM *William Belsham*, who was my Servant 15 or 16 Years, and is a *Quaker*, and one that handed my Certificate above-mention'd in 1683. a Man of known Reputation. FROM *Matthew Belsham*, his Brother, both living well, each having some Estate of their own: He was my Servant about 16 Years, tho' none of them at this time, who, if I were such a Person as some would represent me to be; some, if not all of these, must know something of it. Nay, I do believe I could have had a Hundred of my Neighbours to avouch the same, so far as my Actions have come under their Cognizance: But these being Persons of Credit, and that have had Experience of my manner of Life, may (I think) ballance those Reports, whose Authors cannot be found out: And indeed, were it not for the sake of my Testimony, which the *Quakers* would wound thro' my Sides, I should not have said so much on this Subject, but rather have taken *David's* Patience for my Example; who, when *Shimei* cursed and reproached him in the Day of his Affliction *, yet he bore all patiently: And tho' its true, I am now made to Unmask this *Painted Harlot*, (which will still more enrage her) thereby endeavouring, if possible, that she may see her self, and repent in Dust and Ashes, and be humbled before the Lord; that so she may be Converted and Healed; at least, that hereby others may be caution'd not to imbrace her Pernicious Errors, yet in all this 20 Years time † of my Controversing with the Head of this Sect: I never render'd Railing for Railing (nor do I now) neither have I taken Advantage at their Miscarriages, (a small Sample whereof I have now set forth in the former Chapter) as my Books.

* He came to me in 1676. and has not been from me Three Years.

* 2 *Sam.* 16. 6, 7, 8.

† Tho' about Four Years thereof I was in their Community, labouring for a Reformation, not then understanding their grossest Errors.

Books do manifest, but have handled those Errors which they taught in their Books, which indeed, open the Flood Gates to all their Viciousness *; and with which they are so tainted, as put all Christian Societies together (their Number consider'd) there is not so much Viciousness in any one Society. Tho' if Christ had one amongst twelve, it cannot but be supposed there is in every Society too many that do not, in Life and Conversation, answer their Holy Profession; neither do I bring these Testimonies to excuse my self from my own Infirmities; I am not without Sinful Imperfections, I do acknowledge.

* See a Paper from *Pensilvania*, intituled, *A Brief Admonition to the Elders and Ministers of the People call'd Quakers*.

Here follows the Contents of the several Certificates above mention'd, *Viz.*

First, That he (*Fran. Bugg*) neither is, nor never was distracted or discomposed, since any of us can remember him, or that ever we heard of.

Secondly, That in all his Time he has been moderate, both in his Meat, Drink, and Apparel; and never by any of us known to be drunk, as is reported, nor yet inclined to Drinking, in Excess.

Thirdly, That he ever was a good Provider for his Family, a Lover of his Wife, an Indulgent Father to his Children; forcing none (farther than Perswasion) to a Conformity to his way of Worship.

Fourthly, That we believe he never left his Wife and Son amongst the *Quakers*, to Introduce him to them again; this is a Malicious Report, to render him a Hypocrite, which his whole Life and Conversation has declared the contrary, to his Cost.

Fifthly, The Press being open, and both Parties having equal Priviledge, we look upon it utterly wrong to make use of such Indirect Methods: And some of us are sorry we have no better way to confute his Arguments.

Sixthly, That we are ready to enlarge on any of these Heads to any Man's Face that shall question the Truth hereof.

Subscribed by *William Belsham, Philip Crannifs, Matthew Belsham, Fran. Bugg*, Junior.

Reader, As I could not pass by such Publick Mercies and Benefits as I have received, without some Publick Acknowledgment, without great Ingratitude, both to God and Man; so would I not be too particular, lest thereby I do offend; yet with St. *Paul* I can say, That as Sufferings and hard Usage for my Testimony sake abound, so do not only Inward Consolation, but Outward Benefits abound also *; and as a Proof thereof, I shall add but one Instance more, which is, That since I came to *London*, an ancient Friend of mine, to whom I did owe a certain Debt, upon Bond, who considering the hard Usages I have received from the *Quakers*, (in which

* 2 *Cor.* 1. 5.

which, he himself has had a deep share) and finding me still conscientiously concern'd, without my asking, or once thinking of, or expecting, brought me the Bond, and forgave me the Debt resting due to him upon it, without any Covenant or Promise on my part. Thus hath God opened the Hearts of his Servants, and moved them to Compassion; Blessed be his Holy Name for ever, and Humble Thanks to all, unto whom I have been oblig'd.

CHAP. XVI.

A Word of Encouragement to all who are Sincere amongst the Hearers of the People, call'd Quakers, who begin to be weary of the Yoke of Quakerism, and are willing to embrace the Christian Faith.

FRIENDS,

HAving given you a Brief Account of my Travel in this Pilgrimage, and shewed you the many Turnings and Windings which I have gone through, and the many Quick-sands and Quagmires that I have passed, without sinking, tho' oft-times in great Danger; what by Enemies within, and Enemies without, as also in some Places pointed to *Israel's* Rock, the *Man Christ Jesus*, I am now come to remove one Stumbling-Block, which *Solomon Eccles* has laid in your way, namely, *That there is as great a Gulf fixed between you and the Christians, as there was between Dives and Abraham,* insomuch, that if you would come from them, i. e. *Quakers,* you cannot; his Words are these, *Viz.*

† *Viz*: By Authority greater than the Scripture Truth defending the Quakers, &c. p. 7. by G. W.

I testifie in the Spirit of Truth †, *that there is as great a Gulf between the* Baptists (and consequently other Christians) *that are NOT in Christ*; (that is, NOT in the *Quakers* Light) *and those* (Quakers) *that are in the Truth, as there was between* Abraham *and* Dives *.

* See his Musick Lecture, &c. p. 23.
† The Quakers Challenge, &c. p. 2, 3.

Again, as an Explanation of this Doctrine, he saith, *Come Protestants, Presbyterians, Independants and Baptists, the* Quakers *deny you all:* —— *The Quakers are in the Truth, and none but they* †, &c.

And from this, and the like Doctrine, spring that Aversion in you, that it is impossible to prevail with many of you, either to hear a Sermon, preach'd by the Publick Ministers, or to read their Sermons: So that when the *Quakers* once catch any in their Cobweb, it is very hard and difficult to get you out, unless there be one, that is resolv'd to observe the Apostle's Advice, who said, *Prove all*

* 1 Thess. 5.21. *things, hold fast that which is good* * : And I am not doubtful, but that

that as there has been a Remnant that has taken this Advice, and has forsaken the *Quakers* Errors, so will there many more follow their Example: For this Doctrine of theirs, which alludes to Christ's Parable, is falsly applied; for that Parable relates to the Final Estate of the Blessed, and the Damned, after this Life, as you may read at large, *Luke* 16. And as for the *Quakers* denying all the Professors of Christianity, affirming themselves to be in the Truth ONLY, or the ONLY Church of Christ, as in my former Writings I have made to appear * from their Books; this is all Pride, yea, Spiritual Pride, and Self-Conceit, and ought not to be any Hindrance to you in your Examination and Tryal of your selves; but rather, as a Spur to your Zeal, lest you should be in the Wrong: And if you come once sincerely so to do, I no way doubt but you will soon forsake *Quakerism*. I well remember, that when I first heard it Rumour'd, that G. Fox was looked upon as a second *Moses*, to give forth Laws and Orders for us to walk by, and Methods and Forms of Church-Government, I presently wrote Six Queries touching Church-Government, in the Year 1678 *. which went in Manuscript far and near, as Printed in my Book †; the Tenor of which was:

* *Luke* 16.

* The Picture of *Quakerism*, &c. Part first.

* 20 Years since.
† *De Chri. Lib.* Part 2. Pag. 72, 80.

Query 1. Whether Jesus Christ be Head of the Church, or *George Fox*?

Qu. 2. If you say Christ; then whether he be not Law-giver to his Church?

Qu. 3. If you say, that Christ is both Head and Law-giver to his Church; then whether we ought not to Follow and Obey the Commands and Precepts of Christ, which are laid down in the Scripture, by the four Evangelists, and his Apostles, rather than the Commands and Precepts of *Geo. Fox*?

Qu. 4. If you say, that the Commands and Precepts of Christ ought rather to be obey'd, than those of *Geo. Fox*; then I further Query, whether Christ, or any of his Apostles, ever commanded the Observation of *Womens Meetings*, Apart and Distinct from the Men?

Qu. 5. If you say, That neither Christ nor his Apostles commanded nor left any Example or President for *Womens Distinct Meetings*, to be set up Monthly, any way to intermeddle with the Government of the Church: Then I further Query, where have *Geo. Fox* or you your Power and Authority, to Institute and Ordain such a way of Government? And in whose Name do you compel to a Conformity; and thus to Impose your Ceremonies? &c.

Qu. 6. Whether were not the *Bereans* accounted noble, in that they searched the Scriptures, to see whether what St. *Paul* taught, did accord therewith? And will it not become us to do the like, to see whether what *Geo. Fox* imposes on us, accord with the Scripture?

pture? If not, whether we are obliged to observe his Dictates and Prescriptions, *Yea or Nay? &c.* To which Queries I never received any Answer.

And thus it pleased God of his Infinite Mercy, to give me Courage and Boldness 20 Years since, (for it was some Years before *, that I wrote to their Yearly Meeting, about their forcing their Apprentices to stand bare headed before them, whilst they refuse that Respect to their Superiors) to appear against what I saw to be wrong in them, even whilst amongst them; equally (according to my Understanding) to what I have done since; and methinks I desire no more in the *Quakers* than to be sincere, and that for their own Good too: I mean, to put on Courage, and say; 'What do 'you tell me of G. *Fox,* or *Geo. Whitehead*, or any other Man; I will 'stand by no Man, nor no Principle, nor no People †, farther than 'they are right, at least, in my Apprehension, no farther than they 'agree with the Holy Scriptures: No, I am not yet Far-bored to 'this nor the other Man, Form or Society, for Self Ends, for 'Advantage in Trade, for a Name among Men; no, I am for Truth 'and Righteousness, so far as I know it. I thank God thus it was with me, when I was as Famous amongst them, as since they have endeavoured to render me Infamous; and I desire no more of the *Quakers* than this, let their Errors be never so great, and their Understanding never so clouded, if they be Sincere, and willing to be informed, I could heartily imbrace them, and for which I have great Reason; for I was as Erroneous in many things as the most of them: But when I find that G. *Whitehead* teach them first, *That the Quakers are the True Church;* next, *That they are to believe as this true Church believes* *, and that the People love to have it so, *i. e.* like Teacher, like People, the Blind to lead the Blind, till both fall into the Ditch of Error and Heresie together; this is sad.

But says *Geo. Whitehead, No such Matter; I challenge Francis Bugg, and his Teachers, Abettors, and Congratulators, to produce those Books of the Quakers, with the Pages and Words, wherein we deny the same Jesus that was Born of the Virgin Mary, otherwise Retract and Condemn this Calumnious Aspersion* *.

This bold Challenge has been often answer'd †, and so fully, as I cannot pretend to; yet since this Error of the *Quakers* denying Christ seems to be the Mother of all their other Errors I shall for this Challenge sake, that so his Disciples may see his Impudence, herein also prove, that they (i. e. *Quakers*) do deny the *same Jesus* that was Born of that Virgin *Mary:* And if I do so, I think he is obliged to Retract his Errors, and Condemn the *Quakers* Books, which so teach, by the same Rule of arguing, *Viz.* That both I and my Abettors ought to condemn the Calumny cast on the *Quakers,* by such a Charge, if not true. And now to the Matter: *When Jesus*

---

*Yea, it was May 17. 1675. See Innocency Vindicated, &c. P. 8.

† Such a Man I have not found a-mongst their Teachers. Tho. Upshot came nearest; but when I came to ask him, whether he would justifie their Books? he flew off, saying, No, he would not meddle.

* See his Apost. Incend. &c. P. 3, 16.

* A Sober Expostulation with some of the Clergy, &c. p. 46.
† See *The Snake in the Grass*, 3d. Edit. p. 129, to 145. *Satan D. sobv'd*, &c. p. 8, 9, 13, 14. *Gleanings*, p. 2.

From Quakerism *to* Christianity.

sus came into the Coast of Cesarea Philippi, *he asked his Disciples, saying, whom do Men say that I THE SON OF MAN am*?* Simon Peter *answer'd and said, THOU art CHRIST, the SON of the LIVING GOD †.* Again, *And WE believe, and ARE SURE, that thou art THAT CHRIST, the SON of the LIVING GOD*.*

| *That the outward Person that suffer'd was properly the Son of God, we utterly deny. A Body hast thou prepared me, said the Son. Then the Son was not the Body, though the Body was the Son's.* "A Serious Apology, &c. by *W. Penn*, p. 146.

* Matth. 16. 13.
† Verse 16.
* John 6. 69.

Here you have the Question proposed by Christ himself, *Whom do Men say that I the SON OF MAN am?* You also hear St. *Peter's* answer, which is as plain and as home to the Purpose, as can be; and now you shall hear Christ's Approbation and Confirmation thereof: But you see the *Quakers* Answer is point blank contrary; yea, *W. Penn* does utterly deny, THAT PERSON who suffer'd at *Jerusalem* to be the SON OF GOD. Mark, *Reader,* Christ's Reply to St. *Peter's* Answer to his most Gracious Question, *Viz. And Jesus answer'd and said unto him, Blessed art thou* Simon Bar-jona, *for Flesh and Blood hath not revealed it unto thee, but my Father which is in Heaven *.*

* Mat. 16. 17. and 17. 5.

I think I need say no more, especially since this Point is so largely handled, and so fully proved upon the *Quakers* by that Reverend Author, in the Books above quoted: Only thus much I may add, That if St. *Peter* be Orthodox in this Point, then are the *Quakers* Heterodox; and that herein their utter Testimony is levell'd, that strikes at the very Foundation of Christianity; and as a Reply to G. *W.* I do offer *De Novo,* to prove, and I do now affirm, That the *Quakers* by their Books do deny the same Jesus that was Born of the Virgin *Mary*; THE SAME JESUS, to whom the Voice came from the excellent Glory, saying, *This is my Beloved Son, in whom I am well pleased, hear ye him:* THE SAME JESUS that St. *Paul* preached, *Acts* 17. THE SAME JESUS that St. *Peter* testified, saying, *Let the House of* Israel *know assuredly, that God hath made that SAME JESUS whom ye have CRUCIFIED, both LORD and CHRIST.* And this I offer to prove to G. *Whitehead Vive Voce,* at any convenient time, on Condition he will under his Hand covenant to condemn the *Quakers* Books, which so Teach, when proved upon him, as by his own Argumentation (in the *Challenge* above-recited) he is in Equity obliged too: And if I do not prove it, I will burn my Books, that so charge the *Quakers*; and let this be the Touchstone, to try us both; in the mean time, any *Quaker* that thinks I am in the Wrong, let them look first on *W. Penn's* Book, by me heretofore quoted, as well as this before me; and the Scriptures quoted in the Margin †,

† Luke 1. 26, 31, 32, 33, 35, 2. 10, 11, 12, 13. Matth. 16. 13, 16, 17, 20, 27. cap. 17. 5, 9, 12, 13, 26, 29. cap. 26, 27, 38, 50, 67. cap. 28. 6. Mark 9. 7. John 5. 22, 27. cap. 6. 69. Acts 1. 10, 11. cap. 5. 30, 31. cap. 2. 36. Heb. 5. 9. cap. 12. 2. Rom. 8. 34. 1 Cor. 15. 15. Acts 7. 35, 36. cap. 10. 38, to 44. cap. 17. 3. 31. cap. 18. 5. John 20. 31.

Margin, which I have taken Pains to collect, and he will then certainly find, that I have on my Side the Testimony of the Glorious Angels, Holy Apostles, Blessed Martyrs; yea, the whole Tenor of the Scriptures, and beside all this, a Cloud of Witnesses, *viz.* the Concurrent Testimony of the Ancient Fathers, and all the present Christian Churches to this Day, and that G. *Whitehead* will have none of his Side, but *W. Penn*, and a few of his Brethren; and the Writings of *Isaac Pennington, W. Bayly, W. Smith, Edw. Burrough, Geo. Fox, Ja. Nayler, Christ. Atkinson,* &c. But I knowing, that so soon as your Teachers once espy your looking towards Christianity, they will not only hinder you from reading such Books, that are or shall be wrote against *Quakerism*, but refuse you the Sight of such Books of theirs, as we quote; for so long as they can keep you in Ignorance, so long they may keep you *Quakers*; I shall therefore give you the same Quotations out of some of their Books, which I shall in this Book let you know where to have the most of them, *viz. William Penn*'s *Serious Apology,* &c. p. 146. *W. Smith*'s *Catechism,* &c. p. 57. *W. Smith*'s *Primer,* &c. p. 8. *W. Shewen*'s *Treatise of Thoughts,* &c. p. 35. *Jos. Coale*'s *Works,* &c. p. 93. *News coming up,* &c. p. 33. *The Teachers of the World Unvail'd,* &c. p. 35. *The Sword of the Lord drawn,* &c. p. 5. *Edw. Burrough*'s *Works,* p. 149, 273. *Geo. Fox*'s *Great Myst.* p. 206, 207, 210, 211, 250, 254. *The Quakers Challenge,* p. 6. *Saul's Errand to* Damascus, p. 7, 8. *Some Principles of the Elect People of God,* call'd Quakers, p. 126. *A Question to Professors,* &c. by Isaac Pennington, p. 25, 27, 33. *The Capital Principles of the People call'd* Quaker; *Sol. Eccles Testimony,* p. 24, 25, 41. *W. Penn*'s Part in *The Christian Quaker,* &c. p. 97, 98. *W. Penn*'s *Sandy Foundation,* &c. p. 10, to 30.

<small>Wrote by Dan. Leeds, who has been a Quaker about 20 Years.</small>
I shall now add something out of a Book, intituled, *News of a Trumpet sounding in the Wilderness,* &c. which is come lately out of *Pensilvania,* Printed 1697. and for the Usefulness of it I could be glad that it was reprinted, with this Title, *A Trumpet sounding from Pensilvania, giving an Alarum to the Magistrates & People of* England *to beware of Quakerism*: That so, not only the Justices of Peace, but even our Honourable Patriots, might have one put into their Hands: But all things in their Season, Quakerism had a time to advance, and it must have a time to fall: But as no Heresie, since the Days of Christ, ever rose so fast, prevailed so much, nor carried on with so much Craft, and curious Paint, so none ever fell so fast (as I am perswaded this of Quakerism will do) insomuch, as that in a few Years it will be a Shame, for any Man of Sense, to appear in the Streets, who owns the Principles and Practice of the *Quakers,* according to their Ancient Testimony.

And

From Quakerism *to* Christianity.

And now a Hint out of the *Pensilvanian* Book aforesaid, *viz.* 'Tho' they (i. e. *Quakers*) clash between their Old and New Testimonies, yet we see (says *D. Leeds*) that they have in their late Books dropt here and there some Christian Expressions, more than formerly: And what may we think they intend thereby? Why? *Geo. Whitehead* in his *Counterfeit Convert*, p. 72. says, I may see Cause otherwise to word the Matter, and yet our Intentions be the same. Now is it not admirable that a Man of *Geo. Whitehead*'s Pretences * should be grown so bold in Crafty and Deceiveable Glosses, to deceive his Readers? Is this like the Ancient Simplicity of the *Quakers*, to say, I may see cause otherwise to word the Matter, and yet intend the same? Pray who knows then when such a Man is sincere, or how to believe him in what he says; that thus hides his Meanings, says one thing, and mean another? *&c.* And now I cannot but expect (says *Daniel*, p. 42.) that there will be great Devising, Pulling and Drawing, (Painting and Glossing) rather than make Confession of their Errors, Confusion, and Contradictions herein Manifested and Charged, (as also in other Books, by *Geo. Keith*, *Tho. Crisp*, *Fr. Bugg*, and others) because they have so much accused their Opponents for the same things, (themselves are now justly charged with) surely some curious Wyre drawing, Mincing, Mangling, otherwise Wording and Equivocating †, we must expect; but they having caught themselves in this Net, the more they flutter, the more they'll fetter, insnare, and entangle themselves; for they cannot thus dance in a Net, but some Body will see them: For they are now as easily seen thorough (God be thanked) as they pretend to see through others; yea, this will certainly be the Consequence, till they use the only Christian Means to get out of this Net, which is by Humbly Confessing and Condemning their Errors in their Books, as *Geo. Keith* has done, *&c.*

News of a Trumpet sounding, *&c.* P. 21.

* To Seriousness, to Sincerity, to Reality, to Fidelity, to Constancy, to Infallibility, to Perfection, to Plainness, *&c.* Ibid. 42.

† *G. W.* You must now call your Brother *Ellwood*, and your whole Society of Jesuitical Scribes, for the Alarum is founded in your Pope's Borders.

To all which I cannot but joyn, and wish for their own sakes it may be so, adding, that if ever it so come to pass, then I shall see a great Truth in what *Tho. Ellwood* wrote to his Friends, *viz.* The *way to recover the Deceived, is to discover and lay open the Deceivers.* In the mean time, taking it to be a sound Truth, I have adventured to put his Doctrine in practice, and so I conclude this Passage out of that Useful and Compendious Book, from *Pensilvania*; which had that People receiv'd, my Advice in my Postscript to my Book, intituled, *De Christianæ Libertate*, *&c.* Printed 1682. p. 214. *viz. To frequent the Holy Scriptures, and read them diligently, &c.* this might have been prevented.

Tho. Ellwood's Epistle to Friends, *&c.* p. 72.

And now, to conclude my Advice, lest any should prevent you taking the Advice I gave the *Pensilvanians*, 16 Years ago, as above, I shall, according to my further Experience in this Pilgrimage, tell you,

Y

162   *The Pilgrim's Progress,*

you, that it was the Practice, both of the Church of the *Jews*, and the Christians, (which for Substance are one) to Read and Expound the Scriptures in their Assemblies, (which the *Quakers* call Conjuration) from Morning to Mid-day, and to give the Meaning thereof to the People *, out of the Law of God, given forth by *Moses*; and Christ himself went into their Synagogue, as his Custom was, where he stood up for to read: And when the Book of *Isaiah* the Prophet was given to him, he found (which argues he sought for) a proper place of Scripture; and when he had read, he then, in a Friendly manner, gave the Minister his Book again, and did not fall upon him, and call him Conjurer, Beast, Dog, Witch, Devil, Bloodhound, &c †. but Preached out of what he read, and Expounding it to the People; insomuch, that the Eyes of all the Assembly were fastned on him when they heard his Gracious Sayings *; and at another time, suitable to his own Example, he bad the Jews *search the Scriptures, for they are them which testified of me* †. And after he was Risen from the Dead, how did he appear to his Disciples, and reasoned out of the Scriptures, beginning at *Moses*, and all the Prophets, he expounded unto them in all the Scriptures the things concerning himself, saying unto them, *These are the Words which I spake unto you, whilst I was with you; that all things must be fulfilled which are written in the Law, and in the Prophets, and in the Psalms, concerning me.* Thus did he confirm the Scriptures by his Holy Example; both before and after his Crucifixion, he did not question whether *Moses* or *Hermes* were the first Pen-man thereof; or whether, either or neither, as the *Quakers* do *, in order to Invalidate it, and to overthrow the Divine Authority of it; no, no, he confirm'd them, saying, *The Scriptures cannot be broken* †: Think not (said he) *that I am come to destroy the Law, or the Prophets:* No, no, *it is* (said he) *easier for Heaven and Earth to pass, than for one tittle of the Law to fail, till all be fulfilled* *. And St. *Paul* said, *The Law is our Schoolmaster to bring us to Christ* †: And it was his manner, to go into the *Jews* Synagogue, to Reason with them out of the Scriptures, opening and alledging, that Christ must needs have Suffer'd and Risen from the Dead; proving out of the Scriptures, that the same Jesus which he Preached (who was Prophesied of *, and in due time was Born of the Virgin *Mary*) was the Christ. Read *Acts* 17. read *New Rome Arraigned*, &c. p. 55. to 58. &c.

Here we may see, that neither the Ministers of the Church of the *Jews*, nor Christ, nor his Apostles, call'd the Scriptures, Death, Dust, Beastly Wares, the Husk, Carnal *, Serpents Food, &c. as the Prophane *Quakers* Blasphemously do, as appears from the Books of their Prophets, of greatest Note, *Fox*, *Whitehead*, &c. And if you will look into the Apology of *Justin Martyr*, and the Writings

margin notes:
* 1 Chron. 34. 8, 19, 35. Nehem. 8. 1, 2. Ezra 1. 10, 11.
† As the Quakers does their Ministers.
* Luk. 14. 14, 16, 27, 18, 19, 20, 21.
† John 5. 39.
John 24. 27, 44.
* The Quakers Refuge fixed, &c. p. 17.
† John 10. 35.
* Mat. 5. 17, 18. John 16. 17.
† Gal. 3. 24.
* Mich. 5. 2. Psal. 2. 2. 22. 18. Isa. 61. 1. 9. 7. Deut. 18. 15. Jer. 23. 5. Exod. 12. 46. Numb. 9. 12. 11. 9.
* See the Quakers Plainness, &c. p.

of the Fathers; as St. *Cyprian*, St. *Augustine*, *Origen*, *Chrysostom*, *Isidorus*, *Tertullian*, &c. and into the Practice of our present Church of *England*, you will still find the same: But for your further Instruction in these Matters, I rather refer you to our Reverend Bishops and Clergy, who can better inform you.

Thus having kept nothing back from you, which I think may make a Discovery of the *Quakers* Faith, Doctrine, and Practice, to be contrary to the Faith, Doctrine and Practice of the Jewish, as well as the Christian Church, to that of the Apostles, Primitive Christians, Saints and Martyrs, in all Ages; I shall Conclude this Chapter, begging of God to bless my Labours, to those Ends by me designed, which are best known to him, and my own Conscience; which, whether you believe it or not, is, that you may be thereby helped to understand your Errors; that thereby you may be prevailed upon to beg God's Assistance, to help you out of them, and receive the Benefit of it. *Amen.*

July 30. 1698.

Fran. Bugg.

† Respecting some particular Discoveries, not but there were earlier Pens at work against Quakerism.

To write no more, I long since did intend,
But now, I hope, that Work is near an end:
For abler Men do daily now come in,
To finish what I think I did begin †.

AN APPENDIX.

Discovering a most Damnable Plot, by a United Confederacy, carried on by the chief Emissaries of New-Rome, *against the* Christian Religion, *and* Christian Reputation *of the* Professors *thereof; with a Remedy against it, both Easie and Safe.*

READER,

HAving gone thro' many things (tho' briefly) I do now say, that it was not of my seeking, nor my Choice; I could have been glad to have seen the *Quakers* to have Retracted their Gross Errors, and thereby remove the Cause; but they have slighted all due Methods that are consistent with a Reformation*: For when *Geo. Whitehead* gave forth a Sheet, entituled, *The Quakers Vindication, &c.* saying, Col. 2. P. 3, 4. ' I ' *G. W.* freely offer, and am willing to make it plainly appear before ' ANY Six, Ten, or Twelve Competent Witnesses, who are mode- ' rate Men, of common Sense and Reason, That *Francis Bugg* has ' grosly wronged the *Quakers*, both in Charge, Citation, and Ob- ' servation, *&c.* I then did meet him, and we agreed upon the Preliminaries, upon which we were to debate; but when I came to name Persons, he flew off. Now, by the Contents of his Offer, I had my Liberty to chuse ANY; yea, all the Men, provided they were moderate Men, of common Sense and Reason. But, to avoid his Charge of Partiality, I admitted, that he should have his equal Choice of one part of the Men: And that he might see I would take no Advantage at his Word ANY, whereby I was left free where to make my Choice, as well as who, I offer'd him to chuse out of the Ministers of the Episcopalians, Presbyterians, Independants, or Baptists †; but none would down with him but *Quakers*: Nay, to chuse our Men out of any, or all those Four Christian Societies; which had he been sincere, he could not have denied, since it was his own

* Observe what Proposals I and others have made in our Books.

† I mention this here, because 'tis Rumour'd in Town, that he offered to meet me with the *Baptists*; a horrible Lye.

volun-

APPENDIX.

voluntary Offer: Nay, when he refused to close on this Bottom, as if he feared he could not chuse Six moderate Men of common Sense in all those Societies; I then offer'd him to chuse each of us three Members of the Honourable House of Commons *, and to them we would leave our Matter in contest: But this he refused also; and there being some Gentlemen present, they advised me to send him a Letter to that end, and they would subscribe it, which I did; their Names are as followeth, viz.

* Viz. Whether I had wronged them in Charge, Quotation, or Citation, &c. Febr. 1693.

Samuel Grove,   Henry Symons,   And also
Samuel Plaice,   John Fenn;   Daniel Haffel,

But this Offer G. W. also rejected, which to the Gentlemen above-named, as well as to my self, (and indeed to all that have since understood it) was, and is a Sign of great Guilt and Insincerity in him which indeed is manifest in most of his Answers to several Opposers. Well, I was not yet willing to give over this Meeting, but I offer'd him to lay aside these Men, and the Advantages I had thereby, and to have a Publick Meeting with him, provided he would first engage, under his Hand, to Retract and Condemn what I proved Erroneous, Blasphemous, and Idolatrous, in the *Quaker* Books; but this he also Refused *, which to me is a sufficient Evidence, that he is Self-condemn'd, and Conscious to himself, of the *Quakers* Manifest and Apparent Errors, which he is not able to vindicate, as in an hundred Instances I might mention, but I will only name one in this Place, viz. *W. Rogers* having wrote, ‘ That the *Quakers* ‘ looked upon *Geo. Fox* to be in that Place amongst the Children of ‘ Light in this our Day; as *Moses* was amongst the Children of ‘ *Israel* in his Day, to set forth Methods of Church-Government†, &c. as recited by me herein, p. 20. To this *Geo. Whitehead* replied, saying, ‘ And for *Geo. Fox*, to be in this our Day in that VERY ‘ Place amongst the Children of Light, as *Moses* was amongst the ‘ Children of *Israel* in his Day; this Comparison we own not, &c.

* As at large in my Book, *Quakcrism Withering*, &c. p. 5, 6, 7, 8.

† The Christian Quaker distin &c. part 1. p. 9. part 4. p. 83.

Now there was no Body said, that he was in the VERY Place, upon the VERY Spot of Ground, on which *Moses* stood, at *Mount Sinai*: No, but that G. *Fox* was, with respect to his Power and Authority, to give forth Laws, Statutes and Ordinances in the same Place; that is, endued with a like Authority: And this Sence G. W. did not deny, but only that he might quibble it off, as his manner has been †, and thereby blind the People, for which he has a sore Cup to drink: He that deceives willingly, and of set purpose, as I am certain has been his Custom, what shall we say to such a one, but must leave him to God, the Righteous Judge?

Exod. 1. 9.
† Read *Burrough's Works*, p. 515. and *G.W's Serious Search*, p. 51, 52, 53. and Third Part of the *Quaker's Quibbles*, p. 33, to 44. 85, to 95. And *Dan. Leed's Voice of a Trumpet*, p. 4, to 40.

G. *Fox*, Jun. speaking in the Person of the *Quaker's* Light, viz. ‘ You have in your Imaginations put me afar off, and will not own ‘ me the Light and Life in you: ---- I the Light will overturn King-‘ doms,

APPENDIX.

<small>The Light and Life of Christ within, &c. p. 11.
† News of a Trumpet founded, &c. p. 109, 110.</small>

'doms, Nations, and gathered Churches, which will not own me
'the Light in them: I will make you know, that I the Light
'which lighteth every Man that comes into the World; am the
'true Eternal God, &c. This *Whitehead* vindicates *; yea, if we
'consider what Titles G. *Fox* puts upon himself, as *Daniel Leeas* says †,
'Professing Equality with God. *A brief Relation*, &c. p. 2, 3. *Gr.*
'*Myst.* p. 67. 127. *Saul*'s Errand, p. 6, 7, 8. *News coming up*, &c.
'p. 1. *Quaker's Challenge*, &c. p. 6. And G. *Whitehead* and *W.*
'*Penn*'s Vindication of those Divine Attributes, given to G. *Fox*,
'in their Books, *A Serious Search*, p. 58. *Judas* and the *Jews*, &c.
'p. 44. *Judgment fixed*, &c. p 19, 20. *Innocency against Envy*, &c.
'p. 18. *The Accuser of our Brethren*, &c. p. 40, 41. together with
'*Fox*'s being thus set up a Worker of Miracles too: I say, (says *D.L.*)
'should the *Jews* give equal Credit to the things contained in their
'Books, with the History of St. *Luke*, how shall they know who
'is the Messiah, GEO. FOX, or JESUS OF NAZA-
'RETH; especially, since *W. Penn* denies that Outward Person to
'be the Son of God, which suffer'd at *Jerusalem*, who was called
'JESUS OF NAZARETH? See his *Ser. Apol.* &c. p.
'146. Good Christian Reader, (says *D. Leeds*, yea, and *Fr. Bugg*)
'consider the EVENT and EFFECTS of these things; be (we
'intreat you) otherwise minded, than G. *Whitehead* is, who says,
'he neither consults EVENTS, nor fears EFFECTS in what he
'writes *.

<small>* See his Judgment Fixed, &c. Introd.</small>

Thus then does it appear, not only by what is here quoted, but by what is taken from the Quakers Books, in this, and other of my Books; in *D. Leed*'s Books, in *G. Keith*'s Books, in *Th. Crisp*'s Books, and others, that Quakerism is a Plot against Christianity, and strikes at it Root and Branch.

I cannot but foresee, that my old Friends will be half angry with me, for mentioning *W. Penn*'s plotting to subvert the Government: But this I can tell them honestly, that since the Danger of that is over, and His Majesty has, out of his Gracious Favour, pardon'd him, I should not speak a Word of it, did I not see, that he, and his Brethren, are in a most Damnable Plot against the Christian Religion, of which I gave Notice in *The Pict. of Quak.* p. 72, to 102. But since that Alarum did not sound loud enough, I have already, and shall yet sound a little louder, that so all Ears may tingle, and Hearts may lament, when they see the Honour of our Christian Religion defam'd, and the Holy Profession thereof invaded by these Impostors. But why should they be angry? *W. Penn* has given me a Challenge to it, saying; 'This one open Challenge I make, that if
'amongst the many Plots that have been spoken of, and several have
'been bring'd for; there has been ONE KNOWN QUAKER found
'amongst them: I confess, that the Magistrate is excuseable in his
'Discreet

APPENDIX.

Difcreet Jealoufie over US, &c. But then if one Inftance of a *Quaker*-Traytor is fufficient to juftifie the Difcreet Jealoufie of the Magiftrates over the *Quakers*, as *William Penn* truly fays; then to make up a Pair, I may give a fecond Inftance; namely, *John Yates*, a Quaker, who liv'd at *Hull*, a Mafter of a Ship, who fer carrying Lead into *France* in the time of the late War, had his Eftate feiz'd; but himfelf fled from his Dwelling, and was forced to hide, as his Partner did, or elfe in all Probability he might have been Hang'd alfo; for tho' they cannot fight, (as they fay) yet they can carry Lead to make Bullets for the *French* to kill the *Englifh* with. All which fhews, that the Magiftrates Difcreet Jealoufie over the *Quakers*, is excufable by *W. Penn*'s Allowance, and truly I am of that Opinion too; and not only in that Cafe, but alfo in their moft Horrible Plot againft Chriftianity, which tends directly to fubvert the Faith, in the Crucified Jefus, and therewith the Foundation of Chriftianity; and I pray God to give the Magiftracy a true Senfe hereof, and then to infpire them with an Holy Zeal, to find out a Remedy

For I do fay, that to me it does plainly appear, (and to as many as of late have been Converfant in their Writings, and who have obferved the Tendency of them, together with the whole Frame and Model of their Church-Government) that Quakerifm is a moft Formidable Plot, and a United Confederacy againft both the Chriftian Religion, the Profeffors thereof; together with the Holy Scriptures, and Ordinances of Baptifm and Supper, inftituted by Chrift Jefus, alfo his Death and Sufferings, and that in order to exalt their own Laws and Ordinances, fet up amongft them by their fecond *Mofes*, whom they faid was raifed up to be amongft them in the fame place that *Mofes* was, amongft the *Ifraelites*, tho' not in the VERY fame Place, refpecting *Mount Sinai*, where *Mofes*'s Feet ftood, as above obferv'd: But that I may not impofe upon my Reader, I fhall yet give fome other, or more Inftances, than I have given *. Read *W. Penn*'s Ser. Apol. &c. p. 150. where he thus faith: ' We 'have a Red Catalogue, that fhall ftand recorded againft our *Pref-* '*byterian* and *Independant* Perfecutors; that their Names and Na-'tures too may ftink to Pofterity, &c. read alfo the Books referr'd 'to in the Margin †.

Reader, This is the fourth Warning we have had from the *Quakers* themfelves of this Plot, which they are laying, and which they are preparing for future Ages againft the Chriftian Name and Reputation of the *Englifh* Magiftrate †. And that the *Quakers* Plot is againft the Value of the Death of Chrift; the Exemplary Suffering of the Apoftles, and Martyrs, read *Burrough*'s Works, p. 273. where they fay; ' That the Suffering of the Peó'ple of God (call'd *Quakers*) in this Age, is a greater Suffering, 'and more Unjuft, than in the Days of Chrift, or his Apoftles, or ' in

* Tho' I think I have given fufficient Reafons already.
† *Judas and the Jews*, &c. p. 41. *A Rejoynder*, &c. p. 410. *The Anarchy of Ranters*, &c. p. 42. *A Ser. Apol.* p. 150. *The Picture of Quakerifm*,&c. p. 102, 103. has them at large.

APPENDIX

*Here you see, that the Ten Persecutions, the Bloody Massacres, and Queen *Mary's* Reign, are all less than the Sufferings of the *Quakers* in seven Years time. Oh Monstrous! Oh Horrible!

‘ in any time since *. What was done to Christ and the Apostles, ‘ was chiefly done by a Law, and in great part by the DUE Execu- ‘ tion of a Law: And hereby it appears, the Suffering to be more ‘ Unjust, because what the Persecutors of old time did to the People ‘ of God, they did by a Law, and by the DUE Execution of a Law.

Now, *Reader*, consider what these new Prophets say; and if thou art a Christian, I do solemnly appeal to thee, whether this Doctrine of the *Quakers*, these Impudent *Quakers*, hath not a Tendency, to cause the Names of the Martyrs to stink; in regard it implies they were Criminals, and suffer'd under the Emperors by a Law, and the DUE Execution of their Law; for it could not be a JUST or DUE Execution, unless the Law were Just: Do they not hereby, what in them lies, acquit the hard-hearted Jews; the Barbarous Emperors, and Bloody Papists, of their Bloody Cruelties, and Implicitely Charge both Christ, and his Apostles, and Martyrs, with the Breach of some Just Laws; for which, their Penalties (say they) were DULY Executed: And if so, is not this a Damnable Plot? Not to name other Blasphemies, which lye Couched under this Doctrine; as also, the *Quakers* Pride and Arrogance, thus to exalt their Sufferings, from 1650, to 1657. to be greater than the Sufferings of Christ his Apostles, and Martyrs: And this Plot is still carrying on with Vigour not only against the *Presbyterians*, *Independants*, and *Baptists*, to make their Names and Natures stink in the Nostrils of future Generations, when the surviving *Quakers* bring out their Books of Sufferings, *alias* Martyrdom. But behold this Book of theirs. with the said great Sufferings, greater than that of Christ, and all his Martyrs, since was reprinted *Anno* 1672. and witnessed too by the Approbation of *Geo. Fox*, *Geo. Whitehead*, *Josiah Coale*,

*For what one writ, the other avouch; they speak all one thing, are of one Mind.

Francis Howgill, and their Hireling, *Ellis Hooks* *; so that when they have gathered up all their Sufferings in the Reign of K. *Ch.* II. K. *J.* II. and King *William* III. (for they are still collecting all their Sufferings compleat and full, as in Page 41. herein) no doubt but they will make them to exceed all the Sufferings of the Patriarchs and Prophets, from the Blood of Righteous *Abel*, to the Days of Christ, and from thence to the end of the Chapter, in *Infinitum*. O rare, this will be according to their Ancient Testimony in *Geo. Whitehead's* Sermon, insomuch, that this Hellish and Damnable Plot is against the Patriarchs, Prophets, Christ, and his Apostles, Saints, and Martyrs, in all Ages and Generations. And this is the main Business of their whole Body, in their Convocations, both in their Monthly, Quarterly, Six Week, Second Day, and Yearly Meetings; which ought to be taken Care of, at least Inspected, tho' they have their Liberty of Meeting in those Houses, licensed to Preach and Pray; for at those Meetings there is so many Spectators, that they cannot do that Hurt and Damage to the Christian Religion, they

do

do in thefe Private, Lockt, and Barr'd up Private Conventicles: Thus then it appears, that this Plot is carrying on againſt King, Lords, and Commons; againſt Judges, Councellors, and Lawyers, againſt the Reverend Biſhops, Clergy, and all Proteſtant Miniſters; againſt Sheriffs, Conſtables, and Headboroughs, and indeed, againſt the whole Race of Mankind, that profeſs Faith in Jeſus Chriſt; and therefore how do it concern all Chriſtians, that have any Love to; and Faith in our Lord Jeſus Chriſt, that have any Reſpect to our Martyr'd Anceſtor, who ſuffer'd in the Flames for our Holy Religion, to take Care of the Growth of *Quakeriſm*, as they will anſwer the Neglect of it at the Great and Notable Day of the Lord.

Objection. By this time ſome may be ready to object, ſaying, *Francis,* Does not thy Zeal exceed thy Judgment? What, wouldſt thou have Fire to come down from Heaven, and conſume them, as *Elias* did*? Wouldſt thou have the Government fall upon them, and deſtroy them? 2 *Kings* 1. 10. *Luke* 9. 54.

Anſwer. No; by no means I would not be underſtood ſo; for this I ſolemnly declare, in the Fear of God, and as I hope for Mercy at the Great Day of Account, when both they and I ſhall appear before his Great Tribunal, I do deſire neither; I would not have a Hair of their Head hurt: Beſides, if I did deſire the Growth of *Quakeriſm,* that is the ready way to increaſe them; for they glory in nothing more than to be thought great Sufferers: No; let them have Liberty in their Licenſed Meeting-Houſes, to Preach, Pray, and exerciſe their Talent, equal with others, if the Government think fit: And as this is all that other Diſſenters deſire or expect, ſo if they had not a further Deſign, this would content them, being that which anſwers the Subſtance of all their Petitions and Addreſſes to the Parliament, from one Reign to another, together with not being compell'd to go to any other Worſhip: And they having both granted, I think 'tis all that is neceſſary to anſwer the Ends of all their frequent and endleſs Sollicitations: And nothing of this do I deſire to have them debarr'd of.

Obj. But then ſome may ſay, what other way is there, to put a Stop to the Growth of *Quakeriſm,* if they have this Liberty? Such an Expedient would be requiſite, if ſuch an one were to be found.

Anſw. I have once offered my Thoughts in this Caſe, and ſhall now enlarge thereon: For as I then ſaid, ſo I ſtill believe, that the main requiſite to work a Cure, is to know the Diſeaſe; which, when found out, an ordinary Practitioner may preſcribe a Remedy ſooner than an abler Phyſician, who knows not the Diſeaſe. Beſides this, I have heard, that when a Bill for the Regulation of the well-Tanning of Leather was brought into the *Houſe of Parliament,* one of the Peers of the Lord's Houſe being willing to inform himſelf into the Nature of that Affair, he apply'd himſelf to a *Cobler*; diſcourſes with

APPENDIX.

with him about this, that, and the other Default in Leather, and what Ways might be found to remedy the Abuses thereof, for the Publick Good. The *Cobler* tells his Honour what he knew, by many Years Experience, and told his Lordship how it might with Ease be remedied: Insomuch, that when the said Bill came under Debate in the House, his Lordship was so well skill'd, not only in the Means to be used, but in the Terms of Art, that his Lordship spake like some experienced *Tanner*, who by his Discourse gave Light to the whole House. Now whether this was so or no, I will not determine, but 'tis not Improbable, since the wisest of Men may sometimes improve by such weak Helps, as in other Cases 'tis frequent; such a Vertue is Humility: And thereupon, in answer to the Objection, I shall say thus much.

First, Let *G. Whitehead*, and some others of the *Quakers* chief Leaders, and *Fr. Bugg*, &c. be summon'd by Authority, to appear: And whereas *G. Whitehead*, &c. has given in a Sheet to the Parliament, *Anno* 1693. suggesting, that *Fran. Bugg*, &c. has wronged the *Quakers* in Charge, Citation, and Observation: And if *G. W.* can make it appear so, (for our Law judge no Man before it hear him) let *Fran. Bugg*, &c. be made an Example. Again, on the other Hand, if it appear that *Fran. Bugg*, &c. has not wronged the *Quakers*, nor falsly charged them, either in Book or Page; and that those Points of Doctrine objected against the *Quakers* by *F. B.* &c. be found to strike at the Foundation of the Christian Religion, and to subvert the Faith, then let the *Quakers* be oblig'd to renounce them, and condemn those Books which so teach: THIS, yea, this, would strike *Quakerism* to the Heart *, and give it a Mortal Wound, and preserve the *Quakers* too; and the Books being condemn'd to be burnt, as it would remove the Scandal brought upon the Christian Religion, so would it be a Means to Rescue their Wives and Children from the Jaws of Quakerism, that fatal Mischief to Mankind, and preserve others from falling into it. For now many of them think their Teachers write and speak from the Eternal Spirit; whose so speaking is of greater Authority than the Bible †: And that 'tis as lawful to burn the Bible, as their Books, Papers, and Queries *: Then would those, who are now Tinctured with the Leaven of Quakerism, vomit it up, and forsake their Errors: This I take to be one proper Remedy, and possible might effect the Cure: If not,

* This is the tiring feared by *G. W.* &c. when they cry out, *Fran. Bugg* would stir up Persecution.

† Truth defending the *Quakers*, &c. p. 7.
* Truth's Defence, &c. p. 2. 104.

Secondly, If the *Quakers* would Apologize, that now they believe otherwise than they did formerly; then, as a Proof of their Sincerity and Conversion, let them (having first condemn'd their Books as aforesaid) set out certain Articles of their Faith, in Plain, Clear, and Possitive Words, agreeable to Scripture, (since of late they have so much pretended to be Orthodox therein) and at the Close of them condemn all their other Books, which teach the contrary, particularly by Name.

Thirdly,

APPENDIX.

Thirdly, The next thing requisite, (to make a firm and lasting Cure to them, their Heirs, and Successors) is, to admit each Congregation of *Quakers* to have their Teacher, (or two, if one will not do): And likewise, that these Teachers may attend only their own Flock, and not to range all the World over; at most, not above Five or Ten Miles, to hold forth, lest this Putrified Sore break out again, and the last end be worse than their beginning: And as this, thus granted, is, what other Professors, Dissenters from the Church of *England*, are content with, so will it answer all the just Ends of that Liberty of Conscience, so much by them sollicited for, and so graciously already granted by the Government.

Fourthly, Let them not be permitted to hold Yearly CONVOCATIONS with Doors Lockt, Barr'd, or Guarded by Men, on Purpose to prevent Inspection, in order to make Laws against the Laws of the Land; and with respect to their Subjects, to repeal such Laws as suit not their Design; which shews, that they are a Government within the Government: For as this Practice no Dissenters (*Quakers* only excepted) do desire, (and indeed without his Majesty's Licence, more than the Bishops of the established Church can Legally do) so would it be a Means to work a perfect Cure of this (so much to be lamented) Gangreen of *Quakerism*. *Whose Laws thus made, they keep private, even from many of their own People.*

Fifthly and *Lastly,* That they may not be permitted to teach School Publickly; for thereby they corrupt the Youth, and lay a Foundation for the next Age, for the Seeds of *Quakerism* to spring, and put forth again; for they teach G. Fox's *Journal*, which contains such Doctrine, as tends to undermine the Christian Religion.

Thus having answer'd these two Objections, I shall add no more on this Head, only refert to my former Book *, for more of this Nature, which probably may be of good Use, if the poor Man's Councel be taken †. Read *Joshua* the 9th. at your Leisure. ** The Picture of Quakerism, Part 2. p.121, to 128. † Eccles. 9. 14, 15, 16.*

And now to conclude, with a Word of Encouragement to such who are concern'd in the Discovery of *Quakerism:* Do you not remember the Day, (I am sure I do) how the *Quaker* Teachers went into Churches, and disturb'd the Established Ministers? But now none must disturb them; if they do, the Officer is call'd for, and the Offender prosecuted: A certain Sign what they would do in other Cases, had they Power. I say, do you not remember how they challenged the Publick Ministers to dispute, to answer their Queries? &c. It would take a Volumn to handle this Matter thoroughly; but behold here is a Change with them; you may challenge them long enough, but cannot get them out of their Holes; they see, and know they are discover'd: this makes them Timorous, and as the Scriptures say, Fearfulness surprize the Hypocrites. They see this, that, and the other Book come out against them, which they cannot answer, nor are they able to defend themselves; and now they

APPENDIX.

call out for a Cessation of Arms, and are for an Amicable Conversation; yea, for Peace and Quietness; and 'tis Seditious to challenge them, and remind them of their Errors; this is against *Magna Charta*, say they. *Geo. Keith* hath three times called them out, and challenged them, but they dare not appear, but like self-condemn'd Apostates, lye mute; whereby it's manifest, their Innocency so much boasted of, is not Triumphant *, as *G.W.* says: And therefore, the way to deal with these cunning Sophisters, *G. W. &c.* is still to pursue them with Challenges, to call them into the Field; and thereupon I will pitch my Standard here, on Behalf of the Christian Religion, and Protestant Profession, against *Quakerism*, Head and Tail, and once more challenge G. *Whitehead* to appear on his own Proposition to the Parliament, *viz.* for each of us to chuse four or six moderate Men, of common Sense and Reason, out of the Professors † of the Christian Faith, and let us dispute it out fairly, and aboveboard: And thereupon I shall renew my Challenge, and let it stand here as a Monument of the *Quakers* Cowardice, and Self-Condemnation, if they'd rather lye under this heavy Charge following, than to come out, and make their Defence, *Viz.*

* See his Book, *Innocency Triumphant, &c.*

† I call it his, because he did voluntarily offer to meet me before ANY Six, Ten, or Twelve moderate Men, &c.

First, That they deny Jesus of *Nazareth*, who was Born of the Blessed Virgin *Mary*, who suffer'd without the Gates of *Jerusalem*, to be Christ, the Son of the Living God.

Secondly, That they deny the Scriptures, by their speaking contemptuously of them; calling them Carnal, Death, Dust, Beastly Ware, Serpents Meat, *&c.* and that Preaching out of them, is Conjuration.

Thirdly, That they exalt their own Sayings and Writings above the Scriptures, as being of greater Authority, and of more Certainty; not only in Words, but in Practice.

Fourthly, That they undervalued the Death and Sufferings of Christ Jesus, by granting, they were Inflicted by, or for the Transgression of a Law, and executed in a great Measure (at least) by the due Execution of a Law.

Fifthly, That they exalt their own Sufferings, as greater, and more unjust, than the Sufferings of Christ, his Apostles, and Martyrs; yea, even than all the Persecutions, from the Days of Christ, to the Year of their Rise, namely 1650.

Sixthly, And that (for these and the like Reasons) the *Quakers* Books (which thus reach) are Blasphemous; and their Practices (in their Adorations) are Idolatrous.

This is my Charge, which I have often laid down, and which I now renew, and offer to make good upon them, if he will chuse his Men, and meet me according to his own voluntary Offer, and my Acceptation thereof; or otherwise, because I will give him his

Choice

APPENDIX. 173

Choice of two Methods, *viz.* or on CONDITION*, that he *G. White-*
head, will engage under his Hand to Retract their Errors, if proved
upon them, out of the *Quaker* Books, wrote by their approved Authors, and condemn the Books which teach this Horrible Doctrine,
promising my self also to engage under my Hand to Retract what he
prove erroneous in my Books, or false in Fact, relating to my charg-
ing the *Quakers,* thereby making them publick Satisfaction; and to
burn my Books, if found guilty, as a Testimony of my Injustice *:
And to this I subscribe my Name, *August.* 3. 1698. *Fran. Bugg.*

* At *Oxford* I offer'd *Sylas Norton* to prove the same Charge, against the *Quakers* and their Doctrine.

* A Sign of my not being Conscious of Guilt herein.

This then is my Flag of Defiance, which I hold out to *G. W.* &c.
this is my Standard which I have pitched ON Behalf of my Saviour
Jesus Christ, which the *Quakers* have Contemned, Disown'd, and
Denied to be the Son of God; ON the Behalf of the Scriptures,
which the *Quakers* say are Dust, Death, Beastly Ware, Serpents
Meat, *&c.* ON the Behalf of the Holy Ordinances of Baptism and
the Lord's Supper, which Christ Instituted; ON the Behalf of
the Church of *England*, both Magistrates and Ministers, which the
Quakers have most wickedly Traduced and Abused, as Intolerable
to bear, and Seditious in its own Nature. Let them come forth out
of their Dens and Holes, and acquit themselves like Men, if they
think I wrong them, or else be content to lye under my Charge, as
self-condemned Persons; and let them also know, that my Book, *New
Rome Arraigned, &c.* stands unshaken, and that *G. Whitehead* is
not Triumphant, but forced by the Guilt of his Conscience, to
submit to the Charge above exhibited, which is Ignoble and Base,
on his Part, and will lower his Topsail, to his great Abasement,
Shame, and Confusion of Face, in the Eyes of all sorts of Intelligent
Persons.

Thus having stated the Contest between *G.W.* and me, and advised
my Friends and Fellow-Labourers, not so much to answer the *Quakers*
Books, as to Charge and Recharge them again and again, till they
at last, (being confounded with Shame, Horror and Confusion,)
be forced to come out: But I shall shew *Whitehead's* Fallacy in his
way of answering Books, only by one Instance; for I having in my
Book *New Rome Arraign'd, &c.* p. 47. by way of Retaliation upon the *Quakers,* who call the Publick Ministers, Antichrist's and
Deceivers, and the World's Teachers, I having given Fifteen Instances why the *Quakers* are the World's Teachers and Deceivers,
the second of which was this: *The Quakers, who teach, that the
Name JESUS and CHRIST belong to the whole Body, and every Member in the Body, as well, and as amply, as to Christ the
Head; are of the World, and Deceivers* *. Now this was no Quotation, but a Charge, which rest for me to prove; I grant the Word
AMPLY is by me added by way of Illustration: But the Words
AS WELL, that *G. W.* neither mention, nor disown. *Isaac Penington's*

* *New Rome Arraigned,&c.* p. 47.

APPENDIX.

ton's Words are, *Doth not the Name (*Jesus *and* Christ*) belong to the whole Body, and every Member in the Body, AS WELL as to the* HEAD: ---- *So that the* NAME *is not given to the* VES-SEL, *but to the Nature* IN THE VESSEL†. P. 33. *The Scripture does expresly distinguish between* CHRIST *and the* GARMENT *which he wore*; *between* HIM *that came, and the* BO-DY, *in which he came*; *between the* SUBSTANCE, *which was* VAIL-ED, *and the* VAIL *which* VAILED *it. Lo I come*; *a Body hast thou prepared me*; *there is plainly* HE, *and the* BODY *in which* HE *came*; *there was the* OUTWARD VESSEL, *and the* INWARD LIFE; *this we certainly know* (says *Isaac*) *and can never call the* BODILY GARMENT, CHRIST, *&c.* And whoever read the Scriptures, may clearly see that the *Quakers* are false Teachers, in that they first teach, that the Name JESUS and CHRIST belong to every Believer, AS WELL as to CHRIST THE HEAD, since they can first call him, as you have heard, *A Garment, a Vessel, a Vail, a Body*, but in express Words, they say, they cannot call HIM Christ : But whoever read the Scriptures by me quoted, in the Sixteenth Chapter, I hope they will be convinced. And St. *John* says, *Then Pilate therefore took Jesus, and scourged him*; *Then came Jesus forth, wearing a Crown of Thorns*; *Then the Soldiers, when they had Crucified Jesus, they took his Garments*; *But one of the Soldiers with a Spear pierced his Side : She turned her self back, and saw Jesus: Jesus saith unto her, touch me not, for I am not yet ascended:* Thomas *said, except I shall see in his Hands the Print of the Nails, and put my Finger into the Print of the Nails, and thrust my Hand into his Side, I will not believe : Then saith he* (Jesus) *to* Thomas, *reach hither thy Finger, and behold my Hands, and reach hither thy Hand, and thrust it into my Side, and be not faithless, but believing : And* Thomas *answered unto him, my Lord, and my God : And many other Signs truly did Jesus, in the Presence of his Disciples, which are not written in this Book*; *but these are written, that ye might believe that* JESUS *is the* CHRIST, *the* SON OF GOD: *And that believing, you might have Life through* HIS NAME†.

Thus then it is evident, that the SAME JESUS that was Born of the *Virgin Mary*, the SAME JESUS which suffer'd at *Jerusalem*, is the Christ which the Apostles preached, and which all true Christians believe in : yet as evident, that the *Quakers* do not own him, nor believe in him ; for, as above noted, *Isaac Penington* says, there was the Outward Body, which they can never call Christ : *W. Penn*, he says, *But that the Outward Person which suffer'd was properly the Son of God, WE utterly deny.* Well, but let us hear this G. *Whitehead*, who thus reply'd, saying, *I deny that the Quakers teach that the Name Jesus and Christ belong to every*
Member

APPENDIX

Member in the Body, as amply as to the Head: Where proves he (Fran. Bugg) *as AMPLY?* Says G. *Whitehead*.

Mark, *Reader*, here is a Tacit Confeſſion of the Words AS WELL, tho' he carps at my Word AMPLY, which I put in for Illuſtration ſake, it not being a Quotation, but a Charge, which I ſtill offer to make good, if he will meet me on his own Propoſition; for I take the Word AMPLY to mean no more, but as Plainly, as Evidently, as Apparently; and the *Quakers* ſay, that the Name JESUS and CHRIST belong to every Believer, AS WELL as to the HEAD. This *Whitehead* denies not, this he diſowns not, only carps at the Word AMPLY.

W. Baily's Works, p. 229, 230, 307. The Sword of the Lord drawn &c. p. 5.

And therefore my Advice to all my Fellow-Labourers is, to take this my Method, give *New-Rome* Charge after Charge, as Geo. *Keith* has done *, as Daniel *Leeds* is a doing †, who has been a *Quaker* about 20 Years, and let this be the Teſt between *Chriſtianity* and *Quakeriſm*: If the *Quakers* be Innocent and Sincere, (tho' miſtaken thro' Error) they'll come out; if Inſincere, and Self-Conſcious of their Hypocriſie, they'll not appear, but Rave and Rail like *Rabſhekah* at a diſtance; by this Teſt ſhall the Plot be diſcovered, and the Conſpirators be made manifeſt: And I am not without Hopes, but that what I have ſaid, in Conjunction with my Fellow-Travellers, will be a Means to preſerve ſome from running Headlong (as the Swine did) into the deep Lake of *Quakeriſm*, and to convert others that are miſled, as well as be uſeful to the Church of God in general. Which God of his Mercy grant, for Jeſus Chriſt his ſake. *Amen*.

* *See his Three Narratives.*
† *A Trumpet ſounded out of the Wilderneſs, &c. p. 141.*

Auguſt 4th. 1698.   *Francis Bugg*.

F I N I S.

E R R A T A.

Kind Reader, *I ſhall deſire thee to Rectifie theſe Preſs Errors, which were chiefly occaſion'd for want of Deliberate Examination, thro' ſome Indiſpoſition of Body; which held me great part of the writing hereof.*

Page 4. line 9. for *Fathers* read *Paſtors*, p. 31. l. 19. f. 1696. r. 1676. p. 23. l. 8. r. *many Years*, p. 47. l. 22. f. *and* r. *or*, p. 55. dele *or condemn Actions*, p. 76. laſt Marginal Note, f, 1695. r. 1659. p. 65. l. 12. *after Vomit*, i. e. *Foxonian Quakers*, p. 37. l. 13. f. *dwelt* r. *dealt*, p. 128. l. 7. f. *Scenſes* r. *Scenes*, l. 15. f. *wait* r. *reſerv'd*, p. 129. l. 29. f. *hear* r. *bear*, p. 131. l. 38. f. *I glorifie* r. *I have glorify'd*, p. 139. l. 13. dele *did*, p. 119. l. 26. f. *tho* r. *thorough*, p. 157. l. 8. dele *alſo*, p. 153. l. 14. there wants a Parentheſis, beginning at *I told*, ending at *London*, p. 154. l. 35. f. *Approached* r. *Reproached*, p. 157. l. 16. f. *work* r. *walk*, p. 159. l. 14. f. *non* r. *now*.

A Catalogue of BOOKS, *Writ by* Fran. Bugg, *and Sold by* Walter Kettleby, *at the* Bishops-Head, *in St. Paul's Church-Yard.*

1. DE *Christianæ Libertate,* or Christian Liberty; shewing the Mischief of the *Quakers* Impositions. In *Oct.* bound.
2. The Painted Harlot, both stript and whipt, or the Mischief of Impositions of the *Quakers* further manifested.
3. Reason against Railing; being a Supplement to the Painted Harlot stript and whipt, *&c.* in *Quarto.*
4. Innocency Vindicated, and Envy Rebuked, *&c.* in *Quarto.*
5. The *Quakers* Detected, and their Errors Confuted, *&c.* in *Qu.*
6. A Letter to the *Quakers,* shewing their frequent Addresses to, and Prayers for the late K. *J.* II. and their Non-Address, *&c.* to King *William* III.
7. Battering Rams against *New Rome, &c.* in *Quarto.*
8. One Blow against *New-Rome, &c.* in *Quarto.*
9. *New-Rome* Unmask'd, and her Foundation shaken, *&c. Quar.*
10. *New-Rome* Arraign'd, and out of her own Mouth Condemn'd. *&c.* in *Quarto.*
11. A Sheet deliver'd to the Parliament, *Decem.* 1693. intituled, Something in Answer to the *Quakers* Allegations, *&c.*
12. Quakerism Withering, and Christianity Reviving, *&c. Oct.*
13. Quakerism Anatomized, *&c.* being a Challenge to *Rich. Ashby.*
14. A Sheet, intituled, The *Quakers* Yearly-Meeting Impeached on Behalf of the Commons of *England,* &c.
15. A second Summons to the City *Abel,* by way of Metaphor, to deliver up *Sheba* the Son of *Bichri,* 2 *Sam.* 20. i. e. *Geo. Whitehead* by Name, *&c.*
16. The *Quakers* set in their True Light, *&c.* in *Quarto.*
17. A Brief History of the Rise, Growth, and Progress of Quakerism, *&c.* in *Octavo.*
18. The Picture of Quakerism drawn to the Life, *&c.* in *Oct.*
19. A sober Expostulation with the Hearers of the *Quakers,* touching their Mercenary Teachers, *&c.* in *Octavo.*
20. The Pilgrim's Progress, from Quakerism to Christianity, *&c.* in *Quarto.*

www.ingramcontent.com/pod-product-compliance
Lightning Source LLC
Chambersburg PA
CBHW020245170426
43202CB00008B/230